THE VIRGINIA
ONE-DAY TRIP BOOK

For my daughter Alexis,
an absolute delight from day one!

THE VIRGINIA ONE-DAY TRIP BOOK

From the Mountains to the Sea,
Seven Geographic Centers Offer 101 Scenic
and Historic Delights

JANE OCKERSHAUSEN SMITH

EPM
PUBLICATIONS, INC.

1003 Turkey Run Road   McLean, Virginia 22101

Library of Congress Cataloging in Publication Data

Smith, Jane Ockershausen.
  The Virginia one-day trip book.

  Includes index. 1. Virginia—Description and travel—1981–
—Tours. I. Title. F224.3.S63 1986 917.55'0443 86-13450 ISBN
0-914440-93-4

EPM Publications, Inc., 1003 Turkey Run Road,
  McLean, Virginia 22101

Printed in the United States of America

Cover photography by Everett C. Johnson
Cover and book design by Tom Huestis

Contents

THE VIRGINIA ONE-DAY TRIP BOOK

From the Mountains to the Sea

=================HISTORIC TRIANGLE=================

WILLIAMSBURG

JAMESTOWN

YORKTOWN

=================TIDEWATER=================

NORFOLK

PORTSMOUTH

=================SEA=================

================================PIEDMONT================================

NEED A GOOD VIRGINIA ROAD MAP?

To obtain a free state road map call 1(800)VISIT-VA or write Virginia Division of Tourism, 202 North 9th Street, Suite 500, Richmond, Virginia 23219. Maps are also available at the 10 Highway Welcome Centers and the local/regional information centers listed below.

1 - CLEAR BROOK   6 - BRACEY
2 - MANASSAS   7 - LAMBSBURG
3 - FREDERICKSBURG 8 - BRISTOL
4 - NEW CHURCH   9 - ROCKY GAP
5 - SKIPPERS   10 - COVINGTON

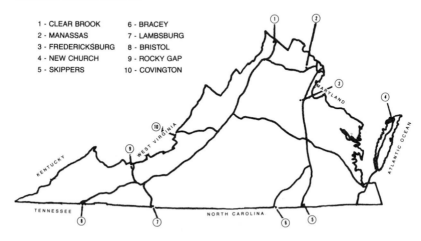

ALEXANDRIA
RAMSAY HOUSE VISITOR
    CENTER
221 King Street
Alexandria, VA 22314
(703)549-0205

THE LYCEUM
201 South Washington Street
Alexandria, VA 22314-3022
(703)838-4994

ARLINGTON
ARLINGTON COUNTY VISITOR
    CENTER
735 South 18th Street
Arlington, VA 22202
(703)284-5096

BIG STONE GAP
TOURISM & INFORMATION
    CENTER
P.O. Box 236
Big Stone Gap, VA 24219
(703)523-2060

CHARLOTTESVILLE
THOMAS JEFFERSON VISITORS
    BUREAU
P.O. Box 161
Charlottesville, VA 22902
(804)293-6789

CHINCOTEAGUE
CHINCOTEAGUE INFORMATION
    CENTER
P.O. Box 258
Chincoteague, VA 23336
(804)336-6161
(Open April–November)

DANVILLE
DANVILLE VISITORS CENTER
P.O. Box 3300
Danville, VA 24543
(804)799-5149

FREDERICKSBURG
FREDERICKSBURG VISITORS
    CENTER
706 Caroline Street
Fredericksburg, VA 22401
(703)373-1776

HAMPTON
HAMPTON INFORMATION
  CENTER
413 West Mercury Boulevard
Hampton, VA 23666
(804)727-6108

LEXINGTON
LEXINGTON VISITORS BUREAU
107 East Washington Street
Lexington, VA 24450
(703)463-3777

LOUDOUN COUNTY
LOUDOUN VISITOR'S CENTER
108 South Street, S.E.
Market Station
Leesburg, VA 22075
(703)777-0519

LYNCHBURG
LYNCHBURG VISITORS
  INFORMATION CENTER
P.O. Box 60
Lynchburg, VA 24505
(804)847-1811

NATURAL BRIDGE
JEFFERSON NATIONAL FOREST
  INFORMATION CENTER
P.O. Box 10
Natural Bridge Station, VA 24579
(703)291-2188
(Open May–October)

NEWPORT NEWS
VIRGINIA PENINSULA TOURIST
  INFORMATION CENTER
13560 Jefferson Avenue
Newport News, VA 23603
(804)872-8000

NORFOLK
NORFOLK VISITOR
  INFORMATION CENTER
4th View Street
Norfolk, VA 23503
(804)588-0404

PETERSBURG
HISTORIC PETERSBURG
  INFORMATION CENTER
P.O. Box 2107
Petersburg, VA 23804
(804)733-2400

PRINCE WILLIAM COUNTY
PRINCE WILLIAM COUNTY &
  MANASSAS TOURIST
  INFORMATION CENTER
2231 A Tackett's Mill Drive
Lake Ridge, VA 22192
(703)491-4045

RICHMOND
RICHMOND VISITORS CENTER
1700 Robin Hood Road
Richmond, VA 23220
(804)358-5511

SHENANDOAH VALLEY
SHENANDOAH VALLEY TRAVEL
  ASSOCIATION
P.O. Box 1040
New Market, VA 22844
(703)740-3132

STAUNTON
STAUNTON-AUGUSTA COUNTY
  TOURIST INFORMATION
  CENTER
30 N. New Street
Staunton, VA 24401
(703)885-8504

VIRGINIA BEACH
VIRGINIA BEACH VISITORS
  INFORMATION CENTER
P.O. Box 200
Virginia Beach, VA 23458
(800)446-8038 or (804)425-7511

WAYNESBORO
ROCKFISH GAP REGIONAL
  INFORMATION CENTER
P.O. Box 459
Waynesboro, VA 22980
(703)943-5187

WILLIAMSBURG
COLONIAL WILLIAMSBURG
  VISITOR CENTER
Williamsburg, VA 23187
(804)229-1000, ext. 2756
(Open March–December)

NEW YORK
VIRGINIA DIVISION OF
  TOURISM
11 Rockefeller Plaza
New York, NY 10020
(212)245-3080

════Discover Virginia!════

In *The Virginia One-Day Trip Book* life-long residents, newcomers and visitors alike will discover daytrips they never expected to find in or near their own backyards. I've been writing about Virginia for 15 years, and I still found attractions heretofore unexplored while researching for this, the fifth, in my series of one-day trip books. The variety and number of attractions prompted me for the first time to focus exclusively on one state.

The book is organized geographically into seven areas so that you can combine nearby attractions when you plan a day trip or weekend outing. Before you set out, I suggest you read all the selections in the city or geographic region you're planning to visit. Keep in mind the total distance you'll be traveling—a daytrip from one end of the state to another may not be practical, especially with small children. Nearly every site described in the book lies within a day's drive—out and back—from Richmond, the capital. That is why all directions to the sites are given from there. Readers in other areas of the state will have to consult their maps to gauge distances and driving time from wherever they are located. I urge you to consult the book's Calendar of Events as well; it will help you choose the attractions best suited to the time of year and to your personal interests.

The calendar will alert you to the birthday celebrations of famous Virginians whose homes can be found throughout the state. You can begin the year on the trail of Robert E. Lee, born January 19, 1807, at Stratford Hall, then visit his boyhood home in Alexandria and his home and grave on the Washington and Lee campus in Lexington. Another Virginian, Thomas Jonathan "Stonewall" Jackson, was also born in January (January 24, 1824). To track him you would start with his home in Lexington and go to his Civil War headquarters in Winchester and finally to the battlefield where he suffered the wound that led to his death. Then, of course, there is George Washington, born in February. You can visit his birthplace in the Northern Neck region, his beloved Mount Vernon and his nearby grist mill. You can also tour the homes of Washington's immediate family: the Mary Washington House and Kenmore in Fredericksburg and Woodlawn just south of Alexandria.

11

You may be surprised, as I was, to learn that one of the best outdoor dramas in the country, *The Long Way Home*, is presented in Radford during the summer months. This harrowing story of a young Virginia woman's escape from Indian captivity is sure to enthrall the entire family. Living history will make you part of the past at Petersburg National Battlefield, Appomattox Court House National Historical Park, the Nelson House, the Yorktown Victory Center and Colonial Williamsburg.

History is only one appealing aspect of traveling in Virginia. The state is also blessed with an abundance of natural beauty. The winding mountain roads of the Blue Ridge Parkway offer a stunning contrast to the narrow trails criss-crossing Chincoteague Island. One of my favorite parks is Prince William Forest Park where during the week you can hike all day without meeting anyone on the trails, though you may spot a shy deer or busy beaver. Wildlife abounds in Virginia from the wild ponies on Chincoteague, to the bald eagles at Mason Neck National Wildlife Refuge and the animal habitats at Maymont in Richmond.

There is so much to see and do that you easily fill your weekends year round. I urge you not to make the mistake of limiting your vacations to long trips once or twice a year but instead plan frequent daytrips. Timing is important, so before beginning your trip read the entire selection. Nothing is worse than arriving to discover the attraction is closed for the day. Hours of operation are given at the end of each selection but these can change, so it's best to double check.

Just remember that yes, Santa Claus, there is a Virginia!

J.O.S.

RICHMOND

Agecroft Hall

15th-Century England in 20th-Century Richmond

You needn't cross the Atlantic to enjoy an old English country house. A 15th-century Tudor manor house built in Renaissance England a decade before Columbus sailed to America now stands above the James River just outside downtown Richmond.

Agecroft was purchased by Thomas C. Williams, Jr., in 1925 when industrialization around Lancashire threatened to destroy the house. Brick by brick, and beam by beam it was taken down, numbered and shipped to Virginia where it was painstakingly reassembled over the next three years.

A 12-minute slide introduction to Agecroft provides details of this amazing move. Special architectural features and unusual furnishings are pinpointed so that you will be sure to notice them on your tour. Your first glimpse of Agecroft's interior is the Great Hall. The enormous mullioned window in this room survived the Atlantic crossing intact—not a single pane was broken!

As you tour the house you'll learn about the life style of the Tudor and early Stuart period, 1485 to 1650. Rushes cover part of the floor in the Great Hall; such long reeds were often left for a month or more in centuries past before they were swept up. Each day more rushes would be added to cover the food and refuse on the floor until they reached a depth of 12 inches or more. The rushes provided insulation and moderated the irregularity of the rough stone floor. When you see the rush lamp you'll learn the derivation of the expression "burning the candle at both ends." Although not literally a candle, the rush was formed into a wick and lit at both ends.

In the withdrawing room there are several unusual chairs. The draught chair was a precursor of the wing-backed chair. A three legged chair attests to the difficulty of balancing on the stone floors. Its massive legs provide a strong point of contact and the stretcher base provides a place off the cold floor to put your feet while seated.

The next room is the eating parlor. Although there are forks on the table these were used only for the dessert course. The apostle spoons on display reveal the derivation of yet another expression

In Richmond you can visit a furnished Tudor manor house built in England in the 15th century. Agecroft Hall was brought to the shores of the James River beam by beam, brick by brick, in 1925.

"born with a silver spoon in your mouth." These spoons were the traditional Christening gift for affluent families and bespoke a comfortable background. The covered cups reveal a less comforting practice. Cups were covered to protect diners from poison, not infrequently employed in Tudor times to remove those who stood in the way of someone else's advancement.

The staircase to the upstairs rooms is a work of art; it is not original to the house but from the priory at Warwick. Upstairs you'll get another view of the Great Hall from the minstrels' gallery. Then you'll see the north bedroom. Here again you'll discover a concern for safety. The Elizabethan bed has an elaborately carved tester; not merely decorative, it also protected the slumberer from bits of falling plaster. Another rare reminder of earlier times is the laundry counter on which the servants kept track of the bedlinens and nightwear they collected from each room.

Each bedroom contains an elaborate and quite different bed. In the second there is a 1629 bed from Bridgewater Castle in Somerset. It is the third bed that is really a stunner, a polychrome bed from the 1600s with its original red, green and yellow paint.

After your house tour you'll step outside to see the exterior architectural features. One window pane at the far end of the terrace contains a royal reminder; on it, on June 12, 1645, King Charles I, used his diamond ring to carve the name William Dauntesey.

Before leaving be sure to allow time to explore the gardens. The sunken garden is copied from Hampton Court. There are three additional gardens you'll want to explore: the knot garden, formal garden and herb garden. The latter contains only herbs grown during the reign of Elizabeth I.

Agecroft Hall is open year round Tuesday through Friday from 10:00 A.M. to 4:00 P.M. and weekends from 2:00 to 5:00 P.M. Admission is charged.

Directions: From Richmond city center take Cary Street west to Malvern Avenue on your right and Canterbury Road on your left. Turn left on Canterbury Road. From Canterbury Road make a right on Sulgrave Road. Agecroft is at 4305 Sulgrave Road. There is free parking on the grounds.

Chesterfield Museum Complex

Go Directly to Jail

A trio of historically significant buildings awaits visitors to the Chesterfield Courthouse complex: a county museum, the jail built in 1892 and a Federal period plantation house called Magnolia Grange.

The **Chesterfield County Museum** is housed inside a replica of the county's 1750 courthouse. This modest museum may have greater appeal for county residents than casual visitors, but it does encompass an important bit of Virginia history. The state's earliest inhabitants, Appomattox and Monocan Indians, are represented by a collection of stone implements and a 17th-century dugout canoe.

The first English settlers in this part of Virginia established themselves at Henricus and Farrar's Island in 1611. The museum has a portrait of the founder of these settlements, Sir Thomas Dale, but nothing else for the enclaves were wiped out by an Indian massacre in 1622.

An historic document from 1749 has a fascinating past. Called the Commission of Peace, it had established the county of Chesterfield. In 1865 Edward Jeffries of the New York Infantry stole it. Then, 90 years later on April 6, 1955, a county resident saw an advertisement for the document's sale. He purchased it and had it returned to its rightful place in Chesterfield.

Three county firsts are commemorated. It was in Chesterfield in 1700 that the French Huguenots established the first coal mines in America. This was also the location of the first iron mines, established in 1619 and eliminated along with the settlements in the 1622 massacre. The first railroad in Virginia was also in this county.

On the lower level of the museum you can watch a 30-minute color film on local history. There is also a well-stocked country store, reflecting the years from 1900 to 1940. Old medicine jars hold long forgotten nostrums. There are such arcane items as a hog scraper, shot gun shell crimper, Cresoline lamps that were the forerunners of vaporizers, cherry seeders and a device for watering baby chicks. On the counter there is a 1922 account book from a general merchandise store; some youngsters are amazed to learn that a store would "carry" a customer.

Downstairs at the jail you'll find the offices of the Chesterfield Historical Society, but you can see the old cells upstairs. They are definitely a crime deterrent—small, dark, cold and totally inhospitable. One prisoner who was determined to escape jumped the jailer. The jailer, who was getting on in years, fortunately had been forewarned by a prison trustee. He pulled his revolver and shot the prisoner dead. He was buried on the sheriff's farm until relatives could claim the body.

The last part of the complex, Magnolia Grange, is across Route 10 from the Court Green. Built in 1822, it is one of the finest Federal period houses in Virginia. It opened to the public in the spring of 1986, newly restored to its original appearance. The architecture and furnishings reflect the Greek Revival influence, except for an upstairs bedroom that is decorated in the Victorian style popular in the 1850s.

The Chesterfield County Museum Complex is open Tuesday through Friday from NOON to 4:00 P.M. and Sunday from 1:00 to 4:00 P.M. Admission is charged to tour Magnolia Grange and donations requested at the museum.

Directions: From Richmond take I-95 south to Chester, Exit 6. Take Route 10 west for 7 miles to Chesterfield Courthouse. The museum is on the right.

The Edgar Allan Poe Museum

Mastering the Macabre

Some individuals—like Edgar Allan Poe—stride across life with great elan. He came by his dramatic flair quite naturally, having inherited it from his father, his mother and his maternal grandmother, all of whom were actors. Poe's biographers believe that David Poe deserted his family before his early death. Poe's mother, Elizabeth Arnold Poe, died in Richmond in 1811 when Edgar was only three. A plaque in St. John's Cemetery commemorates her passing, but the exact gravesite is unknown.

The Edgar Allan Poe Museum in Richmond is a complex of buildings which surround the Old Stone House of 1737–39. This stone house has only a tenuous link with Poe. When the Marquis de Lafayette toured Richmond on his triumphant return to America in 1824 he stopped at this old landmark, and among those who helped to entertain him was Edgar Allan Poe, a member of the Junior Volunteers. Poe's grandfather had served with Lafayette during the Revolution. The Old Stone House is only blocks away from the site of Poe's first Richmond home, no longer there.

To acquaint visitors with Richmond and the Poe connection, the museum's first display is a scale model of Richmond circa 1809–1849. Museum docents retrace Poe's steps around the old city for you. He spent more time here than in any other city. He grew up, married and first gained national recognition for the writing he did for the local *Southern Literary Messenger* in Richmond.

A slide program on his life adds details to the portrait of this tortured genius. In 1826 when Poe entered the University of Virginia, founder Thomas Jefferson was still on hand to greet incoming students. Undoubtedly no remarks were exchanged between these two great American intellectuals, but it is interesting to contemplate their paths crossing.

There is something for everyone in Richmond—including white-water rafting. The only such trip offered in a major metropolitan area, it takes canoeists past the skyline through the heart of the city.

You will learn that Poe was adopted unofficially after his mother's death. His foster father did not give him enough money to cover his tuition and living expenses at the university. He also refused to pay the debts which Poe was forced to accumulate. Consequently Poe moved to Boston and enlisted in the army. Although he gained an appointment to West Point, he deliberately broke minor rules and was dismissed. Poe spent his life fighting the demons of poverty and obscurity.

When Poe left Richmond he was distraught over the forcible rupture of his engagement to Elmira Royster, his childhood sweetheart. His romance with her was to last a lifetime despite his marriage to someone else. Poe's romance with Elmira was rekindled when he returned to Richmond in 1849, about two months before his death. As both of them had lost their first spouses, they became engaged again. He gave his final public reading at the Exchange Hotel and, of course, his popular poem "The Raven," published in 1845, was on the program.

The Poe Museum's "Raven Room" contains a series of dramatic drawings that bring his well-known poem to life. In the adjoining building you will see the few worldly goods Poe possessed at the time of his death: a trunk, his wife's mirror and trinket box, a walking stick and a pair of boot hooks. In the Enchanted Garden, created to complement Poe's poetry, the bust of Poe overlooks a green oasis amid the bustle of downtown Richmond.

The museum is open year round from Tuesday through Saturday, 10:00 A.M. to 4:00 P.M. Sunday and Monday hours are 1:30 to 4:00 P.M. It is closed on Christmas Day. Admission is charged.

Directions: The Edgar Allan Poe Museum is in downtown Richmond at 1914–16 E. Main Street. From I-95 take Exit 9A, go east on Main Street. The Poe Museum will be on the left.

The James River and Kanawha Canal Locks

Locks Link to Past

There are two things you should know about the James River and Kanawha Canal. It was the first canal system built in America, and it is one of the coolest spots in Richmond on a hot summer afternoon. Beneath the 13th Street Bridge, built in 1860, there is a picnic pavilion shaded from the sun and cooled by the canal. Display cases in the pavilion provide background on this historically significant canal.

It was George Washington's dream to have a "Great Central American Waterway" linking the Atlantic Coast to the Ohio River. In order to realize that dream the James River had to be made navigable. From the earliest days, settlers had encountered the obstacle of the James River Falls. On May 24, 1607, ten days after landing at Jamestown, a party of 21 explorers sailed up the James River only to be halted by seven miles of falls. These falls broke the connection between the Atlantic Ocean some 125 miles down river and the 200 miles of navigable river extending into the Alleghenies.

Lots were sold along the falls by Colonel Willliam Byrd II in 1737 and again by his son, William Byrd III, in 1768. This settlement formed the nucleus of the city of Richmond. Although early lot purchasers hoped the James River would be cleared for navigation, it was not until George Washington became President that the work was actually started. With the support of President Washington, the Virginia Assembly in January 1785 established the James River Company with the object of "clearing and improving the navigation of James River."

By the end of 1789 large boulders were removed from the James River, and two short canals were built around the falls. In 1800 an eastern terminus called the "Great Basin" was built in Richmond between 8th, 12th, Canal and Cary Streets. The next step needed to circumvent the falls was to connect the Great Basin in the center of Richmond with Tidewater below Shockoe's Creek—the Tidewater Connection. Between 1810 and 1812, 13 wooden locks were built by Captain Ariel Cooley.

In 1826 Charles Crozet, Chief Engineer of the canal, proposed that Cooley's decaying wooden locks be replaced with stone locks. He estimated the cost at $100,000. By 1854 when the five stone locks and two basins Crozet had recommended were finally open to commerce, the price tag was $600,000.

The canal has not been used since the end of 1870, but you can still see locks number 4 and number 5 of the Tidewater Connection. Each of these large granite locks is 100 feet long and 15 feet wide. A narrated audio-visual presentation plus descriptive plaques tells the story of the canal. This National Historic Landmark is open at no charge from 9:00 A.M. to 5:00 P.M. daily.

Directions: The Tidewater Connection has been preserved by the Reynolds Metals Company. The canal path and lock system have been incorporated into the design of the Reynolds Wrap Distribution Center at 12th and Byrd Streets in downtown Richmond. Parking is available alongside the canal.

John Marshall House

Virginia Is—and Was—for Lovers

In an era when their contemporaries were marrying for wealth and position, John Marshall and Mary "Polly" Willis Ambler married for love. It was a love that was to last a lifetime and influence the career decisions of a major figure in American history.

John Marshall, who was to become Chief Justice of the U.S. Supreme Court, met Polly Ambler when she was a girl of 14. He fell in love and proposed at their first meeting in her family's house. When she burst into tears at his tender proposal, he was taken aback and left in despair. A cousin of Polly's caught up with Marshall as he was leaving and gave him a lock of Polly's hair. This talismen kept Marshall company through the next few years, and when he proposed again two years later, his suit was accepted and the young couple married in 1783.

Along with his good fortune in obtaining the hand of the girl he loved, Marshall also inherited the law practice of Edmund Randolph who relinquished it to run for governor of Virginia.

With a thriving law practice and a growing family, in 1786 John Marshall purchased a one-block lot in the center of Richmond. While their house was being built the Marshalls lived in a small two-story cottage on the grounds. They built a two-story brick house, the only one of their buildings from that period still standing; although during the 18th century there were also a large kitchen dependency, a laundry and Marshall's law-office.

The **John Marshall House** itself has been open to the public since 1913, and it contains the largest collection of Marshall memorabilia in existence. The Marshall silver, returned to the house for his 225th birthday celebration, is here as is the French porcelain purchased by Marshall when he was Ambassador to France in 1797. Utilitarian shutters were used instead of curtains because of Polly's reluctance to have a lot of slaves around. Her invalidism and nervous disorders meant that Marshall did far more of the housework and child care than men typically did in the 18th century. Although Polly did not enjoy entertaining, he frequently invited 30 fellow attorneys for his "lawyer dinners."

His tenure as Ambassador was one of the rare times Marshall accepted an appointment away from Richmond. As Chief Justice, he was able to do much of the case work at home. When you look at the portrait of Polly Marshall at age 33, you can see why he was reluctant to leave her. She was a gorgeous woman despite her ill health and her long years of childbearing. Marshall also had health problems; he had over 1,000 gallstones removed with only alcohol for an anesthetic. Despite their problems both lived long lives, Polly Marshall to age 65 and John to age 80.

John Marshall may well have attributed some of his long life to his wine cellar. He spent a tenth of his income on wine. His Richmond home boasted a superb wine cellar which has been restored. A reproduction of a sundial John Marshall set in place back in the 18th century can be seen on the lawn.

The John Marshall House is open Tuesday through Saturday from 10:00 A.M. to 5:00 P.M. and Sunday from 1:00 to 5:00 P.M.

Admission is charged. A new Court End block ticket provides reduced admission to three houses on a self-guided walking tour which includes ten additional points of interest. The block ticket provides admission to the Marshall House, the Wickham-Valentine House and the John Brockenbrough House which served as the White House of the Confederacy.

Directions: The John Marshall House is in downtown Richmond at 818 East Marshall Street at the intersection of 9th Street.

Maymont

May Be the Place for You

A one-day visit to **Maymont** is a multi-dimensional excursion. You can tour the neo-Romanesque Maymont House, stroll through the Italian and Japanese gardens, explore the carriage collection, drop by the children's farm, see the indoor nature center and the outdoor wildlife habitats, pick one of the four self-guided walks around the estate or treat yourself to the luxury of a carriage ride.

Maymont stands, as does much of Richmond, on land granted to William Byrd in 1675 by the English crown and sold by his grandson to pay his debts in 1769. The land was acquired by James Henry Dooley in 1886. At that time the Dooleys were living on Franklin Street, a fitting in-town address for one of Richmond's most affluent families. Because of the growing noise, pollution, crime and overcrowding in the inner city, however, Dooley acquired 94 acres on the outskirts of the city and later added 11 more.

The 33-room Dooley mansion on this acreage was designed in an early medieval style enjoying a vogue during the last quarter of the 19th century. It is still decorated in the height of fashion—for the 1890s. Furnishings were purchased by the Dooleys on their travels around Europe and were chosen in a mixture of historical and exotic styles.

The ornately decorated rooms in this, the only Victorian estate open to the public in Virginia, make it easy to understand why the late 19th century was called the gilded age. In the library, the first room you will see, there are several unusual items. The Italian Renaissance winged-lion chair the Dooleys may have found in Italy always elicits questions from visitors. The walls feature such Victorian touches as stenciling and strapwork. Stenciling, which originally adorned modest homes in the form of folk art, was later adopted and embellished by the more sophisticated. Strapwork, which had its origins in fine Elizabethan and Jacobean houses, is a ceiling design done with wooden mouldings.

Both the pink and blue drawing rooms utilize French decorative styles. The former is decorated with Louis XV furniture to complement the rococo, 18th-century French architectural details, such as the ceiling frescoes and the 14-karat gold-plated chandelier and sconces. The drawing room has a parquet floor, highly touted in an 1884 edition of *Godey's Lady's Book*. It is said that Mrs. Dooley made visitors put on flannel shoe covers to protect her floor. The pastel stained glass windows demonstrate another favorite decoration of the Victorian period. The blue drawing room is done in the neoclassical style and has Louis XVI furnishings.

The dining room walls are covered with painted canvas "tapestries," very popular during the gilded age. The porcelain is copied from Rutherford B. Hayes's White House china. The enormous, ornately carved mahogany and rosewood cabinet was made in France in 1805 and displayed at the Paris Exposition.

You'll also see the upstairs bedrooms. The most interesting is the Swan Room filled with furniture featuring swan motifs. A large swan bed competes for attention with a table made of silver and narwhal (a single tusk whale) by Tiffany and Co.

In addition to turning the main house into a display of Victoriana, the many dependencies at Maymont have been turned to good use. The first dependency to be built may predate the mansion. Now called the "mews," it serves as a gift shop. The carriage house contains a sizeable collection of 19th-century horse-drawn vehicles. Carriage rides are given from 1:00 to 5:00 P.M. on weekends weather permitting. The old hay barn houses a nature center.

There are also wildlife habitats on the grounds. One of the walking tours covers these animal habitats. The most noticeable member of the grasslands community is the American bison, but you may also spot rabbits, quail, rock doves and cowbirds. Another habitat is the water's edge environment where beavers and muskrats live. The forest edge has its own denizens—raccoons, foxes, chipmunks, elk and deer; and in the forest are black bears, the largest of all wild animals in Virginia. Birds live in all these habitats and also in Maymont's aviary. Domestic animals are at the children's farm.

The gardens of Maymont should not be missed; indeed, they are the primary reason many visitors return. The first of the diverse gardening styles to be observed is the English pastoral landscape that surrounds the house. The objective of this style was to make the grounds look natural even when planted with trees and shrubs that were not indigenous to the area. The

Dooleys imported 185 varieties of exotic trees from six continents.

Between 1907 and 1910 the Dooleys built a three-tiered Italian garden. The garden's multi-level terraces are enhanced by statuary, a formal cascade fountain with terraced pools, a wisteria-covered pergola or arbor plus a promenade overlooking the secret garden.

The cascade fountain continues down into a more natural waterfall in the Japanese garden, a re-creation done in 1976 of the Dooley's Victorian version of a Japanese garden. The current garden includes trained and pruned trees and shrubs, raked sand pools, meandering paths, stone lanterns and delicate bridges.

The many elements of Maymont make for an exciting and full day's outing. Maymont is open 10:00 A.M. to 5:00 P.M. daily November through March and 10:00 A.M. to 7:00 P.M. from April through October. Exhibits are open NOON to 5:00 P.M. Tuesday through Sunday from September through May and 10:00 A.M. to 5:00 P.M. Tuesday through Sunday, June through August. Admission is free.

Directions: From Richmond proper take the Downtown Expressway and exit on Meadow Street, turning left on Meadow Street. Next make a right turn onto Pennsylvania to the Hampton Meadows parking area. If you are coming from north of the city, take I-95 to the Boulevard Exit, Route 161, and proceed south to Columbus Statue. Turn left at the statue and follow Maymont signs through Byrd Park to Hampton Meadows parking area.

Meadow Farm Museum at Crump Park

Confederate Line

With attention focused on agrarian life in these days of crisis for the American family farm, why not plan a timely visit to **Meadow Farm Museum?** In 1975 this 19th-century farmhouse, along with 150 acres of pasture and woodland, was given to Henrico County by Elizabeth Ann Crump in memory of her husband, the late Adjutant General of Virginia, Sheppard Crump.

Reminders of man's interaction with this land date from prehistoric time when Indians camped along North Run Creek. It was acquired by the Sheppard family in 1713. The farmhouse you'll visit was built almost a century later in 1810 by Mosby Sheppard. Earlier in 1800 Mosby had uncovered the details of a planned slave uprising, Gabriel's Insurrection. The idea of a slave revolt terrorized southern slave owners, and encouraged men like John Brown whose Harpers Ferry raid in 1859 was an attempt to get munitions to help slaves seize their freedom.

According to Sheppard family stories, Meadow Farm had its own brush with history one memorable day in 1864. Major General George Custer, with some of his Union cavalry, raided Meadow Farm before continuing on to Yellow Tavern five miles away, where a confrontation occurred that cost J.E.B. Stuart his life.

Your visit to Meadow Farm begins with a 12-minute slide program introducing you to the Sheppard family and a typical pre-Civil War day in the mid-19th century (1845–1855). About 90 percent of the furniture now in the farm house belonged to the Sheppards. The dining room, hallway and upstairs bedrooms were built in 1810. As both family and fortunes grew, a downstairs master bedroom and additional upstairs bedrooms were added. Both downstairs rooms did double duty. A sofa sits in the dining room and the master bedroom also served as a parlor with a much-used piano.

The Sheppards' ten children slept upstairs as did the governess, or tutor, and the boarder. During the prewar years the family had 17 slaves. It's hard to imagine that many people being supported by such a modest farm. John Mosby Sheppard was able to afford his sizeable household because he also had a thriving medical practice. His office at Meadow Farm is typical of most 19th-century doctors' offices.

An 1840 out-building similar to the one used by Dr. Sheppard stands on the site of his old office. Dr. Sheppard's diploma from the University of Pennsylvania Medical College hangs on the wall. The shelves and tables are cluttered with old medicine jars and bandages. Dr. Sheppard mixed many of his own medicines, but did purchase from an apothecary quinine for fevers and laudanum to kill pain. He normally charged his neighbors two dollars for an office visit and four dollars if he had to go out at night. Delivering a baby cost ten dollars. His fees remained substantially the same during his 37-year practice.

After Meadow Farm Museum there are two nature trails to explore. North Run Trail traces the evolution of an old farm field into a forest. You may spot a darting deer or spy a red-winged hawk. The River Birch Trail exposes you to the flora and fauna of the marshy area along the riverbank. You may see nesting water birds or turtles basking in the sun.

There are also picnic and playground areas at Crump Park and special events scheduled throughout the year: the Spring Agricultural Fair and Militia Review in May, Old-Fashioned Fourth, September Civil War Encampment, Harvest Festival in October and a Yuletide Fest. There is a nominal admission for the museum, but the park is free.

Meadow Farm Museum is open Tuesday through Sunday NOON to 4:00 P.M. from the first Saturday in March until the second

Sunday in December. The remainder of December and January the museum is open by appointment only. It is closed during February. Crump Park is open daily from dawn to dusk year round.

Directions: From I-95 just before Richmond take I-295 west toward Charlottesville to Woodman Road South Exit. Follow Woodman Road to Mountain Road and turn right; continue two miles to park entrance on the right.

Philip Morris U.S.A. Tour

Wholly Smoke!

It always gets a laugh: there is no smoking while touring the **Philip Morris Manufacturing Center** in Richmond, Virginia. At the end of the tour, however, adults who want them are given a pack of the Philip Morris brand of their choice.

The Philip Morris plant, nicknamed Marlboro Country, was completed in 1973 at a cost in excess of $300 million. It is considered the largest and most advanced cigarette manufacturing factory in the world. A great deal of thought has gone into providing a well-run and informative tour experience.

No advance notice is required for individuals or groups of under ten. Tours are given from 9:00 A.M. to 4:00 P.M. Monday through Friday. After registering, visitors are provided with what resembles cordless phones so that they can hear a commentary on the artifacts in the Philip Morris Museum. Large free-standing glass cases contain ornamental pipes, decorative snuff boxes, jeweled cigarette cases and hundreds of box-lids and tin tags used to market tobacco products over the years.

After exploring the museum visitors board a tram train for a ride through the noisy plant. Through phones, the guide explains each step of the manufacturing process. There are different cigarettes being made in each of the five bays. The plant operates 24 hours a day five days a week, roughly 6,000 cigarettes per machine per minute. On all those cigarettes, this factory alone pays $3.2 million every day in federal taxes. Combined with its other factories, the company pays between $6.5 and $8 million dollars daily.

From the production tour visitors move to the gallery for an overview of one of the manufacturing bays. The gallery also contains audio-visual displays on tobacco growing and marketing.

The Philip Morris Plant is open year round for free tours except for the week between Christmas and New Year, the week of July 4 and other company holidays.

Directions: Take I-95 to the Richmond area, use Exit 8, Bells Road. Follow the signs for the Philip Morris Manufacturing Center on Commerce Road. It is well marked.

Richmond Children's Museum and Maggie L. Walker Historical Site

Hands Full of Fun

"Let a child be your guide" suggests the **Richmond Children's Museum**. This innovative hands-on museum was established in 1981 to help young people, ages 3–12, find their own way into their futures.

Clothes may not make the man, but a chance to try on the firemen's uniforms, doctors' whites and police badges certainly encourages active involvement in the exhibit, "When I Grow Up." Also contributing to realism is an ample supply of such vocational equipment as cash registers and grocery carts, office phones, an x-ray machine and a video camera. There is an actual working television studio and a real stage on which budding thespians can perform. Each exhibit is designed to be self-motivating and self-explanatory, allowing children to work and play at their own pace.

A variety of workshops expand the museum's educational thrust. Both staff and community experts continue to look for new ways to introduce children to new ideas and interests. Close cooperation with the Richmond Symphony Orchestra, for example, has led to many musical programs. In one year more than 40,000 youngsters will have their imagination stirred and their confidence developed by their experiences at this unusual museum.

The Richmond Children's Museum is open Tuesday through Friday from 10:00 A.M. to 4:30 P.M. Weekend hours are 1:00 to 5:00 P.M. The museum is closed on Mondays, Easter, Christmas and New Year's Day. A nominal admission is charged.

Just a few blocks from the Children's Museum in the Jackson Ward Historic District is the **Maggie L. Walker National Historic Site**. Maggie Walker was the first woman in America to found and become president of a bank. She achieved her success in spite of her sex, her race and her health. In her later years she was paralyzed from the waist down and confined to a wheel chair.

The house at 110½ East Leigh Street was the home for Maggie Walker and her family from 1904 to 1934. The 22-room house is fitted with Walker family pieces and looks as it did in the 1930s. There is no charge for the tour that is given on the hour Thursday through Sunday from 9:00 A.M. to 5:00 P.M. It is closed December 25 and January 1.

The Maggie Walker is just a block away from the park dedicated to Bill "Bojangles" Robinson, who grew up in this Richmond neighborhood. The famed tap dancer is shown in a life-size statue that looks as if he were going to dance down the bronze steps and off the pedestal.

Directions: The Richmond Children's Museum is located at 740 North 6th Street in downtown Richmond north of the Coliseum. For the Maggie Walker House take 6th Street to Broad Street. Take Broad Street to 2nd Street and turn right. Continue on 2nd Street to Leigh Street.

Richmond National Battlefield Park

Double Jeopardy

"On to Richmond" was a battle cry heard with chilling frequency during the War Between the States. Seven Union drives were launched against the capital of the Confederacy. The North wanted the psychological victory of capturing the symbol of Southern independence as well as the military advantage of disabling the principal supply depot for the Confederate army.

Two Federal drives nearly succeeded: McClellan's in 1862 and Grant's in 1864. You can trace them at **Richmond National Battlefield Park**'s Chimborazo Visitor Center with the help of an audio-visual program, exhibits and park rangers. An annotated park map routes you along the 100-mile battlefield trail, and you can rent or buy auto tape tours.

There are five tour stops along the McClellan route (marked in red). The first is Chickahominy Bluff from which General Lee watched the opening skirmish of the Seven Days' Battle. You can see earthwork fortifications that protected his position.

At the next stop, a Federal position, the earthworks along Beaver Dam Creek were part of the three-mile Union line that Lee tried so valiantly to penetrate. Along the short trail at Stop 3, where the Battle of Gaines' Mill was fought, the shallow trenches were used by the same Union forces who had dug in at Beaver Dam. They tried in vain to hold the line against determined Texans and Georgians. A battlefield landmark, the restored Watt House (seen from the exterior only), exemplifies the middle-class farms around which the Seven Days' Battles were fought.

The fourth stop is Malvern Hill where the last of the battles raged. So fierce was the fighting that afterwards a Confederate officer mourned, "It was not war—it was murder."

The last stop along the red route is Drewry's Bluff where Fort Darling protected the James River (and thus Richmond). This Confederate fort even repulsed the *Monitor*, the formidable Union ironclad.

Only an ardent Civil War buff would want to explore both 1862 and 1864 routes on the same day; most people return later to cover Grant's drive (the blue route). If you've stopped before at the Chimborazo Visitor Center you can begin the blue route at the Cold Harbor Exhibit Shelter where there are picnic facilities. There is no staff but park literature and signs guide you along the 1¼-mile auto route. It takes you past well-preserved Civil War trenches that proved impregnable against frontal attack and influenced battlefield tactics. The nearby Garthright House was used as a field hospital. It is not open, but the exterior has been restored to look as it did in the 1860s. Some portions of the house date from the 1700s.

South of Richmond, the action shifts to Fort Harrison where there is another small Visitor Center open daily in the summer and on weekends in spring and fall. During the summer months Fort Harrison offers living history programs. Miles of breastworks connected the forts that surrounded Fort Harrison. A self-guiding trail leads to a splendid panoramic view of the James River and provides information on the fort and the battles.

The last stop on the blue route is Parker's Battery across the James River. This Confederate battery was one of the important defenses of Richmond that enabled the city to hold out until the very end. It was not until after the ten-month siege of Petersburg that the Confederate pullout finally allowed the Union army access to Richmond.

Richmond National Battlefield Park's Chimborazo Visitor Center is open 9:00 A.M. to 5:00 P.M. daily except December 25 and January 1. There is no admission charge.

Directions: From downtown Richmond take Broad Street east to the Chimborazo Visitor Center at 3215 East Broad Street. From I-95 northbound use Exit 10; if you are traveling south, take Exit 10A.

St. John's Church and St. Paul's Church

Chapels of Liberty

Necessity often forced the Founding Fathers to mix church and state. On one historic occasion in 1775 the Second Virginia Convention chose **St. John's Church** as their meeting place because it was the largest public gathering place in Richmond. On the fourth day of their week long convention Patrick Henry

St. John's Church, made famous by Patrick Henry's immortal "liberty or death" oration in 1775, was built by the great-great-great-grandson of Pocahontas in 1741.

delivered his famous "Liberty or Death" speech. (See Scotchtown and Red Hill selections.)

This historic occasion is reenacted on summer Sundays at 2:00 P.M. from the last weekend in May through the first Sunday in September and on the Sunday closest to March 23, the day on which Henry delivered his impassioned plea. Join with costumed actors portraying Henry, Washington, Jefferson and other Virginia delegates as they debate the future of the American colonies. You are indeed where history happened. Later during the Revolutionary War, Benedict Arnold quartered his troops in St. John's while occupying Richmond.

St. John's, 35 years old when the Revolution began, is now the oldest church in Richmond and one of the oldest surviving wooden buildings in the city. It was built in 1741 on land given to Henrico Parish by William Byrd II. Although the church has been largely restored since colonial days, the high pulpit, transept and many of the pews are original.

Guided tours of the church are given for a nominal admission, Monday through Saturday from 10:00 A.M. to 4:00 P.M. and Sunday from 1:00 to 4:00 P.M. St. John's is closed on Christmas Day and New Year's Eve and Day. Sunday Episcopal worship services are held at 8:30 and 11:00 A.M. with a NOON coffee hour and reception. During hours when tours are conducted a Chapel Gift Shop is open in the old Victorian Gothic Keeper's house.

Also historically significant is **St. Paul's Church** at 815 East Grace Street. You can attend services at NOON Monday through Friday and 11:00 A.M. on Sunday at this church where both Robert E. Lee and Jefferson Davis worshiped. The President of the Confederacy was attending service on Sunday, April 2, 1865, when he received word that Petersburg had fallen and the Union army was marching on Richmond. The fear that spread through the congregation was quickly confirmed by Davis's order to evacuate the city. St. Paul's Church is open Monday through Saturday from 10:00 A.M. to 4:00 P.M. and Sunday 1:00 to 4:00 P.M.

Directions: Take Exit 10 from I-95. St. John's is located at 2401 East Broad Street just down from the Richmond National Battlefield Park. For St. Paul's Church take Broad Street to 8th Street and turn left. Make a right on Grace Street.

Science Museum of Virginia

There's Magic to Do

If you want an excursion that's really out of this world, try the Universe in Richmond. The **Science Museum of Virginia**'s Universe planetarium and space theater includes both Digistar and

Omnimax. This is the first time Digistar has been incorporated into a planetarium projection system. Previously it was used to create special effects in the movie, *Star Trek—The Wrath of Khan.* Omnimax is the world's largest projector; even the projection room is an exhibit of interest. Combined, they provide an optimum viewing experience.

You are more than a spectator at Universe—you will feel like a space traveler moving through the heavens. The mysteries of the universe are explored on a dome screen 76 feet in diameter. Images are created by the Digistar computer pinpointing the location. You'll learn how to identify the stars on your own horizon through graphics that connect the celestial constellations. And you'll be given velocities and brightnesses of 6,772 stars visible from earth.

This new wing added in 1983 is only part of the Science Museum of Virginia which is housed in architect John Russell Pope's historic Broad Street Railroad Station. The museum has other special exhibits you won't want to miss: Crystal World; Illusions, Magic and Science; plus The Computer Works.

The museum's first major permanent exhibit, Crystal World, has hands-on exhibits that have grown and been refined through a process of formative evaluation. Scientists have worked with visitors to make sure the displays are understood and perceived correctly. One pod, or display area, takes you inside a crystal, its mirrored walls giving you a look at the internal composition of crystals. Computer controlled lights change the crystal pattern from atoms inside crystal dust to gold crystals, then to common salt crystals and even to the inner space of that hardest of all crystals, the diamond. Other exhibits show crystals growing, teach you to appreciate the diversified use of crystals and dramatize the magic of crystal symmetry.

The exhibit area called Illusion, Magic and Science teaches a number of lessons in a delightful Alice in Wonderland way. In Alice's Parlor where the slanted floor is calculatedly disguised, things are not as they appear. Alice would have appreciated the experiment that lets you put your head on a plate (a sure-fire set up for amateur photographers). Children and adults alike are apt to play 3-D ghost, plus card tricks and optical games. Science in school was never like this!

Computers are fun, too, and you can try your hand at them in another museum exhibit area. All these exhibits take time; you should plan to spend at least 1½ hours exploring the museum, plus another hour for the Universe show. There are admission prices for both, but you can get a combination ticket.

The Science Museum's exhibit areas are open seven days a week between 11:30 A.M. and 8:00 P.M. Universe programs are given Monday through Friday at 1:00, 3:00 and 8:00 P.M. Saturday and Sunday shows are NOON, 1:00, 3:00, 5:00 and 8:00 P.M. Admission for adults, seniors and children varies depending on your choices.

Directions: The Science Museum of Virginia is located at 2500 West Broad Street. Take Exit 14 from I-95/64.

Scotchtown and Barksdale Theatre

Not-So-Canny Country

A man's home may be his castle, but if he plans to build an actual castle something less than grand may be a disappointment. It was a grandiose dream that inspired Charles Chiswell in 1717 to obtain a land grant from the King of England of 9,976 acres in New Kent County, now Hanover County, Virginia. He envisioned an entire transplanted Scotch community with himself as laird of the castle and hired Scotch architects and laborers to build his town.

The main house, mill and a small group of outbuildings were all that were finished when disease decimated the workers and the project was abandoned. A disillusioned Chiswell lived in the main house until his death in 1737.

Scotchtown's next owner, Charles's son John Chiswell, also had his dreams shattered—his by a too hastily delivered sword thrust. Chiswell's intemperate remarks in a tavern in Cumberland County provoked Robert Routledge into throwing his drink into Chiswell's face. Without thinking Chiswell unsheathed his sword and killed Routledge on the spot. He was immediately arrested and, again acting hastily, committed suicide rather than face certain conviction. Perhaps he was correct in assuming the trial would go against him. Feelings were so strong that Routledge's family, suspicious that his death may have been faked, demanded that the coffin be opened before burial to prove he had indeed perished by his own hand.

Things did not run smoothly for Patrick Henry's family either after they acquired Scotchtown in 1771. Sarah Shelton Henry was left at this rural Virginia home with their six children and 30 slaves while Patrick fulfilled his many political commitments. In the seven years the Henry family lived at Scotchtown, he served in the House of Burgesses in Williamsburg, the First and Second Continental Congresses in Philadelphia and the Second Virginia Convention at St. John's Church in Richmond. It was said you could always tell when Henry was approaching the main thrust of his political speeches by his habit of raising his glasses to the top of his head allowing his eyes to pierce his audience. That well-known pose of his is captured on canvas in a portrait hanging at Scotchtown.

Some historians have conjectured that when he delivered his famous "Liberty or Death" speech at St. John's Church his thoughts may have included, in addition to the plight of the American colonists under British tyranny, the unfortunate curtailment of his own wife's liberty. Due to her deteriorating mental condition, she was kept locked in one of the cellar rooms at Scotchtown until her death in 1775 at the age of 36. She was cared for there by Dr. Thomas Hinde and a nurse, as well as by Patrick Henry's mother and sister.

Patrick Henry's second wife, Dorothea Dandridge, whom he married in 1777 while living in the Palace at Williamsburg, did not want to live at Scotchtown and the plantation was advertised for sale in the *Virginia Gazette* in 1778. The years of Patrick Henry's residency are recaptured in this restored plantation house.

The personality of Patrick Henry is imprinted on the house from the Great Hall, where it is said he enjoyed holding dances, to the spinet in the Ladies' Parlor similar to the one he used to play. An enthusiastic, versatile musician, he taught himself to play the flute while recovering from a broken collarbone. One of the most evocative family pieces is the writing desk in his bedroom that is believed to have been made by his father.

Portraits of the Sheltons, his first wife's family, hang throughout the house. Many are primitive paintings, so called because only the head was done from life. There are two portraits of Dolley Payne Madison, wife of President James Madison, who lived at Scotchtown from the age of 11 months until the age of three, while her father rented the property (some historians believe he was the overseer of the plantation).

Eighteenth-century furnishings reveal a great deal about life in colonial America. The carver type rocker in the children's bedroom has two distinct sections on the back enabling either young or older ladies to use it for drying their hair. They would drape their hair through one of the two openings so it would not get the back of their garments wet. It was the custom of the day to take baths only seasonally. Patrick Henry was frequently accused of being untidy; Thomas Jefferson particularly chafed at his countrified ways.

As you wander around the grounds looking at Patrick Henry's old law office and the other outbuildings, it is not hard to imagine the great man himself strolling beneath the trees. Scotchtown is open April through October on Monday through Saturday from 10:00 A.M. to 4:30 P.M. and on Sundays from 1:30 to 4:30 P.M. Admission is charged.

Patrick Henry worked both before and behind the bar. If you are overnighting in the Richmond area don't miss the chance to visit **Barksdale Theatre** in historic Hanover Tavern, where Patrick Henry often helped out in the taproom. As the wine list at this dinner theater proudly claims, they've been "Serving Fine Wines Since 1723." In 1754 18-year-old Patrick Henry married Sarah Shelton, daughter of Hanover Tavern owner, John Shelton. The young couple lived with her parents for three years while Patrick tried to earn a living at store keeping, farming and finally the law.

When the Barksdale Theatre opened in 1953 it was the nation's first dinner theater. You'll dine by candlelight at this tavern that once hosted both George Washington and Lord Cornwallis, though not on the same evening. We know from Washington's diaries that when business or politics brought him to Richmond he often sought dining or lodging at Hanover Tavern. The tavern's Washington Room has a large portrait of Washington over the fireplace, and back in a corner alcove there is a small portrait of Cornwallis, who left without paying the bill for his 18-day stay.

When you make reservations for dinner and the professionally performed play that follows, request a guided tour of the Hanover Courthouse and Old Jail directly across from the tavern. Tours are given at no charge 30 minutes before the buffet dinner. It was at this courthouse that Patrick Henry delivered what is considered by many historians the first attack on the tyranny of George III. Barksdale Theatre is open Wednesday through Saturday, call (804)798-6547.

Directions: From I-95 take Ashland Exit, Route 54. Continue through Ashland for 8½ miles to Route 671 and turn right. Make another right turn on Route 685 for Scotchtown. Parking is available on the grounds and there are picnic tables in a tree-shaded grove. Barksdale Theatre is only 15 minutes from Scotchtown. Take Route 54 past the I-95 intersection to Hanover Courthouse. The courthouse is on the left and the Hanover Tavern is on the right. From I-95 take Ashland Exit, Route 54 east.

Valentine Museum and Wickham-Valentine House

Richmond, This Is Your Life!

The **Valentine Museum**'s three-dimensional chronicle of Richmond's past blends reminders of historical figures with mementos from the daily life of anonymous city residents. This continuing exhibition, "Richmond Revisited," tells the story of

Richmond from the days when Indians camped along the James River to its present renaissance. It also includes a 20-minute film, *Richmond Remembers Two Hundred Years*, narrated by Earl Hammer, creator of the TV series, *The Waltons*.

Supplementing the historic Richmond exhibit are collections of the work of 18th- and 19th-century Richmond silversmiths, firearms, tobacco-related paraphernalia and candlesticks. The museum's fine arts collection of over 1,400 paintings is worth a day's visit in itself. Also of major importance is the textile collection, one of the nation's finest. Needlework, costumes and accessories from around the world are displayed on a rotating basis. Priceless laces, appliquéd bedspreads, rugs, draperies and the tools used to create them are all part of the exhibit. The Children's Gallery, with its large collection of old toys and its re-creation of a 19th-century one-room schoolhouse, is a favorite of youngsters.

The Valentine Museum docents conduct tours of the **Wickham-Valentine House**. They take visitors outside onto Clay Street so that you enter at the front door. John Wickham, prominent Richmond attorney, had this elegant neoclassical, 17-room mansion built in 1812 at a cost of $70,000. It is now designated a National Historic Landmark and houses a treasure trove of Victorian decorative arts.

On entering the house you'll see the 18-inch brick walls overlaid with stucco to look like marble. The cantilevered staircase winds upward to an opening at the top shaped like an artist's palette. The banister is carved with magnolia seed pods, dogwood blossoms and periwinkle. The oval ladies' parlor is unusually beautiful. On its walls are paintings of scenes from Homer's *Iliad*, done during Wickham's residency and subsequently overpainted. Only recently discovered, they are now being carefully uncovered and restored.

Mr. Wickham, the Perry Mason of his day, conducted his law practice from his very masculine library. His most famous case was the successful defense of Aaron Burr in his trial for treason before Chief Justice Marshall at the Virginia State Capitol.

The drawing room was redecorated by the second owner, Mr. Ballard. A noteworthy piece in this room is the large portrait of a young Queen Victoria. Dressed in an elegant gown with shoulders bared, she little resembles portraits done later when she was queen. It is, in fact, one of only four such early portraits.

In the dining room is a portrait of another owner, Mann Valentine, who gave Richmond both his house and his collections of art and archeology to be displayed in the "Valentine Museum" which opened on November 21, 1898. In this portrait he is only eight months old. The dining room also has the original Wickham porcelain dining service shipped intact from China in 1814.

The upstairs bedrooms include period furnishings from 1885 to 1892 and costumed manikins. An open ladies' closet allows a glimpse of plumed hats, beaded bags and delicately decorated shoes, some of the excesses of the day. Form certainly doesn't follow function as far as the bed in the master suite is concerned. It's an old sleigh bed decorated with swans. There are also bedrooms for the 19 children—the nursery plus the girls' and boys' bedrooms.

The garden is the oldest in continuous use in Richmond. It is maintained in accordance with the original landscape specifications. Within the garden you'll find the sculpture studio of Edward V. Valentine, a noted 19th-century artist and brother of Mann Valentine. You'll see the tools of his trade and both completed and unfinished work. Valentine's best known piece is the "Recumbent Lee" that marks the general's tomb at Washington and Lee University.

Now that you have a perspective on Richmond's past, walk down 9th Street to City Hall and take the elevator to the Skydeck. From here you can get a great view of the changes that have occurred, and you can enjoy lunch at umbrella-covered tables.

The Valentinue Museum and Wickham-Valentine House are open Monday through Saturday from 10:00 A.M. to 5:00 P.M. and Sunday from 1:00 to 5:00 P.M. Admission is charged but block tickets can be purchased as part of the Court End Tour that includes the Marshall House, Brockenbrough House (White House of the Confederacy) and Wickham House. (See other selections.)

Directions: Take Exit 10 from I-95, Broad Street west. Continue on Broad Street to 11th Street, then turn right. Follow 11th Street to Clay Street and turn left. Make another left on 10th Street and the museum parking lot will be on your left. From I-64 take Exit 43, 5th Street south. Continue on 5th to Marshall Street and take a left. From Marshall take another left on 11th and left again on Clay Street. Make a last left on 10th Street and the parking lot will be on your left.

Virginia Museum of Fine Arts and The Fan

State of the Art

Richmond's **Virginia Museum of Fine Arts**, America's first statewide arts system, opened in 1936. In December 1985, it effectively doubled its gallery space with the addition of a West Wing, containing the collections of the two gallery sponsors: the Mellons and the Lewises.

The Czarevitch Egg of lapis, diamonds and gold, which con-
cealed a miniature portrait of the Czarevitch Alexis, is in the
outstanding Fabergé egg collection at the Virginia Museum of
Fine Arts. Virginia Museum of Fine Arts

In lofty oversized rooms the Sydney and Francis Lewis collection of Art Nouveau, Art Deco and Contemporary Art is on display. The Mellon's fine selection of Impressionist and Post-Impressionistic Art is hung in smaller, more intimate rooms. These are added to the museum's already exciting collection which spans the past 5,000 years of art. Surrounding the Mediterranean Court, where Sunday concerts are held, are the galleries of the Ancient World, Asia, the Classical Era and Ancient America.

The first century, A.D., life-size statue of the Roman Emperor Caligula is one of the museum's prize pieces. But this is not the work best remembered by Virginia schoolchildren; their favorite is the Egyptian mummy sarcophagus. Another piece in the Egyptian collection, the Seated Scribe, has an interesting story. The two halves of the Seated Scribe were acquired separately, the top part added 13 years after the bottom was purchased by the museum. The figure now looks as it did originally in the years between 663 and 525 B.C. during the Saite Period in the XXVI Dynasty.

Another favorite with visitors is the lovely gallery of Fabergé Easter Eggs and Russian Imperial Jewels. The museum also has a prized set of Gobelin tapestries illustrating the story of Don Quixote. In order to match the splendor of the new wing, the older galleries have also undergone extensive refurbishing at a cost of roughly $100,000 per gallery. Skylights have been uncovered to let in new light on the old masters—Degas, Goya, Matisse, Picasso, Monet, Brueghel, Rembrandt and Gainsborough.

The Virginia Museum also houses Theatre Virginia, one of America's leading professional residential theaters. This 32-year-old, 500-seat theater puts on six Broadway and Off-Broadway plays a year from October through May. During July the museum hosts "Jumpin' in July," a series of Thursday evening jazz and pop music programs in the garden.

The Virginia Museum's Sculpture Garden is itself one of the most beautiful spots in Richmond. It is equally pleasant for a morning stroll, al fresco lunch, afternoon tea or evening concert. The garden's focus is the massive fountain. The sound of the cascading water seems to lower the temperature on warm summer days. The public cafeteria is adjacent to the garden, and trees and umbrellas provide shade for those who enjoy eating outside. Colorful blossoms enhance the sculpture, some of which is on loan from the Whitney Museum of American Art, the Hirshhorn Museum and the Museum of Modern Art.

The Virginia Museum is open Tuesday through Saturday from 11:00 A.M. to 5:00 P.M., Thursday evenings until 10:00 P.M. and on Sunday from 1:00 to 5:00 P.M. It is closed on Mondays and major holidays. Visitors are asked to make a minimum one dollar donation. Seniors and children under 16 are free.

The Virginia Museum is located in the Fan, a district of restored homes, charming cafés, arty boutiques and antique shops. The Fan extends north to Monument Avenue, south to Main Street, east to Laurel Street and west to Boulevard. The once decaying turn-of-the-century townhouses have been reconstructed and are now popular with the faculty and students of Virginia Commonwealth University. One of the favorite neighborhood eateries is Strawberry Street Café at 421 North Strawberry Street. You understand why once you get a look at its cheery red and white tablecloths, stained glass decorative arch, an old-fashioned bathtub with salad fixings and blackboard drawings of café specialties.

Directions: The Virginia Museum is in Richmond's near West End at the corner of the Boulevard and Grove Avenue.

The Virginia State Capitol

Capital Idea!

Age isn't everything, but it is a lot in Richmond. The **Virginia State Capitol** is the second oldest working capitol in the United States (after Annapolis, Maryland). The Virginia Capitol has been in continuous use since it was built to Thomas Jefferson's specifications in 1788. Jefferson modeled this Classical Revival building on the Maison Carree, an ancient Roman temple he admired in Nimes, France.

The Virginia State Capitol does have a dome, as did all of the buildings that Thomas Jefferson helped design, but it is not visible from the exterior. The rotunda dome, 20 feet below the roof, can only be seen from within.

Beneath the skylighted dome stands the life-size statue of George Washington done by French artist, Jean Antoine Houdon. Houdon visited Mount Vernon, and George Washington posed for this work, the only Washington statue done from life. Houdon carved it from Carrara marble and exhibited the statue in the Louvre before shipping it to America in 1796. As you look at the statue you can almost feel the trouser legs gathered into the tight boots. The veins are clearly visible beneath the taut gloves, even the strands of braid on the epaulets can be discerned.

When Lafayette saw the statue he said, "This is the man, himself, I can almost realize he is going to move." How fortunate that he appreciated the work of Houdon because the sculptor also did a bust of Lafayette, which is displayed in the Rotunda. Lafayette and John D. Rockefeller are the only two non-Virginians honored in the Capitol. Encircling the statue of the first president are niches containing busts of the seven other Virginia presidents—Thomas Jefferson, James Madison, James Monroe, William Henry Harrison, John Tyler, Zachary Taylor and Woodrow Wilson.

A portrait of the second honorary Virginian, John D. Rockefeller, who merited this distinction for his work in restoring Colonial Williamsburg, hangs in the Old Senate Chamber. The chandelier-lit chamber has two additional paintings. One depicts the three ships that first brought settlers to Virginia in May 1607: the *Susan Constant, Godspeed* and *Discovery*. The other large painting shows the Revolutionary forces storming the British Redoubt Number 10 during the Battle of Yorktown on October 14, 1781.

The final room on your Capitol tour is the Old House of Delegates chamber, scene of many historic events. The Virginia House of Delegates met here from 1788 to 1906 as did the Confederate Congress while Richmond served as the capital of the Confederacy. In 1807 Aaron Burr was acquitted of treason in a trial before U.S. Chief Justice John Marshall. More than 50 years later on April 23, 1861, Robert E. Lee stood in this room and accepted command of the Virginia armies. A bronze statue of Lee now stands on the very place he stood.

Lee is one of many Virginians honored here. There are busts of such Revolutionary statesmen as George Mason, Richard Henry Lee, Patrick Henry and George Wythe. Some of the Confederate heroes also commemorated are Stonewall Jackson, J.E.B. Stuart, Joseph E. Johnson and Fitzhugh Lee. Two non-Virginians who figured prominently in the destiny of the South are also represented—Jefferson Davis, President of the Confederacy and his Vice-President, Alexander H. Stephens. Finally there are busts of Henry Clay, Matthew Fontain Maury, John Marshall, Sam Houston and Cyrus McCormick.

One item not to be missed in this chamber is the Edwardian-style mace that rests on a table in front of the Speaker's chair. This symbol of government was presented to the Virginia House of Delegates in 1974 by the Jamestown Foundation. The mace was made in England of silver with a 24-karat gold wash.

You can tour the State Capitol any day of the week at no charge. From April through November the hours are 9:00 A.M. to 5:00 P.M. From December through March Sunday hours change to 1:00 to 5:00 P.M.

Directions: The Virginia State Capitol is on Capitol Square between 9th and 11th Streets in downtown Richmond.

The White House and Museum of the Confederacy

FFV

Traditionally attributed to Robert Mills, architect of the Washington Monument, the two-story townhouse of Dr. John Brockenbrough at 12th and Clay Streets in Richmond has survived the vicissitudes of time.

It has not, however, remain unchanged. In the 1850s the Brockenbrough house was architecturally altered to include a third floor and a cupola, and Victorian features were added to the interior. One of the finest in Richmond, the house was purchased by the city in June 1861 for Jefferson Davis, president of the Confederacy. When he would not accept it as a gift, the city rented it to the Southern states to be used as "the **White House of the Confederacy**." The Davis family was in residence until March 1865 when Varina Davis and her four children fled.

During Reconstruction, 1865–1870, the former White House was used as U.S. Army headquarters for Military District Number 1. Alterations were made when it was converted to use as a public school, but by 1890 it was in such sad repair the city considered tearing it down. It was saved by the Confederate Memorial Literary Society, a group that evolved from a ladies' organization devoted to tending the Confederate graves at Richmond's Hollywood Cemetery. The addition of the word "literary" gave justification for the transfer of this former city school to private hands. It also reflected the national interest in the South evoked by the late 19th-century literary movement of Southern authors.

The house was repaired and opened as a museum by the Confederate Memorial Literary Society in 1896. The very existence of this museum prompted donations from throughout the South, and the collection grew.

By 1976 a new Museum of the Confederacy had been built adjacent to the old Brockenbrough House. The personal effects of Robert E. Lee, including the sword he wore at Appomattox, are the museum's most prized pieces. There are military weapons and uniforms belonging to Stonewall Jackson, J.E.B. Stuart, Joseph E. Johnson and A.P. Hill, and many uniforms, letters and mementos from the soldiers who fought the battles the generals planned. Dresses, jewelry and letters from the women who fought the battles at home are also prominently featured.

With the opening of the new museum, work began on restoring the White House to its appearance during the Davis residency. The ground floor houses an exhibit introducing visitors to the

Jefferson Davis family. Above it, on the first floor, will be the public rooms of the Executive Mansion that served as the social center for the political and military leaders of the Confederacy. The second floor will be restored to its use as the Davis family quarters complete with nursery, private office and master bedroom. The third floor contains curatorial and educational facilities.

The neoclassical Brockenbrough House is included in the Court End block ticket (see John Marshall and Wickham House selections). It, along with the Museum of the Confederacy, is open Monday through Saturday from 10:00 A.M. to 5:00 P.M. Admission is charged.

Directions: From I-95 or I-64 eastbound take Exit 10, Broad Street. Go west on Broad Street. From Broad Street turn right onto 11th Street and then turn right again onto Marshall Street. From Marshall turn left onto 12th Street. The Museum of the Confederacy is on the right at the corner of 12th and Clay Streets. There is a parking deck at the end of Clay Street.

Wilton and Tuckahoe

Randolph Riches

Wilton, like neighboring Agecroft Hall, was dismantled and moved brick by brick to a new location. But Wilton's journey was far shorter, a mere ten miles up the James River rather than 3,000 miles across the Atlantic (see Agecroft selection).

Wilton, a Georgian brick plantation house, was built for William Randolph III between 1747 and 1753. William, like others in his family, served in the Virginia militia (he was a Colonel) and was a delegate to the House of Burgesses. William married Ann Carter Harrison of Berkeley (see Berkeley selection) in 1743 and reared seven children at Wilton. Many noted historical figures enjoyed the hospitality of his 2,000-acre plantation.

An entry in George Washington's diary reads, "March 25, 1775. Returned to the Convention in Richmond. Dined at Galt's and went to Mrs. Randolph's of Wilton. 26. Stayed at Wilton all day." One of the bedrooms is decorated to look as it did during Washington's visit. Thomas Jefferson frequently visited his cousins at Wilton. His mother was a Randolph from nearby Tuckahoe.

During the final year of the American Revolution May 15–20, 1781, General Lafayette made Wilton his headquarters. He moved on to Richmond when Cornwallis crossed the James River and headed in Wilton's direction.

Today you can enjoy the hospitality of Wilton, thanks to the efforts of The National Society of the Colonial Dames of America in the Commonwealth of Virginia. In 1933 when Wilton was facing demolition and a museum was negotiating for the parlor paneling, this group under the direction of Mrs. Granville Gray Valentine saved the house. Although Wilton stood empty for years it has now been beautifully restored and furnished with 17th- and 18th-century period pieces, many belonging to the Randolph family.

Your tour begins in the central hallway. The so-called back door was the main, or river, entrance when the James was the main highway between plantations. One of the finest antiques at Wilton is the mahogany tall-case clock in the hallway made in 1795 by Simon Willard. Before you leave the hall be sure to take a close look at the stair railing crafted from a single piece of walnut.

The parlor is included in Helen Comstock's book, *100 Most Beautiful Rooms in America*. The 12 carved pillars are among the most attractive features of the room. The curtained alcoves flanking the marble fireplace add to the parlor's symmetry. The earliest record of furnishings is an 1815 family inventory, but there are several pieces that belonged to builder William and his son Peyton years before then. A secretary made in New York and listed in the inventory is in the library and their desk made in Richmond is in an upstairs bedroom.

In all, you'll see ten family portraits originally painted to hang at Wilton in 1755. They have been loaned to Wilton by the Virginia Historical Society. The Garden Club of Virginia has also made a contribution by landscaping the grounds. Be sure to stroll around the grounds after your tour.

Wilton is open Tuesday through Saturday from 10:00 A.M. to 4:30 P.M. It is closed on Monday (except by advance appointments), national holidays and during the month of August. Wilton also closes on Sunday in July, reopening to Sunday visitors after Labor Day. No tours are given on the second Thursday of the month from October through May. Admission is charged.

After touring Wilton why not head just a little farther out of town to **Tuckahoe Plantation**. You will need to call ahead for an appointment, (804)784-5736. If you feel you recognize the house on your first visit, it is probably because you remember the country scenes filmed here for Williamsburg's orientation film, *The Story of a Patriot*.

Thomas Jefferson lived at Tuckahoe, his mother's home, between the ages of two and nine. The schoolhouse where Jefferson began his studies is matched on the other side of the main house by the plantation office. The rare outbuildings and H-shaped house are according to architectural historian Frederick Nichols, "the most complete plantation layout in North America dating from the early 18th century."

Tuckahoe's interior features some of the most important architectural ideas of the early Georgian period. The house is still a home, and the young couple who live at Tuckahoe conduct the guided tours. They have a wealth of old stories to share with visitors.

Directions: From Richmond center take Main Street to Cary Street (Route 147) west. At the 6900 block of Cary Street turn south on Wilton Road. Follow Wilton Road to the James River. Ample parking is available on the grounds. To reach Tuckahoe from Wilton turn left on Cary Street and continue to River Road. Turn right on River Road. When you pass Parham Road South it is 4.6 miles farther down River Road to Tuckahoe's entrance on the left. The entrance road is flanked by white pillars, and there is an historical marker.

PETERSBURG

Blandford Church

Memorial Day Birthplace

Memorial Day observances began at **Blandford Church** on Well's Hill in Petersburg, Virginia, not on the last weekend in May as it is observed today but on June 9, 1866. It was on that day that Mary Cunningham Logan, wife of General John A. Logan, saw young school girls placing flowers on the graves of slain Confederate soldiers. When Mrs. Logan learned from the girls' headmistress, Nora Davidson, that they intended to hold a "Decoration Day" every year, she urged her husband to propose extending the gesture nationwide. As Commander-in-Chief of the Grand Army of the Republic, General Logan spearheaded the work for the establishment of an official Memorial Day. His objective was achieved when by Act of Congress the occasion was first celebrated across the country on May 30, 1868.

The history of Old Blandford Church does not start with the War Between the States. The church, the oldest building in Petersburg, was built in 1735. The earliest date on a gravestone is 1702, the year that Richard Scarborough died at the age of 87. When the British lost the Revolutionary War the Church of England, or Protestant Episcopal Church as it was then called, lost members. In the year 1799 only six services were held at Blandford Church, one a memorial service for George Washington. The church was abandoned entirely by 1819.

The city of Petersburg added a new roof to the deteriorating building in 1882. But it was not until 1901 that the Ladies

Memorial Association of Petersburg undertook its reconstruction. During the Civil War Blandford Church had served as a hospital for wounded Confederate soldiers. More than 30,000 Confederate dead were laid to rest in the church cemetery. To honor these sons of the south the Ladies Association of Petersburg commissioned Louis Comfort Tiffany to design windows for the rebuilt church, one for each of the southern states plus the three border states of Maryland, Missouri and Kentucky. Each state had to raise the money for its window (about $450). Louisiana's window, commissioned and paid for by the Washington Artillery of New Orleans, was the only regiment represented. All the states paid except divided Kentucky which had already arranged its own memorial. Tiffany donated the 15th window, the "Cross of Jewels." This window, even more than his other works, has the iridescence of jewels. Tiffany, an experienced chemist, developed a unique way for embedding semi-precious stones in the glass so that the refracted light created a kaleidoscope of color. And he added crushed copper, gold and cobalt for special depth and lustre. No one has ever been able to duplicate Tiffany's artistic creations. On the morning after his death, at his direction, his formula and notes were destroyed.

The church contains several memorial plaques. One honors the men who lost their lives in the Battle of the Crater. Their gallant commander, General William Mahone, who led the Crater charge is at his request buried in the churchyard with the unknown Confederate soldier. On a church wall there is a poem written while the church was still in ruins and attributed to the Irish actor Tyrone Power, grandfather of the Hollywood star:

> Thou art crumbling to the dust, old pile,
> Thou art hastening to thy fall,
> And 'round thee in thy loneliness
> Clings the ivy to thy wall
> The worshippers are scattered now
> Who knelt before thy shrine,
> And silence reigns where anthems rose,
> In days of "Auld Lang Syne."

The poetic atmosphere of the historic graveyard has been the scene of more than one duel. On one notable occasion when two suitors, R. C. Adams and James B. Boisseau, were fighting for the affections of Ellen Stimson, they were both mortally wounded. Dr. Ira Ellis Smith, who was called to their sides failed to save his patients, but he saved Miss Stimson by marrying her. On the last Sunday of every month except December, there is a guided walking tour of Blandford Cemetery at 2:00 P.M.

An interpretative center adjacent to the church offers an 18-minute slide presentation that will enrich your tour of

Blandford. You can visit Monday through Saturday from 9:00 A.M. to 5:00 P.M. and on Sunday from NOON to 5:00 P.M. A nominal admission is charged.

Directions: Take I-95 to Petersburg. Take the Wythe Street Exit and go east on Wythe Street for one block, then turn right on Crater Road, Route 301-640. Blandford Church is located on Crater Road.

Centre Hill Mansion and Trapezium House

Front and Centre but No Right Angles

Two totally different homes in Old Towne Petersburg evoke the 19th century. **Centre Hill** overlooking the town is the third hilltop home of the wealthy Bowling family. In 1823 when Robert Bowling was 64 he built Centre Hill for his fourth wife. The architectural eclecticism of Petersburg is nowhere more evident than at Centre Hill, built in the Federal style but remodeled twice. Robert Buckner Bowling who inherited the house from his father in the late 1840s added a Greek Revival look to Centre Hill. At the turn of the century Mr. and Mrs. Charles Hall Davis purchased the house and remodeled it along the then popular Georgian Revival style.

It is the affluent era before the siege of Petersburg that is re-created today at Centre Hill. Your entrance to the house is less dramatic than it would have been in the 1850s. Guests at that time made their way from the river via a tunnel. Despite rumors to the contrary, this was for the convenience of the guests. It was not used for smuggling goods or by escaping slaves.

Centre Hill has some unique furnishings. On the marble mantlepiece are two fire-screens once held by the ladies to protect their wax make-up and a clock commemorating Lord Nelson's victory at the Battle of the Nile. In the dining room is the forerunner of the wet bar, a zinc sink, ideal for wine and beverages. But it is the 24-karat gold-trimmed dinner service that has an interesting story. If you think you have troubles with delivery service today, consider that it took five years for these dishes to get here from the Minton factory in England. The ship on which they were sent had to bypass the Union naval blockade around Petersburg. Then the shipment had to be smuggled past Grant's forces surrounding the city. The dishes finally were delivered during the Christmas season of 1864 and by that time there was no food to serve on them. During that Christmas season there were only "starvation balls."

The President's Room is an upstairs bedroom named in honor of the night in May 1909 when incumbent William Howard Taft stayed here before dedicating the Pennsylvania Monument in Petersburg. He was the third president to visit Centre Hill. John Tyler visited as a personal friend of the Bowlings. Abraham Lincoln stopped once to confer with General George Z. Hartsuff when this was his Petersburg headquarters.

You too can visit Centre Hill from 9:00 A.M. to 5:00 P.M. Monday through Saturday and Sunday 12:30 to 5:00 P.M. except on major holidays. There is a nominal charge. Parking for Centre Hill is located at Tabb and Adams Streets.

The **Trapezium House** just a few blocks away is named for its odd shape. Its owner, Charles O'Hara, an Irish bachelor, was a bit odd himself. There are absolutely no right angles in his house—walls, stairs, floors, windows and even the mantles were all set at an angle. Legend has it that O'Hara built the house in 1816 in response to a warning from a West Indian servant that right angles harbored evil spirits.

O'Hara kept a pet monkey, parrot and white rats. He may well have found the animals more compatible than his boarders. His mistrust of people is obvious from the way he numbered logs beside the fire. This curious house at Market and High Streets can be toured for a small charge 9:00 A.M. to 5:00 P.M. Monday through Saturday and 12:30 to 5:00 P.M. on Sunday except major holidays.

Directions: Take I-95 south to Petersburg, then use Exit 3 onto East Washington Street into Old Towne. Turn right on S. Sycamore and proceed to the end of the street. Then turn right for the Farmers Bank/Information Center parking lot.

Petersburg National Battlefield

Monumental Blow-Up

Do you know where the greatest man-made explosion before World War I occurred? At Petersburg, Virginia, during the longest siege in American warfare. Had the Battle of the Crater turned out differently, the siege would have ended after little more than a month instead of ten long months later. It might even have brought an earlier end to the War Between the States.

General Ulysses S. Grant marshalled his army against Petersburg on June 15, 1864 after a failed frontal assault on Richmond, the Confederate capital. In the early days of the siege a plan was evolved to tunnel under the Confederate lines. Coal miners and other men from the 48th Pennsylvania Infantry began digging a 511-foot tunnel (when you add the two galleries used for powder magazines the total length was 586 feet). At 4:45 A.M.

on July 30, 1864 they exploded four tons of powder beneath the unsuspecting Confederates. The southern troops had heard rumors that the Yankees were trying to dig beneath their lines, but they didn't know where or when. Petersburg had buzzed with tales of the tunnel for weeks.

The gigantic upheaval on July 30th created a 170 × 60-foot crater that was 30 feet deep. The black division selected to lead the charge after the explosion was replaced at the last minute with an untrained force out of fear that the Union command would be accused of needlessly sacrificing black troops. The use of a poorly prepared division brought just such an unnecessary loss of life. Amid the noise and smoke from the eruption that sent men and equipment hurtling into the sky the Union troops, who had entered the Crater out of curiosity and lack of proper management by the regimental commanders, panicked. The Union casualties came to 4,400 while the Confederates against whom the attack was launched suffered only 1,500 casualties.

You can see the Crater and the tunnel entrance on a **Petersburg Battlefield** auto tour. Park at Stop 8 and take the short trail to the Crater. Exhibits and audio stations will provide more details on the action. To obtain a more complete picture of the longest siege any American city has been forced to withstand, be sure to see the map presentation at the Visitor Center. The War Room has a nine-foot, three-dimensional map that traces the action on what was the largest battlefield of the Civil War. After this introduction, walk the short loop trail from the Visitor Center to the Dictator. Although this is not the mortar positioned at Petersburg, it is an original 17,000-pound Seacoast Mortar. The Dictator lobbed 200-pound shells into Petersburg just 2½ miles away.

During the summer months from mid-June to mid-August the park sponsors a living history program. There are artillery demonstrations daily at 11:00 A.M., 2:30 and 4:30 P.M. (except Monday and Tuesday). It's exciting to watch soldiers representing Louisiana's Washington Artillery, with their battleflags flying, gallop up the hill past the earthenwork remains of Fort Stedman. Their six-horse team pulls the cannon and timber. Horses were so vital to the war effort they were always carefully unhitched before the cannon was placed in position. The men fire the 12-pound Napoleon field gun according to standard Civil War drill.

The gun crew carefully explains each step of the firing, does a run through and then suggests visitors hold their ears—the Napoleon makes a mighty noise. You'll learn that the 12-pound balls could travel for one mile. Then you can examine the Table of Fire on the ammunition chest that gun crews used to determine projectory and the amount of powder needed to hit the target. At NOON and 3:30 P.M. the smaller 24 Pounder Coehorn Mortar, which had a ¾ mile range, is fired. Between firings the crew and their horses can be found resting beneath the trees near Fort Stedman.

During the summer other soldiers representing the 200th Pennsylvania Volunteer Infantry are on hand daily from 9:00 A.M. to 6:00 P.M. at auto Stop 3. They'll show you around their camp and talk about camp life. You'll learn that during the summer the infantry men shared dog tents, forerunner of the army pup tents. The name came from the men's claim that they weren't fit for a dog to sleep in. There is also a winter hut of the type that was shared by two officers or from four to six enlisted men. Near the living quarters is a surgical field tent, far more primitive than anything seen in the T.V. show M.A.S.H.; a member of the medical branch of the Union army tells you about the hazards of Civil War field medicine.

It is the maze of connecting earthenwork trenches that fascinate visitors most. It's one thing to read about siege lines and another to walk behind the earth embankments and imagine being under fire with no greater protection than a mound of dirt. There were 70 miles of trenches around Petersburg.

Also in the camp area is the Sutler Store where soldiers could buy supplies and the latest newspaper which meant it was only two weeks out-of-date. Members of the U.S. Sanitary Commission are on hand as they would have been during the long siege to hand out provisions and medical supplies. They were the forerunners of the Red Cross volunteers.

It is certainly more interesting to plan a visit to Petersburg National Battlefield when you can take advantage of these programs which re-create military life in 1864. If you have time you can also join a 20-minute conducted walking tour which begins at Confederate Battery 5, auto Stop 1. The walking tours are given Monday through Friday at 10:20, 11:20 A.M., 2:20 and 3:20 P.M.— also at 12:20 and 4:20 P.M. on weekends. All of these excellent interpretative programs are provided at no charge.

Directions: Take I-95 south, exit on Route 36 and go left on East Washington Street to Petersburg National Battlefield Park.

Quartermaster Museum

Head for the QM, PDQ!

The opening shot of Steven Spielberg's enormously popular *Close Encounters of the Third Kind* shows the crew of a World War II fighter emerging through the swirling desert sand. This mystifying scene suggests the true-to-life discovery in 1960 of the bomber, "Lady Be Good," which disappeared over the Libyan desert in April 1943. The **Quartermaster Museum** at Fort Lee, Virginia, displays rations and gear from that ill-fated mission that were found 450 miles south of Bengazi. There is a quote from a diary found on the body of one of the five doomed crewmen: ". . . could make it," he wrote, "if we had water; just enough to put our tongues to. . ."

The collection of military uniforms, though less poignant, is fascinating. One of the world's most complete collections, it dates from the 1700s to the present and includes boots, helmets and all kinds of special gear such as fearsome looking gas masks and padded dog-training suits.

Many well-known military leaders are remembered. The museum has General George S. Patton's 1944 jeep with its "steamboat trombones" or air horns and General Dwight D. Eisenhower's 1940 mess jacket and his "pinks and greens" dress uniform. Amid the many presidential banners used by Taft, Wilson, Harding, Truman and both Roosevelts is the original 50-star flag presented to President Eisenhower.

The museum reveals the diverse functions of the Army Quartermaster Corps from providing housing, food, clothing and transportation to arranging funerals. You'll learn how much the rations of the U.S. soldier, now considered the best fed in the world, have changed from the fire cakes and water that were standard fare at Valley Forge.

The Corps also quarters and equips animals used by the military. There's a delightful old recruitment poster that tells potential soldiers, "Join the Cavalry and Have a Courageous Friend . . . The Horse is Man's Noblest Companion." The era of the horse soldier is illustrated by a display on the Ninth and Tenth Cavalry, whose black ranks were known as the "Buffalo Soldiers." You'll also see a reconstructed saddler's workshop and blacksmith shop.

In the military funeral exhibit, look for the elaborate black caisson used in the funeral of Jefferson Davis on May 31, 1893, and in 1875 for General George Pickett. There is also the architect's original model for the Tomb of the Unknown Soldier at Arlington Cemetery. A somber black drum used in the funeral cortege of John F. Kennedy causes many a visitor to stop and stand solemnly before it.

There is so much to see that visitors with special interests can spend hours. The Hall of Heraldry alone has thousands of examples of crests, patches, plaques and flags. The QM, as it is called, is open Monday through Friday from 8:00 A.M. to 5:00 P.M. and on weekends and holidays, from 11:00 A.M. to 5:00 P.M. It is closed on Thanksgiving, Christmas and New Year's.

Directions: Take the Fort Lee Exit (signs also indicate directions to the QM Museum) from I-95 just before Petersburg. The QM is located off Route 36, east of Petersburg. The museum is just inside the main gate of Fort Lee. You do not need a special pass; just tell the guard you plan to visit the museum.

Siege Museum

The Echoes Remain

"You can still find the old city if you look, you can hear it if you listen," says Petersburg native Joseph Cotton as he narrates the inspiring movie shown at the **Siege Museum** about the ten months Petersburg was under siege. It was a time of courage and a time of fortitude; no other American city has endured such a long trial.

Petersburg became the Union target because General Ulysses S. Grant believed it was "the key to taking Richmond." He felt the key to taking Petersburg was severing the five railroad lines that fed the city. At the Siege Museum it is the civilians' side of this last great struggle of the War Between the States that is told. They suffered almost daily shelling.

The museum's exhibit of shells reveals that the never ending bombardment left few buildings unmarked. Shells flew so thick and fast they even met in midair, as you will discover. The relatively small size of most of the shells meant that almost all of the damage was repairable.

Personal accounts from diaries and letters lend poignancy to the fear and hunger the townspeople endured. Although they had little to share, ladies smuggled what they could to the men protecting the city. They carried food, supplies and messages beneath their crinolines. Miss Anne Pigman ran the blockade disguised as a poor market woman. Fortunately gallantry was observed by both sides. Had she been required to lift her skirts even an inch, she would have revealed not only smuggled goods but her $60 shoes, a sure giveaway. The expensive shoes are now on display in the museum.

The display on "The City and Its People" re-creates a portion of a typical Petersburg parlor and an office from the Bank of the City of Petersburg. There's also a children's desk and school box indicative of the normal routines the citizens tried to follow.

A more comprehensive look at banking in Petersburg is given at the Information Center located in the Farmers Bank Museum in Old Towne, easily located by following the bright red Petersburg Tour markers. Banks in the 1800s were primarily for the wealthy, so the Farmers Bank was established to serve the common man. The bank museum has a cashier's office with a printing press used to print Confederate money, a teller's office with a small safe made at the Petersburg iron works, plus a bank vault where you can see the hidden chamber beneath the regular vault. You'll learn that when customers applied for a loan, directors would vote with marbles. The black marble indicated a no confidence vote, hence the derivation of the word "blackball."

The Information Center and Siege Museum are located within a block of each other. Except for holidays both are open daily, 9:00 A.M. to 5:00 P.M. Monday through Saturday and 12:30 to 5:00 P.M. on Sunday. There is a small charge for the Siege Museum. On your stroll from one to the other you can browse through the boutiques and antique shops in Old Towne. Along the main street there are two excellent spots for lunch, The Food Shop and The French Betsy.

Directions: From Richmond take I-95 south to Petersburg, Exit 3, Washington Street. Follow Washington Street to the fifth traffic signal and turn right onto Market Street. At the second traffic signal turn right onto Bank Street. The Siege Museum is at 15 W. Bank Street and free public parking is available behind the museum.

HOPEWELL

City Point Unit and Appomattox Manor

Who's Living on the Eppes's Lawn?

During the American Revolution, George Washington received the rank of Lieutenant-General. This rank was not bestowed again until late in the War Between the States, on March 9, 1864, when President Lincoln made Ulysses S. Grant Commander-in-Chief of all the Union armies, with full control over 17 different commands and more than a half million soldiers.

Grant lost 18,000 men at the Wilderness battlefield, another 19,000 at Spotsylvania, where the fiercest 24-hour period of the war occurred at the "Bloody Angle," followed by yet 12,000 more at Cold Harbor near Richmond. These reverses caused Grant to hesitate and not close in when he attacked the Confederate forces in Petersburg in June 1864. A small number of Confederate soldiers, the old, infirm and young, were all that were available to defend the city. The war may well have ended earlier if he had pursued the attack. But Grant's enormous losses made him cautious, and instead of continuing the attack he dug in first at Petersburg then at nearby **City Point**, Virginia.

From City Point he monitored the ten month siege of Petersburg. City Point, at the junction of the James and Appomattox rivers and the terminus of the City Point Railroad, was ideally suited to become headquarters of the Union army. From here railroads, waterways and telegraph lines linked Grant with the capital in Washington, D.C., and with the entire Union army. For a time in 1864 and 1865, City Point was one of the world's busiest seaports. Lincoln conferred here with Grant on two occasions.

His last visit occurred when Petersburg and Richmond fell in March 1865.

When you tour City Point it is fascinating to discover that Grant refused the spacious accommodations available in the Eppes's Appomattox Manor and lived in a tent from June until a crudely constructed officers' cabin was completed in November 1864. The cabin, which for a time stood in Fairmount Park, Philadelphia, has been moved back to City Point.

Appomattox Manor which remained in the Eppes family for 344 years was built in 1763. The east wing and portions of the west wing were added around the central portion before the Civil War. Although there are 23 rooms, only three are currently decorated with original Eppes's family furnishings—the parlor, library and dining room. The attractive porch offers a view of both the river and grounds including several of the original outbuildings.

The City Point Unit, which is part of the Petersburg National Battlefield, is open daily at no charge from 8:30 A.M. to 4:30 P.M. Tours last approximately 40 minutes. It is closed on Christmas and New Year's Day. If you have time you may want to take the Hopewell and City Point Historic District Walking Tour. A map will point out houses occupied by Union generals and several other homes in the community that belonged to the Eppes family.

Directions: From Richmond take I-95 south to the Hopewell Exit. Take Route 10 into Hopewell and follow the Historic Hopewell markers to City Point Unit on the Appomattox River.

Weston Manor and Flowerdew Hundred Plantation

What a Wedding Gift!

Christian Eppes was delighted with her wedding present, but then who wouldn't be happy with a 13-room house overlooking the Appomattox River? The house was rich in architectural details and the land rich in history.

In 1607 around the time Jamestown was settled Captain Christopher Newport led an exploratory party 30 miles up the James River. They were entertained on the banks of the Appomattox River by Queen Opusoquoinuske and a group of Appomatuck Indians. Later in 1635 the land on which they met was included in the 1,700 acres granted to Captain Francis Eppes by crown patent.

The three-story colonial frame farm house that you see today was built in 1735. Only two of these Georgian frame-style houses are still standing. The plantation architecture includes precision-type hand-constructed decorative touches. The woodwork and paneling in the 25-foot entrance hall is particularly attractive. The old heart-of-pine floor still shines despite its long and hard use. If you look closely you can see some of the original wooden floor pegs. One colonial feature that intrigues visitors is the "funeral door" made wide enough to allow access for a coffin. Funerals during this period were held in the home.

Although now beautifully restored and decorated with period reproductions, the house did suffer damage during the War Between the States. The house was shelled by a Northern gunboat. In fact, a cannonball was fired through the dining room window into the ceiling. It may well have served as a reminder of the hazards of war to the officers under General Grant's command who were billeted at **Weston Manor** during the siege of Petersburg. General Philip Sheridan was one of the officers quartered here. Weston Manor may also have been used at least temporarily as a hospital for Federal troops during the time nearby City Point served as supply headquarters for the Union army.

Today this pre-Revolutionary house serenely overlooks the Appomattox River. A community stage has been built on the river bank, and Sunday afternoon concerts are given here during the summer months. Weston Manor is open for tours by appointment; just call (804)458-4829. The tour lasts an hour and a nominal admission is charged.

Just downriver from Weston Manor on the south bank of the James is **Flowerdew Hundred Plantation**, one of the earliest English settlements in North America. This land originally inhabited by prehistoric Indians was granted to Governor George Yeardley in 1618. Secrets from the past are being uncovered by archeologists from the University of California at Berkeley working for the non-profit educational Flowerdew Hundred Foundation. They have been working at Flowerdew since 1971. Sixty-five sites have been excavated and artifacts dating from 9000 B.C. to the Civil War era are on display in the Flowerdew museum.

No plantation house remains although several dwellings from a complex of early 17th-century English style houses are being reconstructed by workers who for added authenticity are using period tools and technology. In 1978 an 18th-century windmill was built to commemorate the original 1621 windmill. At the orientation center you can see a 30-minute film on the mill's history and construction.

Flowerdew Hundred Plantation is open April through November Tuesday through Sunday from 10:00 A.M. to 5:00 P.M. Admission is charged.

Directions: From Richmond take I-95 south to the Hopewell Exit, Route 10. Follow Route 10 into the city. Weston Manor is located near the Hopewell Yacht Club off 21st Avenue on the Appomattox River. There are Hopewell Historic Marker signs to direct you. For Flowerdew Hundred take Route 10 south of Hopewell, then make a left on Route 639. It is off Route 639 five miles east of the Benjamin Harrison Bridge.

JAMES RIVER PLANTATIONS

Berkeley and Westover

Side by Side

The story of Thanksgiving is inextricably linked to the Pilgrims at Plymouth Rock despite the fact that America's first Thanksgiving did not occur in Massachusetts. It took place in Virginia a full two years before the Pilgrims arrived in the New World.

John Woodlief, captain of the 40-ton *Margaret*, landed his small party of 38 settlers at Berkeley Hundred on December 4, 1619. They came ashore and gave thanks for their safe passage reading the message prepared for their landfall by King James I, their English proprietor: "Wee ordained that the day of our ships arrivall at the place assigned for plantacon in the land of Virginia shall be yearly and perpetually kept holy as a day of thanksgiving to Almighty God."

Each year on the first Sunday of November the landing of the *Margaret* and the First Thanksgiving are reenacted at Berkeley. (The house is called **Berkeley**; the settlement, Berkeley Hundred.)

This would be quite enough to secure Berkeley's place in history, but it holds yet another distinction. It is one of only two houses in America to be the ancestral home of a signer of the Declaration of Indpendence (Benjamin Harrison), and two presidents of the United States (William Henry Harrison and that Harrison's grandson, Benjamin Harrison). The second house of the same historic significance is the Adams ancestral home in Braintree, Massachusetts.

Berkeley is credited also with the first distillation of bourbon. In the early days at Berkeley Hundred the colonists worked hard to establish their settlement. George Thorpe, an Episcopal missionary, concocted a home brew to encourage their efforts. His corn liquor proved more popular than their English ale.

The Harrison family acquired Berkeley in 1691, but it was not until 1726 that Benjamin Harrison IV built the Georgian style main house, the oldest three-story brick house in Virginia. Benjamin Harrison's wife was Anne Carter, the daughter of Robert

Berkeley Plantation was the ancestral home of the Harrisons, two of whom became President. The first settlers celebrated Thanksgiving after landing in 1619, before the Pilgrims.

"King" Carter. It was their son, Benjamin Harrison V, who became a signer of the Declaration of Independence and three-term Governor of Virginia. He held elective office for 42 of his 65 years. His picture hangs over the mantle in Berkeley's northern drawing room.

Benjamin Harrison V's youngest son, William Henry, the future president, was born at Berkeley in 1773. He gained fame as an Indian fighter at the Battle of Tippecanoe and became Governor of the Northwest Territory. When William Henry Harrison ran for the presidency in 1840 he initiated campaign publicity. You see examples of his buttons and banners when you tour Berkeley. Although he was born to wealth and social position, Harrison was depicted on his commemorative handkerchiefs as a rude frontiersman standing in front of a log cabin home.

Harrison won the election and became the ninth president. He returned to Berkeley to write his inaugural address in the room where he was born. Harrison had been advised by party leader Nicholas Biddle to "say not one single word about his principles, or his creed—let him say nothing—promise nothing. . ." The opportunity to speak proved too tempting for Harrison; at better than two hours, his was the longest inaugural speech ever delivered. He paid a high price for his vanity; he contracted pneumonia from his prolonged exposure to Washington's cold, wet weather and died within 30 days. His vice president was his Sherwood Forest neighbor, John Tyler, whose smooth succession to the presidency set a precedent for future mid-term transitions. In 1888 Harrison's grandson, Benjamin Harrison, became the 23rd president.

Though Berkeley looks as if nothing had happened to it since colonial days, history tells us otherwise. In 1781, during the American Revolution, Benedict Arnold's troops plundered the plantation. Later in the Civil War, during July and August of 1862, General McClellan made Berkeley his headquarters. The Union Army of 140,000 men camped on the grounds, during which time President Lincoln conferred twice with McClellan here. Linking the past with the present, the current owner of Berkeley, Malcolm Jamieson, is the son of a drummer who served with McClellan's army at Berkeley.

Berkeley's preeminent role in history is highlighted in a slide program that precedes the guided tour of the house. After the tour be sure to explore the grounds and gardens of Berkeley. The plantation is open daily from 8:00 A.M. to 5:00 P.M. Admission is charged.

Next door to Berkeley is **Westover Plantation**. Although the mansion is not open, the views you can get of the house from various parts of the sweeping grounds are worth your time. Westover is considered an outstanding example of Georgian architecture. If Westover looks familiar it is because it is featured in the Williamsburg movie, *The Story of a Patriot*.

There are several dependencies on the grounds, also not open, including the kitchen, smokehouse, ice house and necessary. The formal gardens were reestablished about 1900; within the garden you'll see the tomb of William Byrd II, founder of Richmond and Petersburg, buried here in 1744. Westover's grounds and gardens are open daily from 9:00 A.M. to 6:00 P.M. A nominal admission is charged.

Directions: From Richmond take Route 5 along the James River towards Williamsburg. The drive for Berkeley and Westover, about 22 miles east of Richmond, is well-marked.

Sherwood Forest and Evelynton

Caretakers of the Past

It doesn't seem possible, but **Sherwood Forest** is today owned by President John Tyler's grandson, Harrison Tyler. The tenth president (1841–45) was the first president to gain office by the death of his predecessor. This was also the first and only time neighbors followed each other into this high office, as Tyler's home was next to Harrison's Berkeley Plantation.

John Tyler was 68 when he fathered his youngest son, Lyon, who in turn, at the age of 75 fathered his youngest son, the current owner, Harrison. This direct link with the past is of more than genealogical interest. It enables visitors to see a home remarkably unchanged by time. Few, if any, historic homes have retained as complete a collection of family furnishings, and nowhere else are you as likely to hear as many colorful anecdotes about them as you do here. You learn that when John Tyler and his wife, Julia Gardiner, moved into the White House, Congress would not allocate any funds for redecoration. The Tylers brought their own furniture to the White House and took it back to Sherwood Forest at the end of their term.

The house was under construction from 1660 to 1845. By the time it was finished it was the longest frame house in America, the same length as a football field. One of the last extensions to be built was a narrow ballroom, added specifically for dancing the Virginia Reel. Sherwood Forest is the only James River plantation to have a ballroom. The long hall on the other side connecting the kitchen with the main house was called the colonnade and used as a "whistling walk." Slaves carrying dishes to the dining room had to whistle as they walked, to prove they weren't sampling the fare.

According to family legend one room at Sherwood Forest is haunted by the Gray Lady. The family sitting room, known since

1840 as the Gray Room, is connected by a hidden staircase with the nursery above. The children's nurse customarily brought the youngest child downstairs to rock in front of the fireplace. When the youngster died, the devoted nurse was inconsolable. Since that time a phantom rocker has been heard at night in this room.

Behind the house is a gingko, one of 37 tree varieties at Sherwood Forest that are not indigenous to the area. The gingko was brought to America by Admiral Peary when President Tyler reopened the trade routes to the Far East.

The grounds of Sherwood Forest are open daily 9:00 A.M. to 5:00 P.M. Admission is charged. The mansion is open by reservation only. To plan a visit call (804)829-5377 or write Sherwood Forest, P.O. Box 8, Charles City County, VA 23030.

As you travel Route 5 towards Richmond you'll pass other James River Plantations. One that opened to the public in 1985 after being closed for 20 years is **Evelynton**.

The land on which Evelynton stands was occupied by the Powhatan Indians prior to arrival of the English settlers. It became part of William Byrd's colonial holding and he gave it to his wife, Lucy Parke. It was intended to have been a dowry for their daughter, Evelyn, who died tragically of a broken heart.

Evelynton was purchased in 1847 by Edmund Ruffin, Jr., son of the Confederate who fired the first shot of the Civil War at Fort Sumter in April 1861. The plantation house was burned during the Civil War. During the Peninsula Campaign in 1862 Confederate troops led by Generals J.E.B. Stuart and James Longstreet skirmished with Federal forces on Evelynton Heights. The armies returned to the James River area in 1864 in the last days of the war as the Southern army retreated from Petersburg to Richmond and Appomattox. You can still see breastworks from the 1862 confrontation below the house.

Evelynton Plantation remained in the Ruffin family throughout the difficult years of Reconstruction, although Edmund Ruffin, Sr. did not choose to survive what he viewed as the indignities of Yankee domination. He wrapped himself in the Confederate flag and with one lethal shot joined his dead comrades. In 1935 the current Georgian Revival house was commissioned by Mrs. John Augustine Ruffin, mother of the present owner, Edmund Saunders Ruffin. Constructed of 250-year-old bricks on the foundation of the earlier house, it certainly looks as if it had survived from colonial days. The house stands at the summit of a long cedar and dogwood allée, overlooking the meandering Herring Creek and the James River.

Evelynton underwent a major interior facelift in 1985. The furnishings have been collected by the Ruffin family and include period American and English pieces plus European additions from the early 20th century.

You can tour the house, gardens and grounds. There is a formal English boxwood garden and a fully stocked nursery and garden center. The gift shop, in a century-old corn crib, is filled with mementos of the past and hand-crafted, one-of-a-kind treasures such as dolls and quilts.

Evelynton is open daily from 9:00 A.M. to 5:00 P.M. except Christmas and New Year's Day. Admission is charged.

Directions: From Richmond take Route 5 east towards Williamsburg. Evelynton and Sherwood Forest are on the right; both are well-marked.

Shirley and Edgewood Plantations

Family Trees

It did not take many years for the English who settled at Jamestown in 1607 to discover that one path to the wealth they craved was tobacco. To that end they began spreading out, establishing plantations to grow the golden weed. One of the earliest of these plantations was **Shirley**; the name first appeared on records in 1611, although it would be two more years before the estate was inhabited.

For three centuries and ten generations Shirley has been held by the Hill-Carter family. Though the intricate family tree dates back to 1660, the house was not built until 1724 when Edward Hill III began constructing it for his daughter Elizabeth and her husband John Carter, son of Robert "King" Carter. Architectural historians trace the inspiration for this square shaped home to the Governor's Palace in nearby Williamsburg (see Public Buildings selection), completed in 1720. Rather than the Georgian hyphen and wings design, Shirley has a basement and three stories. Each floor is divided into four squares, a room on each corner. Like the numerous dependencies, the brick house is built in the Flemish bond pattern. On the roof is a carved pineapple symbol of hospitality.

Shirley is noted for its hospitality—to horses as well as presidents. The family silver has been used to serve George Washington, Thomas Jefferson, John Tyler and Theodore Roosevelt. Not one of the presidents, however, had his own silver cup like Nestor, the family's champion race horse. After a victorious race Nestor was offered wine from his cup, reversing the practice of offering the loving cup to the owner.

Family lore abounds at Shirley. One story is told and retold about the frieze over the fireplace in the dining room. It may have

Shirley Plantation has been held by the Hill-Carter families since 1660. Tobacco was being shipped from here seven years before the Pilgrims landed at Plymouth Rock.

been told one too many times. One of the current younger generation at Shirley, after hearing repeatedly about an earlier Carter youngster who whittled all but four acorns out of the carved frieze, decided to make his own mark and eliminated all but one before his mother stopped him in mid-crime.

Fortunately the frieze is not the carved work for which Shirley is noted. That honor belongs to the hanging staircase. This square, not curved, staircase rises without visible means of support, and each tread is gracefully scrolled.

The parlor at Shirley is historically, rather than architecturally, significant. It was here that Anne Hill Carter married Governor Henry "Lighthorse Harry" Lee. Their son, Robert, would spend several boyhood years at Shirley. History also marked this plantation during America's early struggles. Like so many of the James River plantations, Shirley had troops on her soil during both the Revolutionary War and the War Between the States.

Shirley is still a working plantation producing corn, barley, wheat and soy beans. The grounds have a full complement of dependencies—a large two-story kitchen, smokehouse, dovecote, stable and barns. You can visit Shirley daily except Christmas Day from 9:00 A.M. to 5:00 P.M. Admission is charged.

At nearby **Edgewood**, just three miles from Shirley, the family tree is likely to be one of the eight to ten decorated Christmas trees that fill this Carpenter's Gothic house from October well into January. Here the ambience is not Revolutionary or antebellum but Victorian, a delightful change of pace.

The house was built in 1849 by Spencer Rowland, a New Jerseyite who fell in love with the South. His daughter, Lizzie, likewise fell in love with the South, or at least a young Southerner from a nearby plantation, perhaps even Shirley. Lizzie was in her mid-twenties when she moved to Edgewood and lost her heart. Then she lost him to the Civil War. Her ghost is said to haunt the bedroom where she died and her name is etched on the window through which the apparition peers, forever searching for her handsome beau on his spirited horse.

Dot and John Boulware purchased this house in 1978. They have repaired and refurbished the 12 large rooms which evolved into a Bed and Breakfast. Dot conducts tours, and if you call ahead she wears a Victorian dress. The bedrooms are a treasure trove of Victoriana, with old-fashioned clothes laid out casually to enhance the decor. One overnight guest mistook the decor for a gesture and wore the antique nightshirt to bed.

You can visit daily from 10:00 A.M. to 5:00 P.M. except Mondays. To pre-arrange visits or accommodations call (804)829-2962.

Directions: From Richmond take Route 5 for 25 miles to Shirley Plantation on the right and Edgewood on the left.

Smith's Fort, Bacon's Castle and Chippokes Plantation

Surry's Fringe Benefits

Originally part of the Jamestown colony, the land across the James River was included in Surry County when it was established in 1652. The name provided a link with Surrey, England, which most settlers would never see again. And today it offers a chance to see where Virginia's leading crop was developed, where rebels ruled a century before the Revolution, where farm land has been tilled since 1612 and evidence of what may be the oldest formal garden in the United States.

Captain John Smith built and garrisoned a fort in 1609 on the banks of Gray's Creek across from Jamestown. Five years later John Rolfe, who settled in Virginia in 1610 and lost his wife shortly after arriving, remarried. He took as his wife Pocahontas, daughter of the Powhatan chief. The canny Indian chief gave the couple tribal land that the English settlers had already commandeered. Rolfe used the land for experimenting with tobacco strains. Among the varieties he planted was the West Indian blend that became Virginia's number one cash crop.

The house you see today at **Smith's Fort Plantation** was not built until the 18th century. It is noted for its fine woodwork and period furniture. There is a small English garden, and a trail leads to the ruins of the old fort. Smith's Fort Plantation is open Tuesday through Sunday 10:00 A.M. to 5:00 P.M. from mid-April through September. Admission is charged.

Just as John Smith never lived at Smith's Fort Plantation, Nathaniel Bacon never lived at **Bacon's Castle**. This stately Jacobean house, once known as "Allen's Brick House," was built in 1665 by Arthur Allen, speaker of the House of Burgesses and a good friend of Royal Governor Berkeley. The house is one of, if not the oldest brick house in English North America. Although not the fortress its name suggests, it looks formidable with its Flemish gables and their matched triple chimney stacks. The house was extensively renovated both inside and out and recently reopened after a three-year hiatus.

The house became a pivotal stronghold during the full scale rebellion against Royal Governor William Berkeley a century before the American Revolution. The rebels, led by Nathaniel Bacon, burned Jamestown to the ground in September 1676. Bacon then retreated to Gloucester and sent one of his lieutenants, William Rookings, to establish a base of operations in Surry County. On September 18, Rookings and his band of 70 men seized Arthur Allen's house. From there they ruled the county for the next three months until the rebellion was crushed.

Currently the exciting news at Bacon's Castle comes from the extensive archeological work being done on the grounds. Archeologists have uncovered evidence of a 72,000-square-foot garden that may date from 1680, possibly the oldest formal garden ever found in the United States. Although formally arranged in six sections with bisecting and surrounding paths, this was not an ornamental garden with mazes and decorative beds. It was a vegetable and herb garden (some of which flowered). Bacon's Castle is open concurrently with Smith's Fort Plantation from April through October NOON to 4:00 P.M. Tuesday through Sunday.

Another nearby plantation, in **Chippokes Plantation State Park** (named for a minor Indian chief friendly to the early settlers), has a model farm that demonstrates agricultural methods and crops from the 17th century to the 20th century. To gain a better understanding of the work in the fields stop at Chippokes Visitor Center.

Chippokes has both historical and horticultural significance. This land has been in continuous use for more than 300 years since it was first patented by Captain William Powell in 1612. Powell's heirs sold the land to Sir William Berkeley, the Royal Governor.

The antebellum plantation house was built in 1854 on the foundations of an earlier homestead. The mansion and out-kitchen can be toured, providing a look at life on a rural plantation in the days immediately before the Civil War. Behind the house is a six-acre garden, in bloom from spring through fall, with the peak season being late summer when the massed crape myrtle blossom. There are 17th-, 18th- and 19th-century buildings on the grounds. Guided walks on weekends focus on historical reminders as well as the natural environment. An earlier home, River House, built in the 1700s, is not open for tours. Chippokes may be visited daily from sunrise to sunset. The Visitor Center is open only from Memorial Day weekend to Labor Day weekend.

Directions: From Richmond take I-95 south to the Route 10 Exit. Take Route 10 past Hopewell. All three attractions are just a short distance off Route 10. For Smith's Fort Plantation turn left on Route 31. For Chippokes turn left on Route 633 and for Bacon's Castle turn left on Route 617.

Visitors to Busch Gardens learn impromptu Bavarian folk dances in Rhinefeld, the park's German Village.

Historic Triangle

WILLIAMSBURG

Anheuser-Busch Brewery Tour

Six Million Bottles of Beer on the Wall

For the hearty (or the thirsty) the **Anheuser-Busch Brewery Tour** provides a zesty look at the mechanization large companies have introduced to perform age-old processes. The self-guided walking tours are offered from 10:00 A.M. to 4:00 P.M. daily. Although the front door closes every day at 4:00 P.M., later visits are possible from adjacent Busch Gardens.

Your self-guided tour takes you above the action. Through large picture windows you look down to the floor below to watch the process that turns out no fewer than 700,000 gallons of beer a day on which the annual tax is $1,099,400,000. You'll immediately be struck by the fact that there are so few workers on the floor. The process is entirely automated.

Taped messages provide information on each step of the beer making process. First the grain mixture is prepared and cooked for a period of time, then sent to fermentation tanks and finally to the huge lager tanks. The liquid remains in the lager tanks for approximately 21 days before being bottled. Empty bottles on endless conveyor belts feed into a sealed machine and come out full—as many as six million bottles of beer a day. Another area of operations turns out five million cans per day.

Your experience of the brewery process is somewhat sanitized. You get no aromas from the vats and tanks, but you do get a taste. Anheuser-Busch offers all tour participants of drinking age two samples from their many products. Hot dogs, salads and pizza are sold, along with soft drinks, at the Hospitality Center making this an excellent spot for a mid-day break.

Although interesting, the brewery tour is not the major Anheuser-Busch attraction; most of the action is at the adjacent **Busch Gardens**. This 360-acre theme park features quaint European village areas: England with the hamlets of Banburry Cross, Threadneedle Faire, Heatherdowns and Hastings; France, including New France and Aquataine; Germany with the Rhineland and Octoberfest; plus Italy. There are rides a plenty, plus a wide variety of shops, restaurants and shows.

67

Busch Gardens is open daily from mid-May through Labor Day. It is open weekends only from late March or early April until mid-May and again after Labor Day until the end of October. Admission varies according to age and length of stay. The park opens at 10:00 A.M., but closing time varies by season. Call (804)253-3350 to check.

Directions: From Richmond take I-64 to Route 199 and follow signs to Busch Gardens.

Bassett Hall

Putting on the Dog

On November 27, 1926, under an ancient oak tree behind the 18th-century home of Burwell Bassett, nephew of Martha Washington, John D. Rockefeller, Jr., and Reverend W.A.R. Godwin first met to plan the restoration of Williamsburg, the 18th-century capital of the colonies. As they strolled back to town, Rockefeller said if he came back to Williamsburg he'd like to picnic beneath the oak.

It became easy for Rockefeller to picnic at **Bassett Hall** after he purchased the 585-acre estate in 1936. From this comfortable vantage point the Rockefellers watched the rebirth of Williamsburg. John D. Rockefeller, Jr., ultimately spent $60 million on the restoration of the venerable city, and contributions by other family members brought the figure to $100 million.

A tour of Bassett Hall reveals a great deal about the Rockefeller life style. From the moment you enter the informal sitting room, the first room on the escorted tour, one decorative influence is immediately apparent—Mrs. Rockefeller's folk art collection. There are 200 pieces from her extensive collection in this home and 400 pieces at the nearby Abby Aldrich Rockefeller Folk Art Center (see selection).

Bassett Hall represents a mix of decorating styles. In the hall passageway, which in colonial times served as the summer living room, you'll see a collection of Chinese export paintings. The paint was applied on the back side of the glass. Such paintings had to be carefully shipped, for if the glass broke the picture was lost.

In the formal parlor there is another unusual style of painting called mourning pictures. Painted by school girls and much in vogue after the death of George Washington, these depicted graveyard scenes full of tombstones. There are additional examples of these morbid works upstairs, but the master bedroom has stencil pictures with cheerful subjects like flowers, fruits and birds. Throughout Bassett Hall you see objects acquired by Mrs.

Rockefeller's spinster sister, Lucy, on her travels. She purchased the crocheted bedspread in the master bedroom from the Royal School of Needlework in England. Mrs. Rockefeller herself was a talented needleworker, as a trunk full of rugs made by her attests.

In the sitting room of the new wing there is an unusual painting of General Washington crossing the Delaware. The faces of all the men in the boat resemble George Washington.

Back downstairs you'll see selections from the 14 sets of dishes the Rockefellers customarily used. The old 1930s kitchen is flanked by a pantry and garden room where flowers were arranged. Although the dining room is quite elegant, when the heads of state from around the world attended the Summit of Industrialized Nations in May 1983, they enjoyed lunch in the garden overlooking the oak allée.

Explore the grounds before you end your tour of Bassett Hall. There are three original outbuildings: a smokehouse, kitchen and dairy. A modern tea house, or orangery, was added by the Rockefellers.

Bassett Hall is open 10:00 A.M. to 5:00 P.M. Tickets can be purchased at the Reception Center located adjacent to Bassett Hall, right off Francis Street in Colonial Williamsburg.

Directions: From Richmond take I-64 east to Colonial Williamsburg. An alternate route is via Route 5 east from Richmond. You may want to stop at the Visitor Center upon arrival to obtain maps, brochures and tickets.

Carter's Grove and Wolstenholme Towne

Everything Old Is New Again

Your journey to **Carter's Grove** takes you from South England Street in bustling Williamsburg along the eight mile, one-way, one-lane Country Road. As you drive along this old carriage road through quiet woods and across wooden bridges, you can easily imagine the well-dressed burgesses passing the same scenery on their way to an evening's entertainment with Carter Burwell.

Before you visit Carter Burwell's mansion nowadays you stop at a new reception center that traces four centuries of history on this remarkable land. When archeologists were digging in the 1970s for the plantation outbuildings, they uncovered an historical bonanza: the remains of **Wolstenholme Towne**, the 17th-century Martin's Hundred settlement which all but disappeared in 1622.

A group of British adventurers settled at Martin's Hundred and obtained a patent for 21,500 acres from the Virginia Company. Then in 1618 the company sent 220 settlers to Virginia who established a palisaded fort which they named in honor of Sir John Wolstenholme.

The remains of the fort have been uncovered as well as the remains of farmsteads, storehouses, dwellings and graves of settlers, some of whom were buried in haste after the Indian attack of March 22, 1622. The attack cost 58 settlers their lives, 20 more were captured by the Indians, and the homes and fields of almost all were destroyed. It was the end of Wolstenholme Towne.

The short two-year life of the town, plus its abrupt end, makes this an archeological time capsule. Many of the artifacts uncovered, some from sites that survived the massacre, have been of inestimable value. Two closed helmets are unique discoveries; no others have been recovered in America, and these have details not found on helmets exhibited in England. A dish made in 1631 is the oldest dated example of British colonial pottery-making.

After viewing the orientation film, *A Thing Called Time*, you follow a path to the overlook pavilion where you hear the site archeologist, Ivor Noël Hume, narrate a recorded drama about one settlement. Recorded messages are delivered at nine locations along the walk through the site. There is also a detailed painting to help in imagining what the town looked like more than 3½ centuries ago. Because there was not sufficient data to permit a complete reconstruction, only the outlines and partial building facades of the 1620 site have been reconstructed.

In total six sites dating from 1619 to 1645 have been explored. There are still others awaiting excavation including small farmsteads that survived the massacre and date from the period 1650 to 1750, the year when Carter Burwell began building his plantation house.

Burwell inherited the land from his mother, Elizabeth, the daughter of Robert "King" Carter whose vast estate encompassed 300,000 acres. In his will King Carter stipulated that this portion of his land must always bear the name Carter's Grove.

Over a million bricks were used to build Carter Burwell's imposing Georgian mansion. Great care was expended on the carved interior woodwork. Burwell brought an English carpenter, Richard Baylis, with his family to Virginia so that he could devote all his energies and skills to creating the elaborate designs you see today. It took 500 days just to complete the hallway design. Carter Burwell did not have much time to enjoy his completed home (he died six months after it was finished), but it was held by the Burwell family until 1838.

It is furnished with period pieces collected by Mr. and Mrs. Archibald McCrea who purchased Carter's Grove in 1928 and restored it to its colonial elegance. No description of this historic estate is complete without the two legends told and retold about events that are reputed to have occurred here both before and during the Revolution. According to one story both George Washington and Thomas Jefferson had their marriage proposals rejected while courting at Carter's Grove. The Refusal Room is where Washington is supposed to have asked Mary Cary, a Carter cousin, to marry him and where Jefferson is said to have proposed to Rebecca Burwell, his "fair Belinda."

The second legend dates from the Revolution, in 1781 just before the Battle of Yorktown when British Colonel Banastre Tarleton was headquartered at Carter's Grove. Tarleton, believing that the Virginians were looting his supplies, wanted to rouse his sleeping men so he rode his horse up the grand staircase slashing the stair rails with his saber. Though the story may be apocryphal the scars on the stair rails are real.

Carter's Grove is open daily from 9:00 A.M. to 5:00 P.M., and during the summer months it stays open until 6:00 P.M. It can be toured independently, but it is included on the Williamsburg Patriot's Pass. Tickets are available at the Colonial Williamsburg Visitor Center or the Carter's Grove Reception Center.

Directions: From Richmond take I-64 east to Colonial Williamsburg. Follow the signs to the Historic Area and take South England Street which becomes Country Road.

Gardens of Williamsburg

Floral Tribute

Williamsburg's enduring appeal is in its complete evocation of Virginia's colonial capital. Its public and private buildings are seen within the context of the 18th century rather than the hubbub of the 20th century. Brick walks flank the broad streets on which carriages and wagons still travel. As you glance over the picket fences you'll see the gardens of yesterday blooming again.

The town of Williamsburg was laid out by Governor Francis Nicholson in the area called Middle Plantation, established in 1699 on a broad ridge between the York and James rivers. This stockaded outpost provided a line of defense for Jamestown against Indian attacks. After the third Jamestown fire the capital of the colony was moved to Middle Plantation, and it was renamed Williamsburg in honor of King William III. The town grew to a population of 1,800, but this was greatly increased when the General Court and the House of Burgesses were in session.

Nicholson's plan divided the city into one-half acre residential lots; sufficient land for a house, dependencies and a garden. In both the elegant formal gardens of the Governor's Palace and the backyards of private homes they copied the English garden styles popular in the reign of William and Mary, 1687–1709.

Alexander Spotswood, the first of the seven governors to live in the Palace, was determined to make the garden the finest in the colonies, even if he personally had to pay to do it. He succeeded admirably and the garden he envisioned has been reconstructed and replanted. Of enormous help in this restoration was the discovery in Oxford University's Bodleian Library of an 18th-century engraving showing plantings near the Palace. Extensive archeological investigation revealed the location of paths, walls, steps, gates and the parterres (beds). To speak of the Palace garden as a single entity is confusing because there are several separate gardens—the maze, the upper and lower ballroom gardens and the falling garden.

The maze is perhaps the most popular. Young and old delight in tackling the mysteries of this conceit. The prickly leaves of the native American holly used to create this natural puzzle discourage short cuts. The design was copied from Hampton Court's maze, a favorite of the English nobility.

The upper ballroom garden reveals another component of many English gardens, the "Twelve Apostles." These sentinels, cylindrically shaped topiary, keep constant watch over the garden. The extensive use of holly and boxwood means that the gardens remain green all year. Spring and summer bring masses of color to the 16 diamond-shaped beds of the upper garden and the long beds and borders of the lower level. Pleached (interlaced) allées flank the lower garden, making natural tunnels that provide both shade and privacy. The garden was an ideal spot for courting in the 18th century; it was one of the few places a private conversation was possible.

You too might enjoy an escape to the gardens of Williamsburg. Many visitors are so busy trying to see the buildings, they miss the spirit of this remarkable place. The sense of continuity is keenly felt amid the living reminders of the past.

A few of the private homes open their garden oases to the public. A map denoting them is available at the Visitor Center. George Wythe (pronounced like Smith) spent tranquil hours away from disputatious lawyers in the pleasure garden of his home on Palace Green. His neighbor and town mayor, Thomas Everard, added an unusual feature to his garden, a small duck pond. Many of the shops and taverns have gardens. You can enjoy an alfresco meal at King's Arms or Chowning's Tavern.

A garden symposium is held each April. Williamsburg's Historic Area is open daily from 9:00 A.M. to 5:00 P.M.

Directions: From Richmond take I-64 east to Williamsburg. Use Exit 56 onto Route 143 (you'll bear right off I-64). This is quickly followed by a right onto Route 132. You'll turn left onto feeder road Route 132Y into the Colonial Williamsburg Visitor Center.

Public Hospital, DeWitt Wallace Decorative Arts Gallery and Abby Aldrich Rockefeller Folk Art Center

Mind Over Matter

The last of the reconstructed 18th-century Williamsburg public buildings, the **Public Hospital**, opened in 1985, a full century after it was destroyed by fire. When the hospital originally opened in 1773 it was the first institution in America devoted solely as the law stated, "for the Support and Maintainance of Ideots, Lunatics, and other Persons of unsound mind."

During the first year there were only 12 patients who endured the harsh conditions you will become aware of as you tour the Public Hospital. A reconstruction of one of the original 24 primitive cells illustrates conditions prevalent during the Age of Restraint, which lasted from 1773 until 1835. The cell contains only a straw mattress and chamber pot. Patients were manacled; the windows were barred and the doors padlocked. A taped vignette helps re-create the lot of these early victims of mental illness who were treated by cold water plunge baths and harsh drugs.

The opposite side of the viewing room at the Public Hospital has a 19th-century apartment representing the period of Moral Management from 1836 to 1862. This approach was based on the realization that the patient suffered emotional problems, needed kindly and respectful treatment, plus work and recreational activities to fill their time in confinement. A taped dialogue tells how this approach was implemented. The room contains a quilt-covered bed, table, chairs, rug and even a violin and newspaper.

Many of the "tools" of the mental health trade were recovered from the on-site excavations. Exhibited in the museum section of the hospital are a strait jacket; Utica crib, a wire cage-like bed for violent patients; a tranquilizer chair and more benign objects like the sports equipment and games used in later years.

This new addition to Colonial Williamsburg certainly runs the gamut of "pain and pleasure," because after the horrors of the mental ward come the delights in the adjoining **DeWitt Wallace Decorative Arts Gallery**, built with funds contributed by DeWitt and Lila Wallace, co-founders of the Reader's Digest Association. The gallery is reached by elevator or stairs from the hospital lobby. On entering this bi-level museum you go through an introductory gallery that suggests the scope of this incredible collection. More than half of the 8,000 items on display have never, or only rarely, been shown, so it is indeed a new look at some very old items from the 17th, 18th and early 19th centuries.

Around an attractive central court you'll see the master works exhibit with selected pieces from the diverse small study galleries which branch off this core area. The prize pieces are the matched portraits of George III and George Washington which flank a throne-like ceremonial chair. Painted in the same pose, the two pivotal figures present a study in contrasts: the King with his full figure outfitted in elegant finery and the uniformed Washington with his military bearing and piercing gaze.

Study galleries at the museum include textiles, ceramics, glass, metals, prints, paintings and maps plus special rotating exhibits. A major collection of early 18th-century furniture and accessories was donated to the gallery by Miodrag and Elizabeth Ridgely Blagojevich. The 45-minute orientation tour given daily at 1:30 and 3:30 P.M. not only introduces the gallery it also helps visitors appreciate the decorative arts displayed in the homes and public buildings of historic Williamsburg. This important collection contains items too splendid for the modest means of the 18th-century Williamsburg residents. Mr. Rockefeller began his collection in 1933, and by 1969 it was so impressive that Alice Winchester, author and expert in the field said, "the collection at Colonial Williamsburg has grown to such an extent in both quality and quantity that to call it outstanding seems almost an understatement." Now you can judge for yourself. The museum is open daily 11:00 A.M. to 7:00 P.M. Admission is either by separate ticket, Patriot's Pass or a Colonial Williamsburg Museum ticket; prices vary.

The Public Hospital and DeWitt Wallace Decorative Arts Gallery are at 325 Francis Street between South Henry and Nassau Streets. Parking is available at a lot on Nassau Street. A café at the gallery is ideal for lunch, tea or snacks.

If you enjoy the arts you should also include a visit to the **Abby Aldrich Rockefeller Folk Art Center** on your itinerary. Mrs. Rockefeller, mother of the late Governor Nelson Rockefeller, was one of the first to collect American folk art. Her substantial collection serves as the nucleus for this small museum on South England Street adjacent to the Williamsburg Craft House. The exhibited work includes folk painting, decorated household furnishings, quilts, weathervanes, toys, ceramics and signs. The museum is open daily from 11:00 A.M. until 7:00 P.M. You can purchase an admission ticket for this museum, or use a Patriot's Pass or a Museum ticket.

Directions: From Richmond take I-64 east to Colonial Williamsburg following the signs to the historic area.

Williamsburg's Private Homes and Businesses

Tripping That Makes Sense

The smells, sounds and sights of colonial Williamsburg can best be sensed in the private homes and shops. The pungent hot gingerbread cookies at the Raleigh Tavern Bakery, the fragrance of cedar permeating the Cooper shop on Duke of Gloucester Street, the delicate floral scents emanating from the many small gardens half hidden behind the fences and walls of the private yards are all part of the total experience. So also are the sounds that fill the air: the giggle of visitors trying on hairpieces at the Wigmakers, the strident clatter of the blacksmith at work and the rattle and tinkle of the percussive instruments shown on "The Other Half" tour.

The sights of Williamsburg include more than 88 original buildings and an additional 400 reconstructions. You can get a real feel of what it was like to live in this town by visiting just three private homes: the **Peyton Randolph House**, **George Wythe's House** and the **Brush-Everard House**.

The original owner of the Peyton Randolph House was John Randolph, the only colonial Virginian to be knighted. He was first clerk of the House of Burgesses, then the member representing the College of William and Mary and finally Speaker of the House of Burgesses. When Sir John died in 1737 his wife inherited his Williamsburg home; but on her death it passed to his son, Peyton, for whom it is named.

Peyton Randolph's career paralleled his father's. He too studied law in London after attending William and Mary. He too was sent to England on behalf of the colony. He was elected to the House of Burgesses in 1748, and in 1766 he too was chosen speaker. It was up to him to guide the Assembly through the tumultuous debates that led to the Revolution.

The Randolph's home is sectional. The westernmost section of the house, built in 1716, was Sir John's home. He also purchased the house on the adjoining lot. Later the two homes were connected to make one large residence. The furnishings are stylish yet comfortable; it is definitely a home not a museum. The paneled rooms exude a warmth that was enjoyed by two French guests. Count de Rochambeau used this house as his headquarters during the siege of Yorktown. When Lafayette returned to America 50 years after the Revolution he too stayed here. After Peyton Randolph's death, Thomas Jefferson purchased his library, and when the federal collection was burned by the British during the War of 1812 he donated his extensive collection of books to the Library of Congress. Thus the combined libraries of Jefferson and Randolph became the nucleus of the national collection.

If Sir John was the most distinguished lawyer in Virginia in the first third of the 18th century, then another Williamsburg resident, George Wythe, may well lay claim to this distinction in the last third. While his neighbor, Peyton Randolph, was serving the colony in England, Wythe acted as attorney general. Wythe, a member of the House of Burgesses, was a good friend of Governors Fauquier and Botetourt; but when the time came to choose sides, he unhesitantly joined the patriots and signed the Declaration of Independence for Virginia.

The document's author, Thomas Jefferson, was at one time a law student in Wythe's Williamsburg home. And in 1776 the Jefferson family stayed at the Wythe house for several weeks. A popular teacher, Wythe became America's first professor of law at William and Mary in 1779.

Wythe's Georgian mansion was used by George Washington as his headquarters during the Yorktown siege. After the hostilities ended Rochambeau moved here from the Randolph House. Centuries later this historic house became the home of the Reverend W.A.R. Goodwin. Perhaps living here made him more attuned to the urgency of restoring Williamsburg to its former glory. In any event it was he who had the idea for Rockefeller's restoration.

Because George Wythe established a mini-plantation in the heart of Williamsburg, you don't want to miss seeing the outbuildings and gardens. You'll find demonstrators cooking, weaving baskets and making cloth and yarn.

Like the books at the Randolph house those at the Brush-Everard House also have a Jeffersonian connection, though not direct. This library was compiled from a list of 300 basic books Jefferson had recommended to a Virginia planter. The Brush-Everard House represents the middle class life style of the 18th century. A modest frame house, it was built in 1717 by John Brush, gunsmith, armorer and the first keeper of the colony's Magazine (see Public Buildings selection). After passing through the hands of several owners, the house was purchased by Thomas Everard who was mayor of Williamsburg in 1766 and again in 1771. Everard enlarged the house, embellished the interior and added a small pond.

To see how John Brush would have practiced his craft visit the gunsmith shop near the Capitol. It is just one of many colonial crafts you can see demonstrated. There is a milliner, printer, bookbinder, blacksmith, cooper, bootmaker, wheelwright, harnessmaker, cabinetmaker, wigmaker and musical instrument maker. The papermaking demonstration is one of the most fascinating. You'll discover the derivation of "beaten to a pulp" when you watch the papermakers pound cloth rags into fiber. It is impressive to see them turn out six to eight pieces of rag paper a minute.

Added to these ongoing activities are special programs like the musket firing demonstrations (daily except Sunday) on the half hour from 10:00 A.M. to 3:30 P.M. A more elaborate arms demonstration is performed on Market Square at 4:00 P.M. Monday through Thursday, and on Saturday. Reveille is sounded by the Fifes and Drums in front of the Magazine at 8:45 A.M. and the Junior Fife and Drum Corps parades up Duke of Gloucester Street daily at noon. All of these programs are presented during the spring, summer and fall.

For a look at Williamsburg from a different perspective sign up for "The Other Half" tour. Half of the city's population were Afro-Americans and this two-hour walking tour tells you about them. The tour begins at 1:30 P.M. at the Courthouse of 1770—every day in the summer, and on weekends only in the spring and fall. The tour focuses on slave culture, racial interaction, black music and the differences for blacks between plantation and town life.

On the tour you meet memorable characters like Nioto, who talks about his terror in being captured in Africa and being brought to Virginia in chains, and Jesse, a plantation worker who comes into Williamsburg in both fear and excitement. There are free blacks like Betty Wallace who is married to a slave living at nearby Carter's Grove plantation and blacks who have learned a skill or trade like London Briggs and Simon Gilliat who provide musical entertainment for the Palace balls. It is a surprise to learn that the House of Burgesses banned the owning or playing of percussive instruments. You'll learn why as you struggle to play these African instruments.

Admission to all of the homes and shops mentioned here is included in the basic ticket. All are open from 9:00 A.M. to 5:00 P.M. except the Wythe House, the Cooper shop, the Printer & Bookbinder and the Milliner where the hours are 10:00 A.M. to 6:00 P.M.

Directions: From Richmond take I-64 east to Colonial Williamsburg and follow green signs to the Visitor Center. The house and shops are situated along the streets of the Historic Area. Maps are available at the Visitor Center which is open 8:45 A.M. to 5:20 P.M..

Williamsburg's Public Buildings

Officially Speaking

There will always be an England, and on this side of the Atlantic you can find reminders of it in the public buildings of Colonial Williamsburg. The governor, in his Georgian Palace, symbolized the power of the English king in the colony. The Virginia House of Burgesses meeting in the **Capitol** fought, as they had since their first meeting in Jamestown, to receive the rights of Englishmen they considered their due. British Marines were ordered by Lord Dunmore to remove the powder secretly from the Williamsburg Magazine. And Bruton Parish Church was named for an English parish in Somerset that was the home of some of Williamsburg's leading citizens.

The Capitol was built in Williamsburg in 1699 after the seat of government was moved from Jamestown. It had been less than a year since the last of several statehouses in Jamestown had burned to the ground. To prevent a similar fate in Williamsburg the wary burgesses ordered the building constructed without chimneys. There would be no warming blaze, no flickering candles and no smoking of the "noxious weed."

All that was fired up was the temper of the legislators. A constant barrage of complaints forced a reversal, and in 1723 chimneys were added and the ban on smoking and candles lifted. The fate that had been feared occurred on January 30, 1747, when the building was gutted by fire. Rebuilt, it suffered from another fire in 1832 after it had been abandoned by the legislators who moved with the government to Richmond. Although it was the second Capitol building that had echoed to the impassioned words of Patrick Henry and the stirring debate on independence in 1776, it was the first Capitol that was reconstructed by Colonial Williamsburg. Two factors influenced this decision: there were more detailed records available about the first building and it was more architecturally distinct. One wing of the H-shaped building contains the Hall of the House of Burgesses, and the other wing was used by the General Court for their twice yearly sessions. Upstairs there were committee rooms, a Council chamber and a Conference Room where both burgesses and councillors met for morning prayers and held joint conferences.

Absolutely the best way to experience the diversified activities that took place here is to attend "A Capitol Evening" performed during the summer months on Wednesdays at 7:30 and 8:30 P.M. You are even allowed to raise your voice in response to the spirited issues under debate in the Hall of the House of Burgesses. Townspeople are on trial in the General Court and you can evaluate the harsh colonial justice from a new perspective. At the end a short concert of period music is performed in the candlelit Conference Room.

The line between public and private is blurred in so far as the lavish **Governor's Palace** is concerned. It was the private home of a public figure. Seven governors and the first two elected chief executives—Patrick Henry and Thomas Jefferson—lived here.

The Palace was built from 1708–1720 during the term of Lieutenant Governor Alexander Spotswood. The last of the king's men was Lord Dunmore who fled the Palace in early June 1775. It was Governor Norborne Berkeley, Baron de Botetourt, whose tenancy is evoked when you tour the Palace. Botetourt was governor from 1768 until his death in October 1770. A detailed room-by-room inventory taken at that time of the 16,000 objects in the Palace's 61 rooms enabled Colonial Williamsburg to refurnish the Palace as it was then. Additional help came from the daily records that had been kept by Botetourt's butler, William Marshman.

Now when you tour the elegant public rooms and the governor's private quarters the colonially attired guide will help you imagine what it was like to visit the Palace more than two centuries earlier. The outbuildings are more suggestive of a Virginia plantation than a European palace, but the gardens delightfully blend influences of both continents (see Williamsburg Garden selection).

To complete your exploration of the town's public buildings stop at the **Courthouse of 1770**, an original building that now dispenses information and tickets to visitors. Plans are underway to restore this as a focus of local government, 18th-century style. The Courthouse stands on Market Square, one of the community's social, political and economic centers. Townfolk would flock to the square to hear important announcements; this is where they heard the Declaration of Independence proclaimed from the Courthouse steps. Troops were mustered on the square green, and twice each week farmers brought in their produce. Within the Courthouse two courts met regularly, the James City County Court and Williamsburg Hustings Court. County courts acted as the main agents of local government in the Virginia colony exercising both executive and judicial powers. The municipal court, also known as the Hustings Court, exercised civil jurisdiction over Williamsburg.

In front of the Courthouse of 1770 on Market Square Green are the instruments of local justice: the pillory with holes in a wooden frame for the miscreant's head and hands and the stocks that had ankle holes in its wooden frame. Those awaiting trial or in debt were incarcerated at the Public Gaol, described by a colonial chronicler as a "strong sweet prison." Only the General Court could try offenses punishable by death or mutilation. The county and municipal courts levied sentences that subjected the felons to discomfort and public humiliation.

You'll discover that conditions in the Public Gaol were little worse than those in the Public Hospital (see DeWitt Wallace Decorative Arts Gallery selection). In fact, the gaol served for a time as a madhouse as well as a military prison, though the military had their own public buildings, the Magazine and Guardhouse.

The Magazine was the arsenal of the colony, a sturdy brick repository of arms and ammunition. It was built in 1715 at the request of Governor Spotswood and has survived to this day. At the time of the French and Indian War (1754–1763) the Magazine held more than 60,000 pounds of gunpowder. It was at this time that the high protective wall and Guardhouse were added.

On April 20–21, 1775, the Magazine claimed its paragraph in American history. Lord Dunmore, keenly alert in the mood of the Virginians, sent forces secretly to remove the powder from the Magazine, but the irate reaction forced the British to make restitution for the pilfered powder.

Prayers were raised at Bruton Parish Church in 1774 in hopes of averting the division from England. Most parishioners had come to feel that war was the only answer, however, by the time the bells of Bruton Parish Church rang out on May 15, 1776, heralding Virginia's first call for independence. They should have rung yet again centuries later when the rector of the parish, the Reverend W. A. R. Goodwin, conceived the idea of restoring Williamsburg. It was Goodwin who persuaded John D. Rockefeller, Jr. to develop his idea into a reality.

All of these attractions are open 9:00 A.M. to 5:00 P.M. with the exception of the Public Gaol which is open 10:00 A.M. to 6:00 P.M. There are special candlelit organ concerts in Bruton Parish Church Tuesday, Thursday and Saturday at 8:00 P.M.

Directions: From Richmond take I-64 east to Colonial Williamsburg. The Capitol is located at the east end of Duke of Gloucester Street. The Governor's Palace is at the north end of the Palace Green. The Courthouse of 1770 is on Duke of Gloucester Street at Market Square. The Magazine and Guardhouse are directly across the street. Bruton Parish Church is one block west on Duke of Gloucester Street. The Public Gaol is at the east end of Nicholson Street, and there is also a path that led from the Capitol to the Gaol.

Williamsburg's Taverns

Capital Conviviality

During the 18th century there were 40 taverns in the Virginia capital of Williamsburg. Today there are seven offering a variety of tavern experiences. Lodging is available in the historic area at **Brick House** and **Market Square Taverns**. Guided tours are given at **Raleigh** and **Wetherburn's Taverns**. You can dine at **King's**

Arm, **Christiana Campbell's** or **Chowning's Tavern** and take in evening "gambols" at the latter.

Raleigh Tavern, which opened in 1932, was the first Williamsburg reconstruction. The colonial capital was the focal spot of rebellion in Virginia, and a great deal of the action took place at the Raleigh Tavern. When the Royal Governor dissolved the House of Burgesses the members resumed their meetings at the Raleigh Tavern. Often merchants and medical practitioners would arrange their schedules so that they too stayed at the Raleigh while the Burgesses met.

The most expensive piece of tavern equipment was the billiard table in the gaming room where ladies never ventured. You will see one of these old playing tables with ivory balls and hand-carved cues.

Ladies could attend the balls and formal functions given in the Apollo Room. Thomas Jefferson, in his diary, notes that he danced here with his "fair Belinda." The townspeople of Williamsburg gathered in the Apollo Room to celebrate the Treaty of Paris officially ending the American Revolution. Some years later in 1824 Lafayette attended a party at the Raleigh celebrating the American victory at Yorktown. The tavern is open daily from 9:00 A.M. to 5:00 P.M. and is included on the Patriot's Pass and the Basic Williamsburg tickets.

Behind Raleigh Tavern is the bake shop which still employs 200-year-old techniques to prepare gingerbread men and other delicacies for their customers.

Across Duke of Gloucester Street and down about half a block is Wetherburn's Tavern which is also open for tours daily from 10:00 A.M. to 6:00 P.M. The archeological on-site dig helped insure the authenticity of this restoration. Pottery shards and tavern equipment unearthed in the dry wells, the garbage dumps of the 18th century, enabled Colonial Williamsburg Foundation to furnish the tavern faithful to the inventory left by Mr. Wetherburn. Like many of his colonial contemporaries Mr. Wetherburn had two wives. He mourned all of 11 days before marrying the widow of a fellow tavernkeeper, thus securing her inherited goods including a good bit of silver.

As you will readily observe at both the Raleigh and at Wetherburn's, taverns in the 18th century were a combination hotel, restaurant, bar and community center. Unless he paid dearly for a private room a guest was apt to sleep with three or four strangers—not just in the same room, but in the same bed! From this practice comes the expression "sleep tight." Unless the ropes supporting the mattress were tightened each night, all the occupants would roll into the center of the bed. Slaves traveling with their masters slept either on the floor or in one of the dependencies.

Dining in the taverns of Williamsburg today is far different from what it was during the colonial period. The smaller taverns in the 18th century prepared only one meal; few had the luxury of a menu. Now at three taverns you can have a choice of colonial and traditional fare both at lunch and dinner. The fare at King's Arm, the most elegant of the three, features a dinner menu of game pie, oyster pie, Cornish game hen and beef with Sally Lunn bread, Indian corn muffins, assorted relishes, vegetables and old-fashioned desserts to compliment the meal. At Christiana Campbell's, dinner selections include clam chowder, Virginia ham, backfin crab imperial and southern fried chicken. Josiah Chowning's features Brunswick stew, barbecued ribs or pork barbecue; Welsh rabbit is a lunch time favorite. Reservations are a must for these colonial dining experiences, and should be made prior to your visit and confirmed upon arrival. If you stay over in Williamsburg you might want to drop in on the nightly 'gambol' at Chowning's. These evenings of tavern games are very popular. You can play backgammon, checkers, chess, cards or learn such new "old" boardgames as "The Royal and Most Pleasant Game of Goose" and "Bowles' Royal Pastime of Cupid," or "Entertaining Game of Snake."

The Brick House Tavern has been advertising "12 or 14 very good lodging rooms" since 1770. Unlike many taverns of the day, it welcomed women guests. Today 18 rooms are available for any Williamsburg visitors who can get reservations.

Just two blocks away up Duke of Gloucester Street is Market Square Tavern and Kitchen where visitors have found accommodations for three centuries. The 18-year-old apprentice law student, Thomas Jefferson, rented rooms here while he studied with George Wythe. Tavern rooms are available through the Colonial House program at Williamsburg Inn. For information or reservations, call (800)446-8956.

Directions: From Richmond take I-64 east to Williamsburg. Use Exit 56 onto Route 143 (you'll bear right off I-64). This is quickly followed by a right onto Route 132. You'll turn left onto feeder road Route 132Y into the Colonial Williamsburg Visitor Center.

JAMESTOWN

Jamestown Island, Colonial National Historical Park and Jamestown Festival Park

Best of Both Worlds

Side by side in Jamestown are two attractions that tell the same story by very different approaches. One, a national park, lets you use your imagination to rebuild and repopulate the Jamestown settlement. The second park, operated by the Jamestown-Yorktown Foundation, provides a fully realized re-creation of the ships on which the settlers arrived in the New World and the fort they built.

If you arrive at the **Jamestown Island, Colonial National Historical Park** with a proficient 17th-century vocabulary you'll be able to banter with your colonially-attired interpreter on one of the frequent walking tours. Drop a "Heaven forfend," "Shodikans," or "Fie on it;" substitute "nay" or "aye" for "no" or "yes;" use "a" in place of "to" as in "go a town;" or try "me" to replace "I" as in "me feels" and "me thinks" and you'll have a wondrous time.

Visitors to this 1607 settlement are often greeted as if they had just stepped off a ship from England. The settlers at James Cittie wax enthusiastic about the opportunities for advancement in Virginia. They will tell you that the road to riches is tobacco and not gold as the first arrivals so mistakingly believed.

Although only foundations and a crumbling tower from the 1639 church remain from that early era, the Visitor Center helps your imagination rebuild and repopulate the once thriving town. A 15-minute film provides the background on those first intrepid adventurers who set sail from England at Christmastime 1606, on the *Discovery, Susan Constant* and *Godspeed*. After a four-month Atlantic crossing made under difficult and cramped conditions (you can board a reconstruction of one of their ships at Jamestown Festival Park next door to the National Park), they arrived at a land where they had to hunt, grow and build everything necessary for their survival. The site of their James Fort is now beneath the James River, but there is a path along several of the streets of their town. Artifacts that have been recovered are on display in the Visitor Center museum rooms. There is also a gift shop that offers some fine reproductions of the pottery and glassware once made at Jamestown.

Before leaving the park be sure to stop at the Glasshouse, located just inside the entrance. Here, in an open-sided timber

Full-size reproductions of the three ships that carried 104 settlers from England to Virginia in 1607 are moored at Jamestown
Festival Park. The largest, Susan Constant, can be boarded.

and thatch shelter, are reproduced the first "factory-made" exports of the colonies. The green-colored glass, its tint due to the iron oxide in the sand, was sent back to England. You can watch craftsmen deftly blow down a long tube to form a jug or pitcher. A second glassmaker quickly adds a molten piece to form a graceful handle. The glass is at a temperature of between 2,000° and 3,000° when it's first removed from the dome-shaped furnace. As soon as it is shaped it's returned to another oven, an 800° lehr, so that it can be cooled slowly to prevent cracking.

Drive the five-mile loop trail on your way out. This gives you a clear picture of the natural environment the first settlers tamed in order to establish their community. The marsh and woodland is little changed since the early 1600s.

Jamestown Island, Colonial National Historical Park, is open daily, except Christmas, from 9:00 A.M. to 4:30 P.M. with extended hours during the summer months. A nominal admission is charged per car.

Just outside the boundary of this national park is **Jamestown Festival Park** with re-creations that help both young and old gain a deeper and more lasting understanding of the past. It's one thing to read about a confined cabin, rustic fort or spartan Indian village and quite another to climb aboard the *Susan Constant*, to hear the wind whistle through a wattle and daub house, or step inside a Powhatan Indian lodge. Jamestown Festival Park, a privately owned theme park located next to Colonial National Historical Park, offers these options as well as the chance to explore the Old and New World Pavilions.

Starting chronologically, your visit begins in the Old World Pavilion where wax figures represent pivotal characters in the early exploration of North America. Sovereigns and soldiers of fortune, they gambled their country's wealth and their lives to find a route to the east, new territory and the untapped riches of a new land. In the New World Pavilion exhibits depict the early colonial scene and Virginia's role in American history.

A vivid evocation of the Powhatan Indians who inhabited Tidewater Virginia awaits you at the Indian village and its ceremonial dance circle. Youngsters are amazed to learn that eastern Indians did not live in teepees. The seven dwellings in the village are typical of those built by the Paspahegh tribe who lived in the Jamestown area; they were members of the Powhatan empire, a network of roughly 200 tribal villages.

Authentically dressed interpreters explain how the Indians prepared their food and constructed their utensils and tools. Some of the lodges are furnished as they would have been in the early 17th century, with fur-covered ledges along the walls for sleeping, woven mats on the earth and a central fire for warmth and cooking. Extended families shared the lodges. The dance circle was used by the Powhatans to celebrate harvests, hunting expeditions, seasonal changes and other significant events.

The first European settlers in the Jamestown area were sponsored by the Virginia Company of London. Men and company alike were anxious to make fortunes by taking advantage of the natural resources of the New World. The settlers' early efforts were directed toward this goal rather than towards establishing a foothold on the continent. They did not plant crops, but at the insistence of Captain John Smith they did build a rough stockade and crude huts within two months of their arrival on May 14, 1607. Food was obtained by Smith in trade from the local Indians. As winter lengthened Captain Smith was forced to travel greater distances in search of food. These trips enabled him to map much of the surrounding area.

A fire in January 1608 burned the first fort. The harsh winter weather had convinced the settlers that sturdy houses were essential, and the second time they were more careful in their building. They rebuilt the fort, church, storehouse and guardhouse. These and 15 other buildings from the second Fort James have been re-created at Jamestown Festival Park. You'll also see replicas of the three ships that brought the settlers to America. Interpreters dressed in period clothes are at the fort and dock to answer questions.

Jamestown Festival Park is open daily 9:00 A.M. to 5:00 P.M. except Christmas and New Year's. From mid-June to mid-August it stays open until 7:00 P.M. Admission is charged. A combination ticket with the Yorktown Victory Center is available.

Directions: From Richmond take I-64 to the Williamsburg area. Then take the Colonial Parkway nine miles to Jamestown Island. Turn right to reach Jamestown Festival Park. An alternate route is to take I-64 to Exit 57 and turn onto Route 199 west. Drive five miles to the intersection with Route 31 and turn left. The Festival Park is four miles farther on the left.

YORKTOWN

Nelson House

There's Nothing Half-Way About This Nelson

The **Nelson House** in Yorktown, Virginia, is filled not with furniture but with voices from the past. Exemplifying the best traditions of the National Park Service, the free, living history programs performed here bring to life this important American family.

If you've ever wandered through an historic house and thought about the stories it could tell you'll appreciate, *If These Walls Could Talk*. Only two actors perform this mini-drama, but it seems like a larger cast. With minimal costume adjustments they re-create prominent Nelson family members and servants bringing alive the tumultuous days when America sought her independence. The program is given every hour from 11:00 A.M. to 5:00 P.M. except 2:00 P.M. on summer Mondays and Tuesdays.

Alternating with this program is *Visions: The Town, the Man, the Revolution*, which is done Wednesday through Sunday on the half hour, again from 11:00 A.M. to 5:00 P.M. except 2:00 P.M. The second program assumes that visitors are interested in settling in 18th-century Yorktown and would like to hear the Nelson family talk about their daily life.

The Nelsons' family home was built around 1711 by "Scotch Tom" Nelson, an Englishman born near the Scottish border and rumored to be tight-fisted, or "scotch" with his money. Young Thomas Nelson, Jr., just seven when his grandfather died, went on to play a pivotal role in Virginia history. Following colonial tradition he was educated in England at Cambridge University. When he returned to the colonies he served as a member of the Royal Governor's Council. But as the dispute grew between crown and colony, he sided with his fellow Virginians and became one of the signers of the Declaration of Independence.

The Nelson House still bears reminders of Thomas Nelson, Jr.'s military career during the Revolution. As Brigadier General of the Virginia militia he directed his men to fire at his own home. You'll see two cannonballs embedded in the east wall. They were placed in the wall in the 20th century to fill scars left from the siege of 1781.

The revolution not only threatened the very walls of Nelson's house, it also cost him a substantial fortune. He personally outfitted and provisioned his men during the Virginia campaign. Despite his financial reverses, the Nelson family house was the scene of a lavish gala honoring Lafayette on his return in 1824 to celebrate the victory at Yorktown.

Visitors are as welcome now as they were in the 18th century at the "house of two chimneys," open from mid-June to Labor Day and on special weekends from 10:00 A.M. to 4:00 P.M. (hours may vary depending on funding). Before leaving be sure to explore the restored formal English garden. For information on the living history dramas call (804)898-3400, extension 30.

While in Yorktown take the time to stroll along Main Street. Just to the right of the Nelson House are two interesting old homes. The Dudley Diggs House was built in the early 18th century and during the revolutionary years was the home of a council member for Virginia. You'll also see the Sessions House built in 1692 and believed to be the oldest house in Yorktown.

To the left of the Nelson House on Main Street there are five buildings of historical interest. Just across Read Street is the Customs House, reputedly built in 1721. Across Main Street is another 18th-century residence, the Pate House. Next door is Somerwell House, which survived the siege of 1781 to become a hotel during the Civil War. Across Church Street is the Medical shop reconstructed to look as it did during the 18th century. Facing it on Main Street is the Swan Tavern and dependencies, now operated as an antique shop. Swan Tavern was built in 1722 by "Scotch Tom" Nelson in partnership with Joseph Walker.

In summer you can pick up a walking tour map at the National Park Service Information Center on Main and Church Streets. At other times of the year you can obtain information at the Yorktown Battlefield Visitor Center.

Directions: From Richmond take I-64 east to the Colonial Parkway. Follow Colonial Parkway to Yorktown and then follow historical markers.

Yorktown Battlefield

The World Turned Upside Down

The rights proclaimed in the Declaration of Independence—life, liberty and the pursuit of happiness—were grounded in the rights the colonists felt were due them as Englishmen. These rights and privileges were asserted from the beginning; the first permanent settlement at Jamestown had a representative legislative assembly in 1619. At Williamsburg, Virginia, colonists again heralded the cause of man's natural rights in their 1776 "Declaration of Rights." And the final battle to insure these rights took place at Yorktown.

It was the end of September 1781, the seventh year of the American Revolution. Cornwallis had moved his British troops into Yorktown following his campaign through Virginia and the southern colonies. Washington then moved his men from their New York camp down to Virginia, hoping to arrive before Cornwallis escaped by sea with his army.

For three weeks Washington's men dug siege lines around the British who were forced by a French blockade to hold their positions. With his army surrounded and his escape cut off, Cornwallis ran out of options. On October 14 two important British redoubts fell. (A painting in the Old Senate Chamber at the Virginia State Capitol captures this dramatic action. See

Capitol selection.) On October 17 a red-coated drummer appeared on the British inner defense line and beat a parley. The guns were silent at last. On October 18 surrender terms were drawn up at the home of Augustine Moore, and the next day the British army surrendered. It would be another two years before the peace treaty was signed, but the war was, in fact, over.

This Yorktown victory is given depth and substance at the National Park Service Visitor Center at the **Yorktown Battlefield**. A free museum with exhibits and movie provides an ideal introduction to your battlefield tour.

One of the museum's most popular exhibits is the gun deck and captain's cabin from the *Charon*. The *Charon* was a 44-gun frigate the British lost during the Battle of Yorktown. Also on display are their regimental colors surrendered to Washington on October 19, 1781.

Before starting your drive, take the time to view the battlefield from the Observation Deck of the Visitor Center. The seven-mile tour marked by red arrows, includes six main points of interest: British Inner Defense Lines, Grand French Battery, Second Allied Siege Line, Redoubt 9 and 10, the Moore House and Surrender Field.

A second Allied Encampment Tour extends nine additional miles and is marked with yellow arrows. Its significant stops include: the American Artillery Park, Washington's Headquarters, the French Cemetery, the French Artillery Park, the French Encampment Loop and an untouched British Redoubt.

Yorktown Battlefield at Colonial National Historical Park is open daily at no charge. Summer hours are 8:00 A.M. to 6:00 P.M.; spring and fall hours 8:30 A.M. to 5:30 P.M.; and winter 8:30 A.M. to 5:00 P.M. These may vary depending on funding.

Directions: From Richmond take I-64 to the Colonial Parkway. Follow the Colonial Parkway to Yorktown and follow markers to the Visitor Center.

Yorktown Victory Center

The American Revolution: See It, Hear It, Feel It!

The Virginia Peninsula, a 15-mile wide strip, encompasses the Historic Triangle of Jamestown, Williamsburg and Yorktown. On this land the first permanent English settlement was established, the colonial capital of Virginia thrived, and the War for American Independence ended. At the **Yorktown Victory Center** the story of the revolutionary struggle is told, from its beginnings in Boston to its end in Yorktown.

At Yorktown, where the Revolutionary War ended and the United States began, visitors can walk or drive through the battlefields and see re-enactments such as this medical treatment.

You travel through history on Liberty Street. The multi-media exhibits along this mythical colonial street start at the office of the *Tidewater Gazette*. The editor sets the stage as the colonies totter on the brink of war. Special effects re-create the Boston Tea Party; next comes the action at Bunker Hill, and the war begins. The battles leading to the final siege at Yorktown show the mettle of the determined patriots. Displays include a 12-foot reproduction of the Declaration of Independence and a replica of Washington's campaign tent. Inside the tent you'll see a slide presentation showing early action in the Revolution. The exhibit, "The Final Campaign," presents the role of Virginia, and particularly Yorktown, in the war.

Following your walk along Liberty Street you'll see the 28-minute award winning color film, *The Road to Yorktown*. The pivotal sea battles off the Virginia capes, the American armies' strategic efforts to hold the British in place at Yorktown, and the climactic moments of surrender all are brought to life. Watching the British surrender to the tune of *The World Turned Upside Down* will give you goose bumps even though you know the story.

The war at sea is brought even closer as you view the artifacts the Virginia Research Center for Archaeology has recovered from the York River. Just three blocks from the Victory Center off Water Street, divers at the Yorktown Shipwreck Project are salvaging historical reminders from one of General Cornwallis' ships sunk during the Battle of Yorktown. Their finds are displayed along with other exhibits and paintings in the Gallery of the American Revolution at the Victory Center.

The first stage of an exciting expansion project opened in the spring of 1986. A 4½-acre outdoor Revolutionary encampment gives a realistic picture of the daily life of Revolutionary soldiers and the family members who accompanied them to war. The war is seen through the eyes of both soldiers and officers. Camp crafts are demonstrated, and soon to be added is a working-class farm that shows how a family burned out by invading armies survived eight years of warfare. There will also be a middle-class home which will be used as a visitor reception and orientation area staffed by the Center's interpreters taking the roles of characters from Revolutionary times. The chance to observe middle and lower class Virginians of the 18th century lends balance to the portrayal of early American life style, up to now overweighted by depictions of life at the great colonial plantations.

The Yorktown Victory Center is open daily except Christmas and New Year's Day from 9:00 A.M. to 5:00 P.M. From mid-June to mid-August it is open until 7:00 P.M. Admission is charged. A combination ticket is available which includes Jamestown Festival Park (see selection); both are operated by the Jamestown-Yorktown Foundation.

Directions: From Richmond take I-64 to the Colonial Parkway. Follow the Colonial Parkway to Yorktown. Watch for Victory Center markers. Turn left off the Parkway and cross Route 238 into the center's parking lot. An alternate route is to take I-64 to Exit 59. At the end of the exit ramp, turn left onto Route 143. At the traffic light turn left onto Route 238. The Victory Center is four miles farther on the right.

NORFOLK

The Chrysler Museum

Art Is the Driving Force

Though the *Wall Street Journal* considers **The Chrysler Museum** "one of the 20 top museums in the country," its origins were humble. Its roots go back to the years after the Civil War when two Norfolk teachers founded the Leache-Wood Female Seminary.

Irene Leache and Anne Cogswell Wood traveled to Europe each summer returning with paintings and sculpture. Most travelers end up with their mementos stored in the attic, but in 1901 Seminary alumni took steps to find a permanent home for their teachers' collection. This led to the establishment of The Norfolk Society of Arts in 1917. Through the group's efforts the city was persuaded to build a museum which opened in 1933 and was enlarged in both 1967 and 1976.

In 1971 Walter P. Chrysler, Jr., son of the founder of Chrysler Corporation, donated a large portion of his extensive and significant art collection to the Norfolk Museum thrusting it upon the world stage. Mr. Chrysler, who began collecting art when he was quite young, purchased a Renoir landscape when he was 13. His collection spans the continents and the centuries from classical antiquities to modern art. A major $10 million expansion of The Chrysler Museum that will double the space was begun in 1985 and is scheduled for completion in the late summer of 1988. Like so many museums, this one heretofore has kept a large inventory of its works in storage.

Art is subjective and visitors have their personal favorites, but certain pieces merit mentioning. Gauguin's *The Loss of Innocence* has been singled out for attention by John Russell of *The New York Times* who also said the museum's *Bust of the Savior* by Bernini was "one of the greatest single works of art in this country." Bernini was considered by his contemporaries to be Michelangelo's successor. This bust has an interesting history. It disappeared during the 18th century and wasn't identified as being Bernini's long-lost masterpiece until 1971.

Another museum masterpiece is the painting of *Saint Philip* by Georges de La Tour. It is one of only 30 works by this artist whose rediscovery in the 1930s has been called "the triumph of art history." The museum has Renoir's 1882 *The Daughters of Durand-Ruel*, which critics call "one of the painter's most impressive" works. Another crowd pleaser is itself a crowd scene, *The Artists' Wives* by Tissol.

Mr. Chrysler also amassed one of the world's finest glass collections. The museum has nearly 7,000 pieces that provide a comprehensive survey of the history of glass. One of the early pieces, an Ennion bowl, dates from the 1st century A.D. But it is the group of Tiffany lamps that leave visitors exclaiming. These are but a part of the museum's 400 piece Tiffany collection. There is also a comprehensive 2,500 piece collection of American Sandwich glass. Although not part of the Chrysler donation, the Worcester porcelain display is also outstanding.

The Chrysler has a rapidly expanding photographic collection, a decorative arts department and three galleries devoted to exhibits on loan. Visitors with an academic interest in art may want to arrange an appointment to use the 50,000 volume Jean Outland Chrysler Library.

The Chrysler Museum is open 10:00 A.M. to 4:00 P.M. Tuesday through Saturday and 1:00 to 5:00 P.M. on Sunday. It is closed Mondays and major holidays. There is no admission, but donations are encouraged.

Directions: The Chrysler Museum is located in the picturesque Ghent district of Norfolk just six blocks from Waterside. Take I-64 from Richmond and exit at I-264. Continue to the final exit, Waterside Drive. Continue on Waterside Drive as it turns into Dousch Street. Take a left at Brambleton, then an immediate right on Duke Street. The museum is on your left 2½ blocks down Duke Street.

Douglas MacArthur Memorial

Some Soldiers Never Fade Away

When Douglas MacArthur was born January 26, 1880, in Little Rock, Arkansas, the Norfolk, Virginia, paper reported, "Douglas MacArthur was born . . . while his parents were away." This was not a medical first, simply a hometown paper commenting on a local personality. His mother, Mary Pinkney Hardy MacArthur, had been born in Norfolk, and since his father, Arthur MacArthur, was a peripatetic military officer, Norfolk was always their "home by choice."

The General Douglas MacArthur Memorial in Norfolk houses MacArthur's tomb and such historic memorabilia as the surrender papers signed by the Japanese aboard the USS Missouri.

Although General Douglas MacArthur never actually lived in Norfolk, he nevertheless acceded to the city's suggestion of a memorial in 1960 and helped plan the complex you'll see. Norfolk redesigned the 1850 city hall done by Thomas Walter, who is noted for his work on the dome and House and Senate wings of the U.S. Capitol. The **MacArthur Memorial** opened in 1964 on the General's 84th birthday. When MacArthur died on April 5, 1964, he was buried in the rotunda he helped design. Not for him Washington, D.C., where he said he had never won a battle.

Begin your visit at the MacArthur Memorial theater where you'll see a 22-minute newsreel compilation; footage that captures significant events in American history in which the General played a pivotal role. The film gives added life to the still photographs and memorabilia in the 11 galleries surrounding the rotunda.

The first gallery contains gifts the MacArthurs received from admirers around the world. There is a Kutani porcelain plate, a Christmas present from Prime Minister Shigiru Yoshida of Japan. A lacquer chest is a gift form the Empress Nagako. Mrs. MacArthur, who visits the memorial two or three times a year, always stops for a look at her collection of Japanese silver salt and pepper shakers.

In Gallery Two you'll see reminders of the young MacArthur. He had the highest entrance marks to West Point and graduated with one of the highest averages in the academy's history. A Tiffany silver chest that had belonged to MacArthur's father was reluctantly abandoned by the General when he evacuated Manila. The Japanese Ambassador who "acquired" it appreciated the artistry of this silver set, with each utensil individually designed. When the island was retaken the family silver was returned.

Galleries Three through Nine cover MacArthur's service in the Philippines, World War I and II and the Korean War. Photographs, uniforms, weapons, medals and maps help tell the story. Large murals show MacArthur's return to the Philippines, his attendance at the Japanese surrender and his address to Congress in 1951 after President Truman relieved him of command.

The last gallery contains the well-remembered corn-cob pipe, sunglasses and visored cap identified with MacArthur. There are also two large cases of medals presented by countries around the world and by the U.S. government. His Congressional Medal of Honor is prominent among the latter; his receipt of it made the MacArthurs the only father and son in American history to receive the award.

The MacArthur Memorial is open at no charge 10:00 A.M. to 5:00 P.M. Monday through Saturday and 11:00 A.M. to 5:00 P.M. on

Sundays. It is closed Thanksgiving, Christmas and New Year's Day.

Directions: From Richmond take I-64 to Norfolk; then take I-264 and exit on City Hall Avenue and proceed three blocks west. Parking is available on the north side of City Hall Avenue.

Hermitage Foundation Museum

Little Russia

The Hermitage is a museum to be savored. The dark-visaged witches supporting the ceiling, satyrs over the library door, drunken winemakers on the ivory netsuke, multiple secret panels and a thundering organ all combine to delight the visitor who takes the time to look and listen to the tales of the guides who bring this astounding collection to life.

It's hard to imagine a better setting than the Sloanes' English Tudor home. Although it began as a five-room summer cottage for textile millionaire William Sloane, it was expanded into a 42-room mansion. Three master carvers worked 22 years on its elaborate paneling, mantles, beams and custom-designed furniture.

The mood is firmly and loudly established when the guide inserts a roll in the 1935 Moller organ, and music on a grand scale fills the air. It's the perfect accompaniment to the Old World Gothic drawing room. Separating the organ from the drawing room is a rood screen, used in churches to divide the choir from the congregation. Unlike most museums, the Hermitage allows photography—fortunately because the details of this ornately carved wooden screen are well worth capturing. The drawing room is filled with art from around the world: a 16th-century Flemish tapestry, 16th- and 17th-century Spanish religious art and one of two massive limestone fireplaces from Bath, England.

The Sloanes amassed the largest privately owned oriental art collection on the east coast including a linden wood statue of Kuan Yin, goddess of mercy, that is more than 1,000 years old. Other rarities are the Mingchi carved horses buried with the deceased to help carry their possessions into the next world, and a 6th-century Chinese marble Buddha.

The dining room faces the Lafayette River, but it did not always do so. To change the view the Sloanes hired a contractor who had a crane move two rooms in toto, exchanging the location of the dining room with that of the parlor.

This house, like most Tudor mansions, has a Great Hall. It is here that four witches support the ceiling to ward off evil spirits.

Two Tiffany lamps provide muted light. The carpet has the five-toed dragon design, symbol of the Chinese Imperial family. If you want to learn how 15th-century Spanish merchants smuggled, have a look at one of their intricately carved sample boxes (vargueno) displayed here.

In the morning room are displayed perhaps the most intriguing items of all: the lily shoes worn by women to keep their feet from growing. Some feet were tortured to lengths of no more than five inches. The upstairs has additional exhibits not to be missed, including Fabergé creations.

The Hermitage Foundation Museum is open daily from 10:00 A.M. to 5:00 P.M. and Sunday from 1:00 to 5:00 P.M. It is closed on Thanksgiving, Christmas and New Year's Day. Admission is charged, but those under six and service personnel are admitted free.

Directions: From Richmond take I-64 to Route 165 and turn right on Little Creek Road. At the intersection of Little Creek Road and Hampton Boulevard (Route 337), turn left onto Hampton Boulevard. Continue to North Shore Road and turn right. The Hermitage Foundation Museum is one-half mile on the left. Norfolk Tour signs will indicate the route.

Moses Myers House

Jewish Merchant Prince

When Eliza Chapman and Moses Myers were married in 1787 they chartered a boat and moved from New York to Norfolk, Virginia. Myers was the first Jewish settler in the Tidewater area. Within four years he had established a five vessel fleet for his import-export business and built a classic Georgian townhouse.

The oldest four-square portion of the house was constructed of 18th-century English ballast bricks. In 1796 the **Moses Myers House** was expanded from 8 to 15 rooms. From the outside you can clearly see the difference between the English and American bricks. Five generations of Myerses lived here and 70 percent of the furniture is original. Moses Myers was a community leader and his home reflects his successful life style.

Myers was president of the city council; a major in the Virginia militia; consul from the United States to France, the Netherlands and Denmark; founder of the Junior League; manager of the 1817–18 Assembly Ball; superintendent of the Bank of Richmond; and collector of customs.

From the moment you pull the old English bell to gain entrance you'll be intrigued by this remarkably well preserved old city mansion. The Myerses did not require exterior door locks;

servants were always on hand with a massive one pound key to unfasten the English triple box lock. The entrance hall still has the original four-inch native heart pine floor boards and a decorative snowflake pattern plaster ceiling. In the formal parlor you'll see Gilbert Stuart's portraits of Moses Myers painted when he was in his early fifties and Mrs. Myers when she was in her early forties. The parlor's Portuguese tole chandelier is a curiosity; the light prongs surrounding the eternal flame bear the likeness of Christopher Columbus. The mantle decoration around the parlor fireplace also reveals the visage of an important historical figure. George Washington gazes out from the rosettes flanking the fireplace on this unique mantle. The mold the mantle was made from is included in the American Wing of New York's Metropolitan Museum.

The dining room is regarded as one of the most beautiful in all the south. Here the Myerses entertained the Marquis de Lafayette, President James Monroe, Daniel Webster, Stephen Decatur, Henry Clay and General Winfield Scott. In the china cabinet you'll see the apricot Spode dishes that date from Mrs. Myers's first marriage. The white, grey and silver decor combines with the black and white patterned canvas matting on the floor to create a surprisingly modern look.

The Myerses were all musical, and their music room has both a pianoforte and harp. The family reputedly had the largest collection of musical books in early America, with George Washington a close second. The three Myers daughters wrote the musical scores in quite a number of the books. On the music stand you'll see one of the volumes the Myers girls copied.

Displayed in the upstairs hallway is the dueling pistol James Barron used to kill Stephen Decatur. Another room has a seven lock iron money chest which Myers anchored to the floor with thick iron chains. There is also a grand harmonicon. Only five of the 25 glass bells have survived, but it is enough to give visitors a look at an instrument for which both Beethoven and Mozart composed.

The curtain treatment in the south bedroom is unusual; plaster rods are shaped like giant fiddle ferns. Over the Myers's bed is a carved acorn, symbol of fertility. It obviously was effective; they had 12 children. In Mrs. Myers's bedroom you'll see her oriental sewing box. The back bedroom has a six-foot modified sleigh bed.

Before ending your tour be sure to visit the outside kitchen, the garden and the gift shop. Hours, April through December, are 10:00 A.M. to 5:00 P.M. Tuesday through Saturday, and NOON to 5:00 P.M. on Sunday. From January through March the house is open NOON to 5:00 P.M. Tuesday through Saturday, closed Sunday and Monday and on major holidays. This is one of the few historic homes that celebrates Hannukah, the Jewish Festival of Lights, which occurs in December. Candles are lit in an antique brass menorah for each of the festival's eight days. Admission is charged.

Directions: From Richmond take I-64 to Norfolk, then follow I-264 east to the Waterside Drive Exit. Take Waterside Drive to St. Paul's Boulevard, then turn left on Market Street and right onto Bank Street. The Moses Myers House is at the corner of Freemason and Bank Streets.

Norfolk Botanical Gardens

Gardens-by-the-Sea

Glide on a trackless train along meandering wooded paths brightened by colorful azaleas, rhododendrons and bright annuals, or float along the wandering canals for a different view— either option is available at the **Norfolk Botanical Gardens**. Each 30-minute ride provides a perfect introduction to the 20 focal spots at this 175-acre garden. Once you gain an overview you can enjoy a closer look along the 12 miles of walkways.

Norfolk Botanical Gardens claims "there is something always in bloom," but undoubtedly the best time to visit is in April and May when the more than 200,000 azaleas bloom. What began as a WPA project in 1936 has grown into one of the best azalea gardens on the east coast. Since 1954 Norfolk has hosted the International Azalea Festival the third week of April to salute the North Atlantic Treaty Organization. Blooming concurrently with the azaleas in May are the more than 150 varieties of rhododendron. Banks of these lovely spring bushes line the canals, train paths and walkways. Tulips, daffodils and spring bulbs add to the seasonal show. For a panoramic view climb to the top of the Hill of Nations Observation Tower.

The award-winning Bicentennial Rose Garden is in bloom from mid-May through October. There are more than 250 varieties of roses and roughly 4,000 bushes representing all the colors of the rainbow. The fragrant blossoms, enhanced by sculpture and fountains, can be enjoyed from the pedestrian terrace, overlooks and garden walkways.

Although there are random blossoms to be seen in January and February such as the witch hazel, wintersweet and pyracantha, it is in March that the first major garden area, the camellias, comes into bloom. Norfolk, with some 700 varieties, has one of the best collections in the country. This is particularly true since the more northern collections have suffered severe damage from sub-zero winters.

Other specialty areas are the Japanese Garden, Fragrance Garden, Colonial Garden and the 17½-acre Flowering Arboretum. The Norfolk Botanical Gardens also has two scenic fishing piers. Children under 16 and seniors don't have to have a license, but anyone else must obtain a city fishing permit. Norfolk Botanical Gardens is open daily 8:30 A.M. to sunset. Admission is charged.

During summer, you can extend your day by heading over to Norfolk's **Ocean View Beaches** which paradoxically overlook the Chesapeake Bay. Both visitors and natives enjoy the calm waters and uncrowded beaches. Beach parking, often a problem, is solved here by large free public lots at both 9th Street and Ocean View Avenue and 6th Street and Ocean View Avenue. Boardwalks provide beach access. Other pluses at Norfolk beaches are the gently sloping sandbars, free of undertow, where youngsters can swim and play in safety and deeper water free of buffeting waves for adults. Only occasionally will a northeast wind churn up the waves and currents. In late July and August you do get an influx of jellyfish but no more than you'll find at nearby ocean beaches. Lifeguards are on duty from 11:00 A.M. to 7:00 P.M. There are also restrooms and shaded picnic areas. Two commercial fishing piers with bait shops and tackle rentals are popular with both fishermen and crabbers. For boaters there is a ramp at 13th Ocean View which is open at no charge year round. If you plan to bring your boat to Norfolk call (804)441-2222 for docking information.

Directions: From Richmond take I-64 to Norfolk. The Norfolk Botanical Gardens are off Route 170 on Azalea Garden Road. For Ocean View Beaches take Bay View Boulevard off I-64, which will intersect with Ocean View Avenue (Route 60).

Norfolk Naval Base

Nautical but Nice!

The **Norfolk Naval Base**—the world's largest naval base—certainly demonstrates the magnitude of America's military strength. The long line of destroyers, aircraft carriers, submarines and support ships tied up at Norfolk is truly an impressive sight.

Norfolk's naval significance dates from the Civil War when the famous battle of the ironclads, *The Monitor* and *The Merrimac*, occurred in Hampton Roads harbor. Today there are 130 ships, 45 aircraft squadrons and 67 shore based activities in the South Hampton Roads commands. The Norfolk Naval Base extends over 3,400 acres and provides a great deal of interesting information and sights.

Tours leave daily between 10:00 A.M. to 2:00 P.M. from the Naval Base Tour Office at 9809 Hampton Boulevard. They leave on the half-hour and take about 90 minutes. There is a charge, but no reservations are required.

As you enter the base you'll see that the Marine Corps stands security for this naval installation. Norfolk has the largest Marine barracks in the United States. More than 460 Marines are quartered here to provide security for the base and personnel.

It seems everything is bigger here! The Naval Supply Center is, as the sign says, "The World's Largest Store." It is open daily year round and employs 3,600 civilians and 71 military personnel. It's easy to see why this Norfolk facility has a $3.5 billion federal payroll.

Near the top of the military payroll are the Flag Officers. Along "Admiral's Row" you'll see replicas of famous homes from various states built in 1907 for the Jamestown Exposition, and all now used as officers' homes. For example, the Georgia House is a copy of the summer home of Franklin Delano Roosevelt's mother, known for a time as the Little White House. A typical colonial homestead represents Delaware. A lovely porticoed Virginia plantation house is the quarters of Admiral McDonald, Supreme Allied Commander of NATO. Along this fascinating drive there is also a scaled-down replica of Independence Hall which houses the Hampton Roads Naval Museum open from 10:00 A.M. to 4:00 P.M. on weekdays (until 5:00 P.M. on weekends).

Ten percent of the Navy's aircraft is home based out of Norfolk. There are 147 aircraft plus overhaul and repair facilities. Also based here are Sea King, Sea Knight and Sea Sprite helicopters. All weather early warnings, surveillance coordination, search and rescue missions and numerous other functions are carried out by the Eighth Carrier Airborne Early Warning Squadrons home ported at Norfolk. You are sure to see some of the Hawkeye planes they fly.

What's a military installation without confusing shorthand? On the tour you pass both the FASOTRAGRULANT and the NAVCAMSLANT. The former is a sophisticated flight simulator facility. The latter is the largest and most complex communication station in the world.

All of the above is just icing on the cake as far as most visitors are concerned. They come to see the ships, and there are plenty to see! As you enter the two-mile waterfront area the first you see, berthed along the Pier 12, are the world's largest warships. You'll learn how to tell the difference between the nuclear powered and conventional powered ships. (Just a hint: it has to do with the color of the antennas.) You may see a nuclear powered aircraft carrier such as the *Nimitz* or the *Eisenhower*. These massive ships are 18 stories high and as long as three football fields plus an extra 100 feet at both ends. The size comes into focus when you learn that each link in the anchor chain weighs 350 pounds. The warships carry more than 6,200 men each. By act of Congress, women may not be stationed aboard any ship meant for combat.

Next, at the Cargo Ship Pier, you'll see 23 types of boats and ships: destroyers, cruisers, amphibious ships, helicopter ships, fleet oilers and tugs. On weekends from 1:00 to 4:30 P.M. there are usually two ships that you can board although these rarely include aircraft carriers and submarines. The final part of the harbor portion of the tour takes you past the workhorses of the Atlantic Fleet—more destroyers and cruisers plus submarines and submarine tenders.

Directions: From Richmond take the I-295 loop around Richmond and pick up I-64 east to Norfolk. After you cross the Hampton Roads Bridge-Tunnel you turn right on Bellinger Boulevard for the Norfolk Naval Station.

Willoughby-Baylor House

All in the Family

In 1754 when William Willoughby built one of the first 20 brick townhouses in Norfolk his family's roots in this Virginia community extended back to the earliest days of the colony. His great-great-grandfather, Thomas Willoughby, had come to Virginia in 1610 at age nine. By 1636 Thomas had obtained a patent for 200 acres of Tidewater land on which Norfolk was later built. Thomas already owned the 500-acre Willoughby Plantation that is now Ocean View.

When William, prominent retail merchant and contractor, repurchased the old family acreage, Norfolk was struggling to recover from the massive fire damage caused by Lord Dunsmore's bombardment in 1776. The home William Willoughby built reflects both Federal and Georgian design. Furnishings are in keeping with the 1800 inventory filed with the will at George's death. Hard use over the years resulted in the loss of all the original furnishings.

In the front parlor you'll notice that the handkerchief table, card table and the tilt-top tea table all fold up. Furniture in the 18th century had to be both versatile and movable to allow maximum use of space. The pair of Queen Anne mirrors that hang opposite each other, one in the parlor and the other in the adjoining dining room were designed to reflect candlelight not images; called mirrors when used downstairs, they were listed on inventories as looking glasses when used upstairs. The dining room table was once owned by James Madison's mother and was used in the White House during the Madison administration.

In the upstairs hall you'll find a sword chair, designed so that a man could sit and work while wearing his sword. There's also a dressing room with a gentlemen's basin stand. The shaving cup is an ingenious contrivance with a saucer that held alcohol. The alcohol was lit and by the time it burned off, the water in the cup would be hot enough for shaving.

In the master bedchamber there is a curious device used for making inkles, the braided linen tapes used to secure clothes during the 18th century. Clothes were adjusted by inkles at neck, wrist and waist so that one size fit all. These small inkles prompted the expression, "don't have an inkling," meaning smallest idea. The last room on the tour is the children's room, in which you'll see a narrow chimney closet. The pattern on the children's dishes matches artifacts of china discovered during excavation.

The Willoughby-Baylor house is open April through December from 10:00 A.M. to 5:00 P.M., Tuesday through Saturday and Sunday from NOON to 5:00 P.M. From January through March hours are NOON to 5:00 P.M., Tuesday through Saturday, closed Sunday, Monday and major holidays. Admission is charged.

Directions: From Richmond take I-64 to Norfolk and then I-264 east. Exit on Waterside Drive and take an immediate right at St. Paul's Boulevard. Take a left onto Market Street, then the next right onto Cumberland Street. The house is at the corner of Cumberland and Freemason Streets.

PORTSMOUTH

Portside

Deserves a Bow

They no longer charge a bale of hay for the ferry ride across the Elizabeth River; now it's 50 cents. That's still an inexpensive way of getting out where the action is—the busy Norfolk-Portsmouth harbor.

This waterway has been important since the earliest days of the Virginia colony. An exploration party led by Captain John Smith sailed up the Elizabeth River in 1608. Adam Thoroughgood, who arrived in 1621 as an indentured servant, operated the first ferry service in 1636. (See Adam Thoroughgood House selection.) Adam owned a small skiff and had two oarsmen who would take passengers across the river. Stories were told that his helpers would hide in the marsh grass until enough passengers arrived to make it profitable, but then the stories also claimed that Adam was paid in bales of hay.

Ferry service between Portsmouth and Norfolk, the oldest continuous public ferry service in the country, reached its zenith in the 1940s when there were six diesel ferries for passenger cars. Once the tunnel had connected the two cities in 1955, the ferry service was discontinued. The recent resumption of service has proved popular. The ferry runs on Monday through Thursday from 10:00 A.M. to 10:00 P.M., Friday through Sunday from 10:00 A.M. to MIDNIGHT and weekday mornings from 7:00 to 9:00 A.M. The ferry leaves Portside on the hour and the half hour and Waterside in Norfolk at 15 and 45 minutes past the hour.

The *Carrie B* offers 1½-hour afternoon cruises and three-hour sunset sails. The *Carrie B* is a replica of a 19th-century Mississippi river boat. It cruises past the world's largest working shipyard, the Norfolk Naval Shipyard, founded in 1767 when Virginia was still a British colony. During the Civil War when Federal troops had to abandon the Norfolk navy yard, they sank the U.S. frigate *Merrimac*. The Confederates raised the ship and in 1861–62 reconstructed the ironclad *Virginia* upon the hull of the *Merrimac* in drydock here. This is the nation's oldest drydock, but technology has kept pace with the changes in ship design. The navy sends many of its modern supercarriers, submarines and missile ships here for repairs.

The *Carrie B* leaves from Norfolk, stopping at Portside 15 minutes later. From mid-April through November and from Labor Day through October, cruises sail at NOON and 2:00 P.M. June through Labor Day there are also cruises at 10:00 A.M. during the week and 4:00 P.M. daily. Sunset cruises are at 6:00 P.M. from June through mid-September daily except Monday.

Whether you opt for the brief ferry trip or the longer cruise your interest in nautical matters is likely to be piqued. Portside has two museums to satisfy your curiosity. The Portsmouth Lightship Museum at London Slip is located in a ship that never sailed but gave long service. Lightships combined attributes of both lighthouses and buoys; their lighted masts resembled the former and they floated like the latter. They had an additional benefit in that they could move from place to place. As they changed locations they frequently changed names. The lightship now permanently docked at London Slip was first called *Charles*, then *Overfalls*, *Nantucket Relief*, *Stonehorse* and just before retiring in 1964 it was called *Cross Rip*. In addition to seeing the inside of one of these old lightships you'll see Coast Guard equipment, uniforms and old photographs. You are welcome aboard at no charge Tuesday through Saturday from 10:00 A.M. to 4:45 P.M. and Sunday from 2:00 to 4:45 P.M.

Open during the same hours is the adjacent Portsmouth Naval Shipyard Museum. One of this museum's most interesting displays is the 1776 map of Portsmouth. An audio-visual program uses the map to acquaint you with life in colonial Portsmouth. You'll also see the plans of John L. Porter for the conversion of the *Merrimac* (these are the plans he hid in his home nearby; see Portsmouth Walking Tour selection). Old tools, weapons, ship models and uniforms fill the cases at this maritime museum.

During the summer months you can enjoy an al fresco meal at Portside's Olde Harbor Market. Seafood is the specialty at many of the stalls—steamed shrimp, crabcakes, clams and oysters vie with more traditional fare. If you prefer a restaurant take the ferry across and explore the more than 100 shops and restaurants of Norfolk's Waterside. (See Norfolk Naval Base & Harbor selection.)

Directions: From Richmond take I-64 to the Norfolk-Portsmouth area. Exit on I-264 for Norfolk's Waterside. Take the Berkeley Bridge to Portsmouth. Turn right on Crawford Street to High Street. Go right one block on High Street to the waterfront area for Portside and the museums.

Portsmouth Walking Tour

Harboring a Spirited Past

Portsmouth boasts the largest concentration of antique houses between Alexandria and Charleston, South Carolina. You'll see more sites on the National Register of Historic Places here than in any other Virginia city. It is not quantity, however, that captivates visitors on a walking tour of Olde Towne; it's the diversity of architectural styles.

The old English city checkerboard pattern was laid out in 1752 by Colonel William Crawford, prominent merchant and ship owner. You can follow the red brick sidewalks into America's past on the Olde Towne Lantern tour. Portsmouth plaques on the street lanterns indicate stops on the walking tour. You get the tour map by stopping at the Portside Visitor Center.

Begin your walk on London Boulevard at 108, the Cassell House that Captain John McRae built in 1829. You'll want to pay close attention to the details of these old homes. The Cassell House features a handcarved arched frame door with a fanlight and stone lintel. The gabled roof indicates the Dutch influence.

The house at the corner of London Boulevard and Crawford Street has two names. The first, Murder House, does not recall a heinous crime but the pronunciation of the owner's family name, the Murdaughs. Since the Civil War it's been called by its second name, the Pass House, because the Federal adjutant general headquartered here granted passes to enter and leave Portsmouth. This is the first example you'll see of the above ground basement homes copied from Hull, England, that were ideally suited for this low-lying location.

The now respectable office building at 216–218 London Boulevard was once a sailor's tavern called The Red Lion. Recent renovations uncovered a cockfighting pit in the cellar.

Move up London Boulevard to Middle Street and turn right. Several visitors have heard, but only one has seen, the ghost of the Ball-Nivison House at 417 Middle Street. According to that eyewitness, a professor in academic gown carries not his books but his head under his arm. John Nivison, prominent Portsmouth attorney, certainly kept his head when he bought this Dutch Colonial home in 1784. It is one of the many "tax dodger" homes in town, so named because the British taxed only full floors, leaving the dormer floor tax free.

When the Marquis de Lafayette returned to Portsmouth in 1824 50 years after the Revolution he stayed at the Ball-Nivison. Lafayette was 19 when he joined the fight for American independence. He returned, an elderly statesman, to a hero's welcome. The Lafayette Arch at Crawford Street and London Boulevard commemorates his visit.

The Gothic Revival House at 370 Middle Street is full of gingerbread touches like the wooded lattice and patterned bargeboard gables. Victorian woodwork, called jigsaw, is featured on the porch at 371 Middle Street. Just a few steps down the street is another elaborate porch at 365.

Continue up the 300 block of London Boulevard to the corner of Court and Queen Streets and you'll see the pink granite Court Street Baptist Church, considered by some architectural historians to be one of the four best examples of Romanesque design in the country. The words "In God We Trust" were added to our money at the suggestion of Mark R. Watkinson, a former pastor of this church.

The corner of Court and High Streets was Towne Square on William Crawford's plans. On the four corners there was a church, a market, a court house and a jail. This took care of both moral and practical needs. Only Trinity Church remains; it is Portsmouth's oldest church dating from 1761.

Norfolk burned during the American Revolution but not Portsmouth. The city was saved by Lt. John Dickey of the British Royal Navy. He had been captured and brought to Portsmouth, but instead of spartan imprisonment he enjoyed the hospitality of Tory sympathizers. Dickey repaid the city by intervening when Lord Dunmore was ready to turn the British guns on Portsmouth. General Cornwallis, too, spent time in Portsmouth. He was headquartered here before his ill-advised move to Yorktown. British supporters made him welcome, but he decided the town was difficult to defend. The Revolution might have lasted longer had Cornwallis remained in Portsmouth. It is from the British "constable on patrol" in the old colonial city that we derive our present day usage of "cop."

At 420 Court Street, a Victorian house built in 1870 has stylish floor length windows with semi-elliptical arched tops. Be sure to notice the ironwork, particularly where it crests over the porch. The 400 block of London Boulevard looks like a Currier and Ives print. The small frame house at 412 will remind you of Williamsburg. A row of colorful cottage style houses built in the mid-to-late 1800s have a wealth of architectural details. Along Washington Street you'll find another group of 19th-century homes. Smuggled medicines destined for the Confederate army were hidden beneath the hearthstones at 412 Washington Street.

Turn right on North Street. At the corner of North and Dinwiddie Streets is the Federal style house built in 1799 by Colonel Dempsey Watts. During the Black Hawk War the chief of the warring tribes was brought to Portsmouth to see the "big canoes" and hear the "big boom" of the *U.S.S. Delaware* cannons. Impressed, the Black Hawk Chief returned to the Watts House where he was entertained as a guest of the nation.

Turn left on Court Street to explore the 300 block. Like many of the English basement houses, 336 has been lowered so that the main floor is close to street level. The ghosts at the Maupin House, 326, are pet bull terriers.

The Harth House at 320 Court Street is reputedly the oldest house in Portsmouth still faithful to its original design. This early 19th-century basement house has a Greek Revival portico. Notice the door's transom light with rectangular panes and the brass door knob and knocker.

The William Peters House at 315 Court Street, with its Classical Revival look, suggests the Battery homes of Charleston, South Carolina. The Porter family lived here during the Civil War. When Union General Benjamin Franklin Butler, who was in charge of this Confederate city, appeared to inspect their home one of the ladies tripped him on the stairs. This was not as ill-advised as you might think. The general's nickname was "Spoon" Butler; he had a habit of purloining the family silver. When Miss Porter tripped him silver spoons bounced out of his uniform pockets as he tumbled down the stairs. Only Butler's dignity was harmed, but luckily for the Porter family he did not return to complete his inspection.

John L. Porter had hidden his plans for the conversion of the salvaged Union ironclad *Merrimac* into the Confederate ship *Virginia* in the wall of his home. Years later when Butler ran for President on the Radical Reconstruction ticket a campaign banner was hung in Portsmouth recalling the general's Civil War victory. To the slogan "Butler Hero of Five Forks" a local opponent added, "and the Lord only knows how many silver teaspoons."

On the corner of Court and North Streets is the Bain House, built on one of William Crawford's original lots. The old Elks Club across Court Street is built in the Romanesque style. The 300 block of North Street has another group of mid-19th-century basement homes. The first city mayor, George W. Grice, who served from 1858 to 1861, lived at 314 North Street.

The Hill House, 221 North Street, was built in the early 1800s by Captain John Thompson. His nephew, John Thompson Hill, the second owner, gave his name to the house, and it remained in the family until 1962. Many original 19th-century pieces still fill the house which is open for tours Tuesday through Sunday from 2:00 to 5:00 P.M. Admission is charged.

The Grice-Neeley House, 202 North Street, suggests New Orleans with its wrought iron balcony and graceful stairs. To complete your walking tour turn right on Crawford Street. You'll pass three mid-19th-century homes, the Benthall-Brooks Row. Brooks, a sea captain, built these homes in the 1840s, one floor at a time. He built the basement story for all three and waited a year; then built the second floor and waited another year. He finished the three houses the third year. Perhaps he knew what he was doing; the row houses have survived more than 150 years.

On weekends in the spring and fall and daily during the summer you can take a 45-minute trolley ride through Olde Towne Portsmouth. If you are visiting with youngsters be sure to stop at the 1846 Court House at Court and High Streets for the hands-on Children's Museum. The Portsmouth Fine Arts Gallery is located on the floor above the children's museum. It is open Tuesday through Saturday from 10:00 A.M. to 5:00 P.M. and Sunday 2:00 to 5:00 P.M. A nominal admission is charged. Next door, at 420 High Street, is the Virginia Sports Hall of Fame where you can see such sports memorabilia as Sam Snead's golf hat and Arthur Ashe's tennis racket. Hours are the same except an hour earlier opening on Sundays. There is no admission charge.

Directions: From Richmond take I-64 east to Norfolk and connect with I-264. Then at the Elizabeth River take the Berkley Bridge to Portsmouth.

The Casemate Museum

Roommates and Casemates

Edgar Allan Poe, tired of army life after spending the dark winter months of 1828–29 at Fort Monroe, sold his enlistment for $75 ending his career as an army artilleryman. After wandering through the gloomy chambers of **The Casemate Museum** you may wonder if he hadn't just decided that he had enough inspiration for his tales of horror. Casemates, the damp, dungeon-like artillery vaults within the fort's mammoth stone walls, make a perfect setting for a Poe story. They also make a good setting for exhibits on the people and events in the history of Fort Monroe.

If Poe found the casemates inspirational, Robert E. Lee more than likely found them educational. Lee, an army engineer, worked from 1831 to 1834 on the construction of Fort Monroe. During the Civil War he was careful not to attack the "Gibralter of Chesapeake Bay." The name was well deserved. Fort Monroe was the largest stone fort built in North America. At the time it was completed, it was also the largest enclosed fortification in the United States. The designer, General Simon Bernard, had been trained to think big as aide-de-camp to Napoleon Bonaparte.

The fort's impenetrable stone walls imprisoned Jefferson Davis at the conclusion of the Civil War. He was charged with plotting to assassinate Lincoln, mistreating Union prisoners and treason. After his capture on May 22, 1865, the former president of the Confederacy spent five months in casemate cell 2. For the first five days he was kept manacled in leg irons, but even after these were removed his dank, spartan cell was a bitter home for a man who had just led a country, albeit to defeat. After five months Davis was transferred to better accommodations in Carroll Hall; its location is marked on the Fort Monroe Walking Tour. Davis was released on $100,000 bail May 13, 1867. Two years later all charges were dropped.

Though Davis was a most reluctant resident, some Federal officers made comfortable homes in the casemates. Photographs from the 1900s show four such living quarters. You wonder as you look at the piano in the re-created casemate parlor if the fort kept a tuner on the payroll.

Another major exhibit focuses on the four-hour Civil War battle that occurred just off Fort Monroe in Hampton Roads between the ironclads *Monitor* and *Merrimac* (though the traditional spelling is without a "k," naval historians prefer Merrimack, after the New England river for which it was named). The museum models, battle plans, weapons and uniforms tell the story of this great naval battle.

Scale models of weapons from the army's Coast Artillery branch are also exhibited here. The Coast Artillery School was located at Fort Monroe, which served as the headquarters for the defenses of the Chesapeake Bay during World War II. Fort Monroe has an extensive collection of artillery pieces. On the walking tour you'll see a 15-inch Rodman gun that was named for President Lincoln and used to bombard Confederate batteries on Sewell's Point. You can also drive along Fenwick Road on the Chesapeake Bay and see Fort Monroe's seacoast batteries.

The Casemate Museum is open at no charge 10:30 A.M. to 5:00 P.M. daily, closed Thanksgiving, Christmas and New Year's Day.

Directions: From Richmond take I-64 to Hampton, exit for Fort Monroe immediately before Hampton Tunnel.

The Mariners' Museum

A Model Museum!

You know the feeling. You read a book, hear a joke, eat a fine meal—and can't wait to share your find. That's the reaction you'll have when you visit **The Mariners' Museum** in Newport News. Although the museum was founded in 1930, it's still a relatively undiscovered treasure.

The treasures here are the varied ships that ride the seas. The "jewels" of the collection, spotlighted in a darkened room, are the 16 miniatures crafted by August F. Crabtree. These exquisite models cannot be oversold; each is a work of art. They represent the labor of a lifetime. August Crabtree was born into a shipbuilding family in 1905 in Oregon. He worked for a time in a shipyard in Vancouver but enjoyed carving models more than building full-size ships. When Crabtree worked in Hollywood, he created the model of Lord Nelson's ship in the movie, *That Hamilton Woman*.

The Mariners' Museum purchased Crabtree's models in 1956. On Sunday afternoons at 2:00 P.M. visitors can listen to Mr. Crabtree discussing his craft. His work is exact in every detail. To outfit the tiny prehistoric men on the raft and dugout canoe Crabtree trapped a mouse for its fur. The models reveal the

Gracing the entrance to the Mariner's Museum in Newport News is this 1½-ton gilded eagle figurehead from the U.S. Navy frigate Lancaster. It has a wing span of 18½ feet.

artistry inherent in the construction of ships like the one from Queen Hatsheput's Egyptian fleet, circa 1480 B.C., or the Roman merchant ship, circa 50 A.D.

Some of the models have historical significance such as the *Mora* on which William the Conqueror invaded England in 1066 and Christopher Columbus's *Santa Maria* and *Pinta*. Others are so intricately carved you need to use the magnifying glass attached to the display case to see the details. The hull on a 1687 English 50-gun ship is carved with 270 human, animal and mythological figures. An 1810 American brig is noted for its elaborate rigging.

The last of Crabtree's models was the first of Cunard's red-and-black funneled passenger steamers, the *Britannia*. One of the early passengers was Charles Dickens who claimed his cabin was "an utterly impracticable, thoroughly impossible and profoundly preposterous box."

Entrancing as the models are they fill only one of the museum's 14 galleries. The museum is also noted for the board room models done on a scale of one-quarter inch to a foot. These models were made by the shipbuilders for the ship owners' board rooms. Many cruise ships are represented including the *S.S. Rotterdam* and the *Queen Elizabeth I*. The latter is done on a scale of three-eighth inch to the foot and is over 32 feet long. The room where these board models are shown has as its centerpiece the still operating light from the Cape Charles lighthouse; only a foghorn could add to the ambience.

A wood carver works several days each week in the Carving Gallery surrounded by over 20 lifelike figureheads including one of Jenny Lind, the famous singer. The museum has quite a collection of these carved symbols that once graced the bows of tall ships. As you enter the museum you'll see one of the most striking: the 1½-ton gilded eagle with an 18½-foot wing span from the U.S. Navy frigate *Lancaster*. There are some unusual figures among the more traditional buxom female figureheads, among them an imperial-looking Queen Victoria, a threatening Hindu with a spear and even the Apostle Paul. When the Paul figurehead was purchased in Providence, Rhode Island, it was transported in an open rumble seat. The figure, wrapped in a blanket to prevent damage, looked so real that passersby took it for a dead body and called the police.

It takes a separate building to house the small crafts, the most complete international collection in the western hemisphere. The oldest range from primitive skin boats to dugouts from Louisiana, Jamaica and the Congo. There are experimental racing yachts like the *Dilemma*, Dutch yachts called jotters, a Brazilian raft, a Chinese sampan, a Norwegian four-oared boat, a Venetian gondola, a Spanish sardine boat and a Portuguese kelp boat.

The museum owns more than 25,000 items, most on permanent display. There are many decorative pieces with nautical themes; Liverpool creamware, Staffordshire figures, Sèvres and Derby ceramics and lovely scrimshaw work. Photographs, weapons, uniforms and ship models tell the story of important military confrontations at sea. The Chesapeake Bay Gallery covers fishing and boating on the bay since European settlers first arrived.

For those with a scholarly interest in the sea the museum has a 60,000-volume library as well as maps, journals and some 250,000 photographs. It is an amazing facility set in a 550-acre park and wildlife sanctuary. Within the park is 165-acre Lake

Maury. There are fishing boats, athletic fields, picnic tables and walking trails around the lake and through the woods.

The Mariners' Museum is open Monday through Saturday from 9:00 A.M. to 5:00 P.M. and on Sundays, from NOON to 5:00 P.M. It is closed on Christmas. Admission is charged.

Directions: From Richmond take I-64 to exit 62-A at Newport News and Route 17 to the museum entrance. The route is well marked.

The Northern Neck

Planters' Paradise

On the western shore of the Chesapeake Bay lies Virginia's **Northern Neck**, first charted in 1608 by that intrepid explorer, John Smith. During the colonial period it was the port of call for many trading ships on their way to the West Indies and England.

The patriarch of one of America's first families arrived on one of those early trading ships. John Washington, great-grandfather of George, was a mate on an English ship that was trading for tobacco in 1657. It ran aground near Mattox Creek while sailing down the Potomac River on its voyage home. John Washington was so impressed with the land, the southern hospitality and the daughter of his host, Colonel Nathanial Pope, that he decided to remain. When he and Anne Pope were married, they were given 700 acres of choice land, Pope's Creek Plantation, and an American dynasty was begun.

It was here that George Washington was born on February 22, 1732. The site is now the George Washington Birthplace National Monument. Because both progress and wars have bypassed this region, the grounds of the Washington plantation and the surrounding countryside look much as they did in the 18th century.

The natural beauty of the meandering Pope's Creek, the broad views of the Potomac River and the gently rolling fields all can be enjoyed as you stroll along the park's trails. The land's historical significance is captured in the excellent film, *A Childhood Place*, shown at no charge at the Visitor Center. Fall leaves and migratory birds, quiet snowy farmland, spring planting and summer wildflowers speak quietly and eloquently of the same seasonal shifts that influenced young George Washington. These natural rhythms form a bond between those who visit and those who once lived here.

George Washington lived on this family plantation until he was 3½ years old when the family moved to Little Hunting Creek Plantation, now known as Mount Vernon. After his father's death when George was 11, he often returned to his early childhood home, inherited by his half-brother, Augustine.

The family home was destroyed by fire on Christmas Day 1779, while George Washington was commander of the Revolutionary army. Oyster shells now delineate the foundations of the original home. A memorial house, erected in 1930–31, represents a house typical of the kind the moderately wealthy Washingtons could afford. Although most of the furniture is over 200 years old, only a small tea table and an excavated wine bottle are from the original house.

Both birth and death are remembered here. As you enter the grounds you'll see the miniature Washington monument, a simple granite shaft erected in memory of George Washington in 1896. Nearby is the family burial grounds where George's father, grandfather and great-grandfather are all buried.

But it is the rebirth of nature that brings the long ago days to life. George Washington in his later years remembered fishing along Pope's Creek. You can easily imagine the young boy making his way to the river and perhaps glimpsing an ocean-going trading ship from the shore. Today the National Park Service owns 538 acres of preserved shoreline, woods and pasture at Pope's Creek Plantation. Fields are still planted and tilled by 18th-century methods. During the summer months special demonstrations are given on sheep shearing; tobacco planting, harvesting and curing; soapmaking; candlemaking; dyeing and weaving. There are also colonial music programs featuring the spinet and other instruments.

The George Washington Birthplace National Monument is open at no charge daily from 9:00 A.M. to 5:00 P.M. except Christmas and New Year's Day. There is a picturesque picnic area overlooking Pope's Creek. You can also picnic at nearby Westmoreland Park. While at the park, you may want to take advantage of the Olympic-size pool or even spend a relaxing hour on the beach.

After a mid-day respite you can continue exploring. The Washingtons were not the only family of prominence to have their roots in the Northern Neck. James Madison, James Monroe, the father of John Marshall and the Lee brothers were all born in the region. The Washingtons and the Lees were virtually neighbors. Richard Henry Lee, who became a signer of the Declaration of Independence, was born the same year as George Washington, on January 20, 1732. His brother and fellow signer, Francis Lightfoot Lee, was born two years later on October 14, 1734. It is provocative to imagine the mutual influence these young men might have had on one another had they grown up together.

The Lee family home, Stratford Hall, is far grander than the Washington home. It once encompassed 4,100 acres and even now includes 1,580 acres. Like Pope's Creek Plantation, it is still a working farm. The house itself was an architectural anomaly in colonial America. It was not designed in traditional Georgian manner but in the Italian style with the major living quarters on the second floor. The design features an H-shaped Great House with two clusters of four chimneys each. The Great Hall forms the center of the H, and it is considered one of the 100 most beautiful rooms in America. Like the rest of the house, it is furnished with 18th-century pieces. Visitors like seeing the bedroom where Robert E. Lee was born. The adjoining nursery contains a fireplace with two bas relief winged cherubs said to be favorites of the young Lee.

Stratford Hall is open 9:00 A.M. to 4:30 P.M. except Christmas Day. Admission is charged. If you decide not to picnic, try the log cabin dining room that is open from 11:30 A.M. to 3:30 P.M. from April through October.

Directions: From Richmond take Route 301 north. Turn right on Route 3. The George Washington Birthplace is 1.7 miles off Route 3 on Route 204. For Stratford Hall return to Route 3 and continue east to Lerty. Turn left on Route 214 for Stratford Hall.

Tangier, Chincoteague and The Barrier Islands

Virginia's Islands in the Sun

In 1608 Captain John Smith, who charted so many of Virginia's waters, stopped at an island in the Chesapeake Bay and named it **Tangier** after the Moroccan coast he felt it resembled. Located 15 miles from the Maryland shore and 20 miles from the Virginia mainland, Tangier was a hunting and fishing ground for the Pocomoke Indians. It was bought from them in 1666 for two overcoats by an Englishman named West. In another two decades John Crockett, who was drawn by the rich oyster and crab grounds, bought part of the island from West and settled in Tangier with his family. Even today the fewer than 1,000 residents of this isolated island retain an old English accent more reminiscent of 17th-century Elizabethan England than 20th-century Virginia.

It is hard to imagine 12,000 British soldiers on the tiny 3½-by-1-mile island, but this was their staging area for the attack on Baltimore in the War of 1812. The beach from which they embarked has now been reclaimed by the sea. Erosion, an ever-present threat, has made the islanders put their small white frame houses well back from the shore. There are no trees and only three cars. Visitors may take tours by golf cart on the narrow roads or bring their own bikes. Inquire about arrangements when you make reservations for the island trip (call (804)333-4656).

Getting to Tangier is half the fun. During the summer months the ferry, *Captain Thomas*, leaves from Reedville at 10:00 A.M. (a two-hour drive from Richmond) and returns at 4:15 P.M. Reedville is the center of the Chesapeake Bay menhaden fishing industry, and on your way across the Bay you're likely to see fishermen settling their big nets around huge schools of fish. It's an hour-and-a-half trip to Tangier, but the breeze off the water makes it pleasant even on the hottest summer day.

Though the ferry's schedule allows you only a brief three hour visit you won't want to miss having lunch at Mrs. Crockett's Chesapeake House. Many passengers return just to enjoy the family style meals. Enormous platters of crab cakes, clam fritters, Virginia ham, hot corn pudding, fresh vegetables and homemade rolls and pound cake are washed down with pitchers of iced tea. Those who want to stay can find overnight accommodations at the Chesapeake House, but reservations are required well in advance (call (804)891-2331).

Tangier Island can also be reached from Crisfield, Maryland. The *Steven Thomas* leaves the dock at 12:30 P.M. and returns at 5:15 P.M. from Memorial Day through October.

A more accessible island with a very different appeal, **Chincoteague** is linked to the mainland by bridge. Chincoteague, in the path of the Atlantic Flyway, is a regular stop of migratory birds on their flights north and south. Binoculars and a field guide to the birds are a must; all but the most avid Audubon enthusiasts will see waterfowl they'll need help identifying. More than 275 species of birds have been sighted at the Chincoteague National Wildlife Refuge. Brochures at the National Park Visitor Center include drawings of only the most frequently seen varieties.

You'll need no book to identify Chincoteague's wild ponies, although Marguerite Henry's children's novel *Misty* makes excellent family reading before your trip. The wild ponies are believed to be descendants of ponies that survived the wreck of a Spanish galleon. The ponies may approach stopped automobiles, but they should not be fed or petted. One look at their uncombed manes, shaggy coats and forelocks over their eyes tells you that these are not domesticated animals. The best place to spot the wild ponies is from the observation platform near the Pony Trail. There are roughly 130 head on the Virginia portion of the island so you are quite likely to spot one of the roving bands. They travel together in groups of 2 to 20 animals. One of the most popular events in this part of Virginia is the annual pony swim and penning held on the last Wednesday in July. The Virginia ponies are herded across Assateague Channel to Chincoteague.

Their refuge home can be explored along automobile routes and hiking and biking trails. Many visitors enjoy walking along the unspoiled shore where for miles and miles there is no sign of man's intrusion. After making your own collection of shells you may want to stop at the Oyster Museum in Chincoteague to see their unusual and extensive array. Hours are 11:00 A.M. to 5:00 P.M., and there is a nominal admission charge. The Refuge Motor Inn offers accommodations, wildlife safaris through the center of the refuge not ordinarily accessible by car and sunset cruises around the island.

If Chincoteague and Tangier make you yearn to get even farther away from it all, then the day trip for you is a cruise along Virginia's **Barrier Islands**, the Atlantic's last frontier. The Nature Conservancy sponsors 25 to 30 boat trips for the hardy explorer. Neither the boat nor the islands have public facilities, and there is no protection from the elements. The open boat, however, makes it easy to spot the plentiful waterfowl and migratory birds as do the island hikes. The 35,000 acres of sandy islands and salt marshes are a breeding ground for geese, loons, ibises, egrets, hawks and even the rare peregrine falcon. Trips leave from the Virginia Coast Reserve Headquarters at Nassawadox around 8:00 A.M. and return at 3:30 P.M. It is a long day but an exciting one for nature lovers. Write the Virginia Coast Reserve, Brownsville, Nassawadox, VA 23413 to obtain a schedule of trips and workshops planned for spring, summer and fall, or call (804)442-3049. Reservations must be made early.

Directions: From Richmond take Route 360 to Reedville for the Tangier Island cruise. For Chincoteague and the Barrier Islands take I-64 east past Norfolk and then take Route 13 north through the Chesapeake Bay Bridge Tunnel all the way up to Nassawadox for the Virginia Coast Reserve Headquarters. For Chincoteague continue up Route 13 to Route 175 and go east on Route 175 which leads directly to the Chincoteague National Wildlife Refuge.

Virginia Beach

Surf-Fire Fun

There is more than sun, sand and surf at **Virginia Beach**, Old Dominion's ocean playground. If you like the ocean but don't like to lounge on the beach then you may enjoy the 27 miles of hiking and biking trails within the 2,770-acre Seashore State

Park or a drive into the park to see some of the more than 336 species of trees and plants. During the summer the yucca plants, which provide oases of greenery on the park's mountainous dunes, blossom with bell-like white flowers.

The park, a Registered National Landmark, is open year round. The entrance is on U.S. Route 60, Shore Drive. There is a Visitor Center and Museum where you obtain maps of the trails fanning out from the center. Many trails are sturdy wooden walkways that permit access to the swampy areas. If you set out in late afternoon, do apply insect repellent.

Across Shore Drive at Fort Story on Cape Henry are several historic reminders. The First Landing Cross commemorates the spot where the Jamestown settlers touched the shores of the New World on April 26, 1607. Easter Sunrise Service is held here each year, and on the April Sunday closest to the landing date, the Order of Cape Henry makes a pilgrimage to this National Historic Landmark.

One of America's first lighthouses, built here in 1791, provides mute testimony to the dangers of these waters. Funds for the Old Cape Henry Lighthouse were authorized by the First Congress. It was built with stones mined at Aquia Quarries, which also provided stones for The White House, the U.S. Capitol and Mount Vernon. During the summer months for a small admission you can tour the inside of the lighthouse. The Old Cape Henry Lighthouse is off Shore Drive via the West Gate of Fort Story, or you can enter the East Gate at the end of Atlantic Avenue.

One ship that went down despite Cape Henry Lighthouse was the Norwegian bark, *The Diktator*, which was wrecked off the shores of Virginia Beach in 1891. The citizens of Moss, Norway, gave Virginia Beach a statue, *The Norwegian Lady*, to perpetuate the memory of the ship lost here. A second statue stands in the Norwegian city. The Virginia Beach statue is at 25th Street and Oceanfront.

An exhibit detailing this maritime tragedy can be seen at the Virginia Beach Maritime Historical Museum. Since Virginia Beach grew up around the U.S. Life-Saving Coast Guard Station much of the town's early history is captured at this museum, which also includes maritime memorabilia from around the world. The museum, at 24th Street and Oceanfront, is open Monday through Saturday 10:00 A.M. to 9:00 P.M. and Sunday NOON to 5:00 P.M., from Memorial Day through September. From October to Memorial Day its hours are Tuesday through Saturday 10:00 A.M. to 5:00 P.M. and Sunday NOON to 5:00 P.M. It is closed Christmas, New Year's Eve and Day. Admission charged.

The **Virginia Museum of Marine Science** on General Booth Boulevard opened in 1986. It features the natural marine en-

The Adam Thoroughgood House, circa 1637, is considered the oldest standing brick house in America built by early English settlers. It was the home of a man who came as an indentured servant.

vironment, encompassing four marine habitats and live vegetation, fish and birds. In the Coastal Plains River Habitat birds fly freely through the trees. From a sunken seating area you can watch the activity in a running stream encapsulated within a 10,000 gallon aquarium. In the Chesapeake Bay Hall you get an up close, personal look at such creatures as a horseshoe crab and a starfish. A simulated deep sea dive enlivens the Deep Ocean Habitat Room. In it you peer through portholes as you descend (via illusion) 2,500 feet. In the Man and Marine Environment you can test sea water for pollution and control waves in a giant tank. Admission is charged. (Hours are still being established.)

The wide variety of things to do in Virginia Beach extends from museums and military installations to historic homes. There are two brick homes that have survived from the colonial period. The **Adam Thoroughgood House**, circa 1637, is considered the oldest standing brick house in America built by early English settlers. It was built by a young man who came to Virginia as an indentured servant in 1621. Three years later, at the age of 22, he was his own man and his hard work had provided him enough capital to become a man of property. Thoroughgood married a girl of 15 and built his brick home in the English style. The house is furnished with 17th-century antiques. Guides in period attire give tours from 10:00 A.M. to 5:00 P.M. April through November and from NOON to 5:00 P.M. December through March. It is closed on major holidays and on Sundays and Mondays. Admission is charged. Because the Adam Thoroughgood House is owned by Norfolk, it is included on the Norfolk Automobile Tour, but is located in Virginia Beach. The house can be reached via Route 225, Independence Boulevard, off the Virginia Beach-Norfolk Expressway (Route 44).

Lynnhaven House, built between 1725 and 1730, is very much like the Adam Thoroughgood House, but the crafts and furniture represent the 18th century. Lynnhaven House is just off Route 225, at Independence Boulevard and Wishart Road, and is open for a nominal admission Tuesday through Sunday from NOON to 4:00 P.M. from April through November.

If the present piques your curiosity more than the past, the **Navy** offers you much to see. There are no tours of the Oceana Naval Air Station, but you can watch the Navy's most advanced aircraft while enjoying a midday picnic at either of two parks: Observation Park on Oceana Boulevard or London Bridge Observation Park.

At Little Creek Amphibious Base you can actually board one of the home-ported ships. This is the largest base of its kind in the world and each weekend one of the ships has an open house. You can also visit the Amphibious Museum from 1:00 to 5:00 P.M. on weekends. Passes onto the base are available at the Main Gate 4 off Shore Drive between Independence Boulevard and Diamond Springs Road.

For information on these and other Virginia Beach activities stop at the Virginia Beach Visitors Bureau at 19th and Pacific Avenue. It is open daily from 9:00 A.M. to 5:00 P.M. with extended hours during the summer months. Before visiting call (800)446-8038 for information.

Directions: From Richmond take I-64 east to the Virginia Beach-Norfolk Expressway (Route 44) and go east to Virginia Beach. Turn left onto Route 60 for Shore Drive. For the Amphibious Base, exit I-64 onto Route 13 north (Northampton Boulevard) to Route 615 (Independence Boulevard), and then go left on Shore Drive (Route 60) to the base gate.

Historic Sully in Chantilly looks almost as it did in 1794 when it was built by Richard Bland Lee, the first Congressman from Northern Virginia.   FAIRFAX COUNTY PARK AUTHORITY

Colvin Run Mill Park and Sully

Down by the Old Mill Stream

Just past the commercial bustle of northern Virginia's Tysons Corner is a bucolic reminder of the past—**Colvin Run Mill**. The mill was built between 1794 and 1810 along Difficult Run which ran beside the Leesburg Turnpike. Even in the 19th century this turnpike was a major artery from Shenandoah Valley farms to the bustling port in Alexandria.

Local businessman Phillip Carper designed Colvin Run according to the recommendations of Oliver Evans, whose book, *The Young Millwright and Miller's Guide*, suggested substituting waterpower for manpower in all steps of milling grain except weighing.

Water from Difficult Run was drained into a lagoon and millrace; then it flowed over the waterwheel to power the milling process. On each floor of the mill a different process was performed. Grain moved by elevators, chutes and sifters from floor to floor and process to process. This smooth, efficient operation was necessary for large merchant mills like Colvin Run that produced flour for foreign markets: Europe, Canada and the West Indies.

Colvin Run Mill Park includes several additional restorations. The Miller's House, built by Phillip Carper on a shaded hill overlooking the mill in 1820, now serves as a museum with an exhibit on "The Millers and the Mill" detailing the lives and times of the families who milled at Colvin Run. Craft programs are held at the mill on spring, summer and fall weekends. The restored barn is used for interpretive exhibits and demonstrations. The General Store, an original structure, served the local community during the early 20th century. Today you can purchase flour products ground at the mill as well as candy and handicrafts.

Throughout the year Colvin Run Mill Park sponsors special events: an Old-Fashioned Fourth, a ghostly and ghoulish gathering for All Hallows Eve and a traditional Christmas party which features a taffy pull. Colvin Run is open daily 11:00 A.M. to 5:00 P.M. mid-March through December and weekends only from January through mid-March. It is closed Tuesdays, Thanksgiving and Christmas. Admission is charged.

While in the area you should plan to visit nearby **Sully** which, like the mill, is also operated by the Fairfax County Park Authority. This Virginia country home was built by Richard Bland Lee in 1794. Lee combined two architectural styles he had grown to love; the Georgian colonial of his native state and the Philadelphia frame exterior he had admired while serving as northern Virginia's first Congressman.

The Philadelphia influence helped make his wife feel at home. Elizabeth Collins was the daughter of a prominent Quaker merchant in Philadelphia. The Haights, second owners of Sully, were also Quakers from the north. Their pacifist beliefs did not protect them during the Civil War. The men were forced to leave their southern farm and retreat behind the Union lines. Haight's children stayed at Sully and protected their home from the foraging armies of both North and South.

Today Sully is restored and decorated with Federal furnishings. After touring the main house you can see the dependencies: the kitchen-laundry, smokehouse and stone dairy.

Sully also hosts special events; perennial favorites are Plantation Daily Life in May, the Quilt Show in August and Harvest Days in October. Sully is open daily from mid-March through December from 11:00 A.M. to 5:00 P.M. and on weekends January through mid-March. It is closed Tuesdays, Thanksgiving and Christmas. Admission is charged.

Directions: From Richmond take I-95 to the Washington Beltway, I-495. For Colvin Run Mill Park take Exit 10B, Route 7, west for five miles. Colvin Run is on the right. For Sully take Beltway Exit 9, Route 66 west. Continue on Route 66 to Route 50 west and proceed for 5.5 miles to Route 28. Turn right on Route 28 and go ¾ mile to Sully.

The Flying Circus

Old Stuff Still the Right Stuff

The Flying Circus is an old-fashioned barnstorming extravaganza that re-creates the halcyon days of aviation. It proudly claims to have "the authenticity of a museum with amusement park thrills."

All across America small towns used to look forward to the excitement of the visiting barnstorming show. Town folk would run out into yards and fields when the new-fangled flying wonders buzzed their community. The Flying Circus near Bealeton is one of the last examples of this highly popular form of entertainment.

Shows are given at 2:30 P.M. on Sunday afternoons from May through October by an enthusiastic group of aviation buffs, including an architect, a clergyman and airline pilots. As one airline pilot said, "The Circus gives you freedom to enjoy what you're doing. At 200 feet, you can feel your speed, see the ground go rushing by under you. At 35,000, you feel like you're standing still."

Many of the flyers at the Circus have rebuilt their own biplanes; planes with double wings. Among the vintage planes here, found nowadays mostly in museums, are a 1940 De-Haviland Tiger Moth, Stearman, Waco and two 1929 Fleets. Like the barnstormers of old, the pilots take them through all kinds of aerobatics (stunt flying). The audience gasps seeing these biplanes made of cloth, wood and wire turn somersaults, fly upside down and plummet dangerously close to the ground.

Young and old are impressed when a pilot breaks a series of balloons with his plane's propeller blades. As a stunt flyer explains, "First impression is that all you have to do is hit the balloons with the airplane, which is no big deal, but if you don't slice it with the last four to six inches of the propeller, it won't pop." Another popular stunt is slicing a falling ribbon three times before it hits the ground, an incredible demonstration of the maneuverability of biplanes.

The Flying Circus parachutist can land on a dime; or at least an airshow equivalent, the tiny platform directly in front of the cheering crowd. The top crowd pleaser is the wing walker. Exactly like less sophisticated audiences of the 1920s and 30s, today's visitors hold their breaths when the daredevils climb out of the cockpit. Without parachutes they stand on the wing while the plane loops and barrel rolls. The biggest applause comes when the wing walker hangs by his heels as the plane makes a low pass across the field. One welcomes a chance to relieve the tension by watching the clowns and the tethered hot air balloons.

The barnstorming show itself lasts about 90 minutes, but visitors (picnickers included) may come as early as 11:00 A.M. when the field opens. After the show you can view the biplanes up close and talk to the pilots. The announcer does warn, "Don't touch the planes, though you can occasionally fondle the pilots."

For an experience you'll never forget, try a ride in one of the vintage planes. It's worth the fee, especially if you're willing to indulge in a bit of aerobatics. Passengers ride in the front cockpit, and once you put on the helmet and goggles you'll feel like a flying ace. There are also hot air balloon rides.

Plane models can be purchased in the wooden hangar that serves as a small museum. A stand sells snacks and cold drinks.

Admission is charged. Special events include model airplane competitions, antique car meets and the annual Hot Air Balloon Festival in mid-August. For additional information call (703)439-8661.

Directions: From Richmond take I-95 north to Fredericksburg. Continue north on Route 17 for 22 miles. The Flying Circus is just off Route 17 on Route 644 near Bealeton; watch for signs.

Manassas

War and Peace

Soldiers from the Union and Confederate armies met on the battlefield at **Manassas** more than twice. Of course, the First and Second Battles of Manassas are the occasions you read about in the history books. The opening salvos on July 21, 1861, were the first of the many major battles that would be fought by the Blue and Gray. And the Confederate victory at Second Manassas gave the South the momentum to carry the struggle into the North. Manassas National Battlefield Park has an audio-visual presentation, electric map program, battlefield maps and rental tapes for automobile tours, any one of which gives details of the two pivotal battles.

The less well-known meetings are also filled with human interest and historical significance. In the years after the great struggle soldiers from both armies often visited this battlefield. They came to remember fallen comrades, reflect on the battles they survived and perhaps relive the times they could not forget. In the 1920s, before the Manassas battlefield came under the jurisdiction of the federal government, Mr. Adoniram Powell was caretaker.

Mr. Powell would do the honors at the battlefield, and there were occasions when veterans from both sides joined forces to help him retrace the action. Imagine the difficulty of guiding those who had fought one another and had quite different memories. During one such awkward tour Mr. Powell pointed out the land where, he said, Jeb Stuart had led his First Virginia Cavalry in a sudden and violent attack that broke through the ranks of the New York Fire Zouaves. "Tain't so!" snorted a grizzled Union veteran. "That ain't the way it was. I was there, and I know." With trepidation because the mood of his mixed audience was unpredictable, Mr. Powell explained that according to the stories he had heard, the resplendent Zouaves retreated. The old warrior proclaimed, "We didn't retreat. We ran like hell."

Mr. Powell is long gone, as are the veterans of this bitter struggle, but rangers still provide walking tours of First Manassas on the hilly ground surrounding the Visitor Center. During the summer months there are special living history programs around the Old Stone House that served as a hospital during both battles.

The story of the first peaceful meeting between Union and Confederate soldiers at Manassas is one that is all too frequently overlooked. It was called the National Jubilee of Peace and took place 50 years after the first confrontation on July 21, 1911. The day began with soldiers of the Blue and Gray once again lined up facing each other. This time, instead of responding to the order to fire, they slowly closed the gap between the lines and solemnly clasped hands in friendship. This is, according to knowledgeable scholars, the only such gesture of peace ever made by opposing armies on the very land over which they once fought.

The Peace Jubilee continued in town with a speech by President Taft which, according to a letter his aide Major Archie Butt wrote, was "a flubdub speech about the Blue and Gray which brought tears to the eyes of veterans of both sides and smiles to the faces of politicans." At the base of the stone monument are cannons and naval anchors (contributed by Assistant Secretary of Navy Franklin Delano Roosevelt) standing in front of the former Prince William County Courthouse to commemorate the Jubilee.

The Peace Jubilee Monument is one of the points of interest on the tours (either walking or driving) of Old Town Manassas. There are two museums: the City Museum and Rohr's, adjacent to Mayor Edgar Rohr's old fashioned variety store. The latter houses a collection of antique cars including a custom-made 1933 Rohr sedan, as well as a rare 1905 Paragon. Other cars are a 1917 Detroit Electric and a 1957 Thunderbird. The second floor of Rohr's Museum has everything from toys and dolls to light bulbs and license plates.

The Manassas National Battlefield Park is open daily. Visitor Center hours are 9:00 A.M. to 6:00 P.M. in the summer and 9:00 A.M. to 5:00 P.M. the rest of the year. It is closed on Christmas Day. The Manassas City Museum is open 10:00 A.M. to 5:00 P.M. Monday through Saturday year round. Rohr's Museum is open 2:00 to 5:00 P.M. on summer Sundays and by appointment at other times. To arrange a visit call (703)368-3000 or 368-6000. Admission is charged.

Directions: From Richmond take I-95 north to Dumfries-Manassas, Exit 51, Route 234. Go west to Manassas. This will take you through Old Town Manassas. You can stop at Manassas City Museum, 9406 Main Street, for a Walking and Driving Tour Brochure. For the battlefield continue on Route 234. After you drive under I-66, look for signs to the battlefield Visitor Center on your right.

Morven Park and Oatlands

Band Box Perfection

The two lavish country estates, **Morven Park** and Oatlands, on either side of Leesburg on Route 15, would appear at first glance to create a problem of choice. Both of these grand houses are white and have a columned entrance area, but their differences make it worth visiting both.

Although Morven Park may suggest Scarlet O'Hara's Tara from the outside, the opulent interior is more reminiscent of William Randolph Hearst's San Simeon. The mixture of architectural styles—the Renaissance grand hall, French drawing room and Jacobean dining room—is matched by furnishings collected from around the world by the 20th-century owners, Governor Westmoreland Davis and his wife.

The house the Davises purchased in 1903 had changed dramatically over the years. Originally the land was farmed by Pennsylvanians who settled in the area in the late 1700s. An unpretentious stone house was built here around 1781. In 1808 Thomas Swann acquired the land and built a Federal style home which he enlarged after he retired. It was Swann who added the Greek Revival four-columned entrance portico. Swann named his estate after the Princeton, New Jersey home of Commodore Robert F. Stockton, who was flattered by his gesture but suggested that he add "Park" to the name because of the vast acreage (roughly 2,562 acres at that time).

After inheriting his father's estate, Thomas Swann, Jr., was too involved in business and politics to spend much time at this Leesburg estate. His position as president of the Baltimore & Ohio Railroad made it necessary for him to spend time in Baltimore. While living in Annapolis as governor of Maryland and in the Washington area as a five-term congressman he maintained Morven Park as a summer residence. Despite the claims on his schedule, he still exerted a great deal of influence on Morven Park. It was Thomas Swann, Jr., who embarked on the last major building program, integrating the three separate buildings into the one imposing mansion you see today.

If the exterior reflects Governor Swann, the interior reflects the taste of Governor and Mrs. Davis. They filled the house with treasures from Europe and Asia. Six wall-size tapestries woven in Flanders in 1640 line the great hall, and their grandeur is matched by the red velvet thrones from the Pitti Palace that sit beneath them. The ornately carved dining room furniture is reflected in huge rococo mirrors.

The house tour is just the beginning. There is a great deal more to see such as the recently opened Museum of Hounds and

Hunting that traces fox hunting in America from George Washington's day to the present. The estate was bequeathed the Winmill Carriage Collection that provides a mini-history of transportation in the 18th century. Names you may only have encountered in books take on fascinating form, as you examine the landaus, sulkies, breaks and phaetons as well as the more easily recognized carriages, sleighs, carts, coaches and buggies in the 125-vehicle display.

Nature lovers will find an extensive garden. The Marguerite G. Davis Boxwood Garden has the largest living stand of boxwoods in the United States. Spring bushes and bulbs add color and in the summer months roses, dahlias and crape myrtle are in bloom.

Morven Park is open Memorial Day weekend through Labor Day weekend, Tuesday through Saturday, from 10:00 A.M. to 5:00 P.M. and on Sunday 1:00 to 5:00 P.M. Admission is charged.

Oatlands traces its lineage back to Virginia's early days. The land was purchased by the Carter family from Lord Fairfax as part of the 11,357-acre Goose Creek Tract. It wasn't until 1804, a quarter of a century after the purchase, that George Carter, who had drawn close to 5,000 acres in a lottery held by his father for his ten surviving children, built his post-colonial country estate. George Carter married a 39-year old widow, Elizabeth Grayson Lewis, when he was 60. He died after only nine short years of wedded life.

Elizabeth and their two sons briefly abandoned Oatlands at the start of the Civil War. The boys served in the Confederate army and the house served as a billet for Confederate troops. After the war the Carter family had difficulty maintaining the house. They took in boarders for a time but eventually were forced to sell the family home and 60 acres.

The Greek Classical Revival house has a three-story pavilion flanked by two-story wings. In a break with tradition, it has a staircase on each end of the house rather than one in the center. Oatlands, like Morven Park, did undergo some remodeling over the first 20 years, 1804–1829. When the vogue for octagonal rooms caught on, a square-shaped room was converted to an eight-sided drawing room. One of the most distinctive features of the interior design is the elaborate plasterwork done in the 1820s.

The house and garden you will see today were reclaimed from years of neglect by Mr. and Mrs. William Corcoran Eustis. He was the grandson of the founder of the Corcoran Gallery in Washington, DC. They furnished the house with American, English and French pieces. The dessert plates you'll see on the dining room table once belonged to George Washington.

The Eustises restored the boxwood garden laid out by George Carter, reclaiming and expanding to create what is now considered one of Virginia's finest historic gardens. Mrs. Eustis, in describing the garden, said it was noted for "mystery, variety and the unexpected." It is the only garden in the country to use boxwood for the pleached, or tunnel, walk. The wisteria walk is a springtime delight. Specialty areas include a rosarium and an herb garden.

Oatlands is open April through December 21, Monday through Saturday 10:00 A.M. to 5:00 P.M. and Sunday 1:00 to 5:00 P.M. Admission is charged.

Directions: From Richmond take I-95 north. Just past Fredericksburg go northwest on Route 17 until it merges with Route 29-15. Turn right on Route 29-15 and continue north. Past Warrenton Route 29-15 divides. Take Route 15 north towards Leesburg. Oatlands is off Route 15 on the right just before Leesburg, and Morven Park is off Route 15 on the left just past Leesburg.

Occoquan, Tackett's Mill and Potomac Mills

A Trail of Three Mills

One explanation for the country saying, "mean as an old dog," is that it derives from the irascible temperament of the Dogue Indians who once lived in Virginia. The name **Occoquan** comes from a Dogue word meaning "at the end of the waters."

Occoquan, at the head of the Tidewater and the foot of the Piedmont region, was established as a milling community in the early 18th century. In 1734 the Virginia Assembly chose Occoquan as the location for a public tobacco warehouse.

Though its early existence was industrial, it is now a picturesque artisans' community. Within a four block square, designated a Virginia Historic District and included on the National Register of Historic Places, are 97 retail shops. Many of the artist-owners teach their craft as well as sell their work. At the Country Shop on Mill street, Milly Lehto teaches quilting, sells a wide selection of fabrics and quilting supplies and advises the White House on the quilts they acquire.

At the Basket Case you can learn to weave baskets or purchase some locally made, creatively designed baskets. Classes are given at both the Occoquan Gallery and The Undertaking Artists' Co-op. The latter, originally a funeral home, is just one of several shops that, according to local lore, is haunted. In the late evening brisk steps echo through deserted corridors; artists in residence call their unseen companion the conscientious undertaker. The last Indian in Occoquan is said to haunt the Occoquan Inn, one of several dining spots. A reflection of the tall Indian with the long black hair is reported to have been seen in an upstairs mirror. The Dogue Indians lived in peace with the European settlers, and this last shadowy reminder is said to be a peaceful presence.

Most shops in Occoquan are open daily, but some do close on Monday. For more town history stop at the Historic Occoquan Museum on Mill Street, open June through September daily except Monday. Hours are Tuesday through Saturday, 11:00 A.M. to 4:00 P.M. and Sunday 1:00 to 5:00 P.M. The museum is also open on weekends during April, May and October.

After you have visited the ghosts and galleries of Occoquan you can head up the road to another shopping area that is situated around a working 18th-century mill. **Tackett's Mill** overlooks a five-acre lake with a fountain and covered bridge. Its millhouse serves as a Prince William County Visitors Information Center. The 50 specialty shops around it give the village the look of a New England coastal town. Several restaurants overlook the lake, and a glass elevator provides several visual vantage points as well as access to various shop levels. The shops are open Monday through Friday 10:00 A.M. to 8:00 P.M.; Saturday 10:00 A.M. to 6:00 P.M.; and Sunday NOON to 5:00 P.M.

While at the Information Center you can obtain information on other spots of interest along the I-95 corridor in Prince William County. Heading down I-95 you'll come to **Potomac Mills**, billed as the world's largest factory outlet mall. Over 170 stores offer discounted prices in a far from warehouse-like environment. Colorful graphics, easy-to-locate neighborhoods plus a computerized directory, make it easy to explore the 1.3 million square feet of retail space. Off-price retailing has never been more upscale than at Potomac Mills. Anchoring the mall are Waccamaw Pottery, Ikea of Sweden which claims to be the world's largest home furnishings retailer and Cohoes, an apparel shop from New York State.

A food court with 14 eateries, ten movie theaters and the Elvis Presley Museum provide respites for shoppers. This is the first officially licensed Elvis Presley Museum outside of Graceland. It received its imprimatur from the estate of the late singing idol. The museum owner, Shelley Husta, has access to the largest private collection of Elvis memorabilia. Fans will enjoy seeing the 1973 white stretch Lincoln Continental which Elvis purchased after he saw it in the movie, *Shaft*. Another white car in the collection is his 1969 Lincoln Continental convertible. Furs, jewelry, costumes and furniture from Graceland will delight followers. The admission price is less than you'd pay to see an Elvis Presley movie.

Potomac Mills is open Monday through Saturday from 10:00 A.M. to 9:30 P.M. and Sunday from NOON to 6:00 P.M.

Directions: From Richmond take I-95 north. For Potomac Mills take Exit 52 west, then follow Route 784 west to Gideon Road (the first stoplight). Make a right on Gideon, then cross Smoketown Road and turn into the Potomac Mills parking lot. For Occoquan and Tackett's Mill continue north on I-95 to Exit 53, Route 123. For Occoquan stay on Route 123 which takes you into the historic town. For Tackett's Mill turn left on Davis Ford Road. Proceed for less than two miles on Davis Ford Road through the entrance to Lake Ridge. One block past the entrance turn left on Harbor Drive and go one block to Tackett's Mill.

Prince William Forest Park

Plus Marines and Weems-Botts Museums

If the idea of hiking all day through a woodland watershed, passing only a few fellow nature lovers, appeals to you, then visit **Prince William Forest Park** across from the U.S. Marine Corps Base at Quantico.

The 35 miles of trails and fire roads crisscross the north and south branches of the Quantico Creek. The land now reclaimed by the forest was once farm land. In 1756 Scottish settlers established a port in Dumfries which rivaled any in the New World. It is from Dumfries that historians believe William Ramsay barged his home up the Potomac River to his lot in the new town of Alexandria. Poor farming practices led to soil erosion, and the harbor at Quantico Creek became silted. It eventually became an unpenetrable marsh. Now whistling swans winter over along Quantico Creek at Dumfries.

The land on which Prince William Forest Park stands was originally acquired by the federal government as the Chopawamsic Recreation Demonstration Area in 1934. The Civilian Conservation Corps began the process of restoring this land to its natural state. The National Park Service has managed the land since 1939. As you follow the forest trails you'll see old orchards, building foundations, overgrown cemeteries and an old pyrite mine site.

Today the woods are populated with songbirds, raptors, whitetail deer, foxes, ruffled grouse, flying squirrels, wild turkeys and beavers. You are more likely to see signs of the beavers' presence than any of these shy animals. Throughout the woods across the meandering streams there are dams under construction as well as old decaying edifices. If you have a fishing license you can try your luck catching the bass, bluegill, perch and catfish found in the park's streams. To get a license park rangers will direct you where to go.

There are four self-guided trails. The Pine Grove Forest Trail, at the Pine Grove Picnic Area, is paved to provide access for strollers and wheelchairs. Taped messages at audio stations tell about the animals to be found here. At the Oak Ridge campground, which has 113 campsites, the Farms to Forest Trail shows the process of reclamation from cleared land to forest land. At the Travel Trailer Village, which has hookups for recreation vehicles, the Living Forest Trail stresses nature's interactions within the woods. The Crossing Nature Trail at Telegraph Road Picnic Area features the natural and human history of the park. For trail maps, stop at the National Park Service Headquarters or the Nature Center.

While in the area be sure to stop at the newly revamped **Marine Corps Air-Ground Museum** across Route 1 from the park. You need no advance reservations. The Marine guard at the sentry booth will check your driver's license when you enter the base and issue you a Visitor's Pass.

Formerly the museum was limited primarily to Marine aviation. The addition of ground equipment and weapons has broadened its scope. Currently there are two hangars open to the public: the first covering the "Early Years" of the air-ground team (1900–1941) and the second covering World War II. A third hangar on the Korean War is being planned.

Quantico's association with aviation goes back to the Civil War when hot air balloons were used for reconnaissance missions. In 1896 America's first flying vehicle was launched over the Potomac River near Quantico. Dr. Samuel Pierpont Langley launched a 25-pound, 13-foot flying model from the roof of a wooden houseboat moored in the river. He believed the water would make recovery of the craft more likely. Langley models were the forerunner of the Wright brothers' airplane. Langley did try two unsuccessful manned flights before the Wright brothers succeeded at Kitty Hawk.

Although Langley's flying machine is on display in the main lobby of the National Air and Space Museum in Washington, the Marine Corps Air-Ground Museum does exhibit some early models in the "Early Years" hangar. These include an early Curtiss airplane "Pusher" and two World War I vintage aircraft: a Thomas-Morse "Scout" advance trainer and a DeHaviland D.H. 4B fighter bomber of the type flown by Marine pilots in France. There are also two Boeing fighter planes from the late 1920s and 1930s as well as a Stearman N25-3 primary trainer. A Wright J-5 "Whirlwind" engine on display is the same type that powered Lucky Lindy's "Spirit of St. Louis."

In addition to the airplanes there are tracked and wheeled vehicles, artillery, small arms, uniforms, personal equipment, photographs and art—all parts of the story of the Marine Corps' air-ground attacks and defense.

The museum is open April through November from 10:00 A.M. to 5:00 P.M. Tuesday through Sunday. It is also open on holiday Mondays, but closed during Easter and Thanksgiving holidays. Guided tours are provided for groups by prior arrangement; call (703)640-2606. No guided tours begin after 4:00 P.M.

One other museum in the area is the **Weems-Botts Museum** just up Route 1 in Dumfries. Parson Weems was not a preacher but a traveling book salesman. In the early 1800s, under his full name, Parson Mason Locke Weems wrote a book on George Washington. His apocryphal anecdotes, including the cherry-tree story, have become part of America's folklore.

Weems purchased this story-and-a-half house in 1798 to use as a bookstore. In later years Benjamin Botts used the house as a law office. An addition built around 1850 now houses the Botts memorabilia. Benjamin Botts was the youngest lawyer on Aaron Burr's defense team in his 1807 trial for treason. It is well that Botts achieved fame early for he met a tragic death along with his wife, the Governor of Virginia and 162 other patrons who perished in the Richmond Theatre fire of 1811. The museum hours are 10:00 A.M. to 4:00 P.M. Tuesday through Saturday.

Directions: From Richmond take I-95 north to Quantico-Triangle, the Prince William Forest Park (Exit 50). Take Route 619 east for about a mile to the Marine Corps Air-Ground Museum, head west for ¼ mile to the park. For the Weems-Botts Museum return to I-95 and go north to the next exit (Exit 51 Dumfries), then follow signs to the museum.

Waterford

A Fair-ly Long Run

Waterford has for diverse reasons—philosophic, economic and geographic—remained isolated over the centuries. This distancing has enabled Waterford to survive. The houses, shops, churches, schools, barns and fields all evoke a simpler way of life and preserve the unspoiled image of a 19th-century village.

Waterford was settled in 1733 by Quakers from Bucks County, Pennsylvania, who established a community of small farms. They were soon joined by Scotch-Irish craftsmen, also from the Pennsylvania colony, whose skills were responsible for the elab-

The Quaker village of Waterford, which began its restoration with a weekend fair some four decades ago, now offers house tours and 250 craftspeople annually at the state's "fairest of fairs." ALLEN STUDIO

orately carved interiors of many of the Waterford homes. The community remained largely Quaker, however, and few took part in the American Revolution. Those who did fight were read out of meeting (see South River Meeting House selection). After the war and on through the early part of the 19th century Waterford prospered. Many of the homes and shops you'll see date from this period. It is interesting to discover that the only organized troops in Virginia to fight for the North were the independent Loudoun Rangers, a group formed by Samuel Means, the local miller. After continued Confederate harassment, Mr. Means abandoned the Quakers' principles of non-violence and organized the fighting brigade. The town also came under Union fire because of its southern location. This crossfire resulted in numerous farms being torched by both sides.

Its geographical isolation left Waterford behind when the railroad brought new business to the nearby town of Leesburg. Many commercial establishments in Waterford failed because the town could only be reached by a narrow dirt road. The Depression also took its toll.

Restoration was attempted on a small scale in the 1930s, but the real impetus to improvement came in 1943 with the establishment of the Waterford Foundation. For 42 years the Foundation has been sponsoring an annual fair held the first weekend in October. It started small with the villagers gathering together to sell their handicrafts. Now it's called "the fairest of fairs," is the oldest in Virginia and is one of the best on the east coast; a three-day event featuring more than 250 craftspeople, entertainment and the popular house tours. Fair time is the only time during the year that residents open their doors to visitors, and each year eight or nine private homes can be explored. The fair admission is used to continue the Foundation's renovation and restoration work. Efforts thus far have been successful, as you will discover. The Foundation has been rewarded by having Waterford included on the Virginia Historic Landmark Register and the National Register of Historic Places. In 1970 the entire village and the surrounding farmland became a National Historic Landmark.

Although fair week in October is the best time to visit, there are two homes in Waterford, often featured on the house tours, that operate Bed and Breakfast inns. The Pink House in the center of town was once used to billet troops during the Civil War; it now offers art, antiques and a pretty garden. (To arrange a visit call (703)882-3453.) The James Moore House on the Big Hill was built by a descendant of Thomas Moore who persuaded his neighbors to change the town name from Milltown to Waterford after the Irish city. The Moore house is now owned by a professional quilter, and her distinctive hand-made quilts decorate the bedrooms. (For reservations call (703)882-3342.)

Waterford's tree-shaded streets are ideal for an old-fashioned walk. This town is not a museum; it's a community and visitors get a warm welcome. It's nice to know towns like this still exist. **Directions**: From Richmond take I-95 north to Fredericksburg. Then take Route 17 north to the intersection with Routes 29-15. Follow this around Warrenton toward Manassas and when the road splits take Route 15 to Leesburg. At the Route 7 bypass around Leesburg take Route 7 north four miles to Route 9. Take Route 9 for one-quarter mile to Route 662, and turn right on Route 662 for Waterford.

ALEXANDRIA

Gadsby's Tavern and Stabler-Leadbeater Apothecary Shop

Bottled Remedies

Even the patronage of such illustrious colonial gentlemen as George Washington, George Mason and the Lees did not preclude an evening that would, by today's standards, be considered unruly. At 18th-century dinner parties, such as those held at **Gadsby's Tavern** in Alexandria, breakage was typically figured in the cost of the evening.

A tavern bill from a 1778 party for 270 gentlemen included a charge for breakage of 96 wine glasses, 29 jelly glasses, nine glass dessert plates, 11 china plates, three china dishes, five decanters and a large inkstand! This excessive damage is perhaps explained by reading the listing of alcoholic beverages consumed by yet another party of 55 at a 1787 dinner party. The 55 revelers were charged for 22 bottles of Porter, 54 of Madeira, 60 of claret, eight of Old Stock, eight of cider, eight of beer and seven large bowls of punch.

They don't have parties like that any more. They do, however, still serve lunch, dinner and Sunday brunch at Gadsby's Tavern, the "finest publick house in America." The 18th century is evoked by the menu, service and surroundings in the three restored tavern rooms.

Even if you don't stop by for a taste of the past, you should stop for a tour of Gadsby's Tavern Museum. The tavern consists of two buildings; the 1770 tavern and the 1792 City Hotel acquired by John Gadsby in 1796. Gadsby's Tavern was the center of Alexandria's political, social and cultural life. Here the colonial leaders met both before and after the Revolution. One of the grand events of the year was George Washington's birthday ball, first held in 1787 and still a popular Alexandria event. The tavern tour includes the restored ballroom where Washington enjoyed dancing. There are also restored bedrooms to give you an idea of tavern accommodations. Guided tours of Gadsby's Tavern are given daily at quarter of and quarter after the hour from 10:00 A.M. to 4:15 P.M., and on Sunday 1:00 to 5:00 P.M. For dinner reservations call (703)548-1288.

In the same year that City Hotel was built, 1792, a new shop opened in Alexandria, the **Stabler Apothecary Shop**. It is the second oldest drugstore in the United States, predated only by a shop in Bethlehem, Pennsylvania.

Although it is often called George Washington's drugstore there is no documentation of any personal visits from him. A note from Martha dated April 22, 1802, reads: "Mrs. Washington desires Mr. Stabler will send by the bearer a quart bottle of his best castor oil."

The Alexandria lot on which the store stands was originally purchased in 1752 by Washington's neighbor, George Mason of Gunston Hall. It was purchased later in 1774 for $17 by Philip Dawe, who built the three-story brick building that still stands. He leased it to Edward Stabler who ran an apothecary shop until 1852. At that time his son-in-law, John Leadbeater, took over the shop. This drugstore served the community for 141 years until it closed in 1933, a victim of the Depression.

The shop has the largest and most valuable collection of medicinal glass in North America. Long wooden shelves border the narrow store. Since many customers were unable to read, color was used to convey warnings. Poison was always put in blue bottles deliberately roughened so that even in the dark their message could be read by touch. Another warning was conveyed by the large apothecary jars in the shop window; when they were filled with red liquid it meant danger—an epidemic in town. Green liquid meant "all clear." Many of the containers of this repository of the past still contain their original potions.

According to local lore, Robert E. Lee was making a purchase at the Stabler-Leadbeater Shop on October 17, 1859, when Lieutenant Jeb Stuart hurried in to bring orders that would take both him and Lee, two young Marines, to Harpers Ferry to quell John Brown. The two Southerners ultimately resigned their commissions to fight in the Confederate army. You can visit this shop at 105 S. Fairfax Street from 10:00 A.M. to 4:30 P.M. Monday through Saturday. Entrance is through the adjoining antique shop. Donations and sales at the shop support the museum for which there is no admission.

Directions: From Richmond take I-95 north to the Washington Beltway. Go east on I-95 (which is part of Washington Beltway

I-495) to U.S. 1, Exit 1. Take Route 1 north into Alexandria. Turn right on Franklin Street, left on Washington Street, then right onto King Street to Royal. Gadsby's Tavern is one block to the left at 134 North Royal Street. For the Apothecary Shop continue down King Street one more block and then turn right onto South Fairfax Street.

Gunston Hall and Mason Neck National Wildlife Refuge

Eagle Eye

George Mason built for the future; both his words and his house endure. With his words, in the 1776 Virginia Declaration of Rights, he built a framework of freedom. "That all men are by nature equally free and independent and have certain inherent rights . . . namely, the enjoyment of life and liberty, with the means of acquiring and possessing property, and pursuing and obtaining happiness and safety." His immortal document served as the model for the U.S. Declaration of Independence, Federal Bill of Rights and the French Declaration of Rights of Man. After being copied in many emerging democracies, it also served as the framework for the United Nations' Declaration of Human Rights.

Mason's concern for detail, so evident in the careful choice of the right words in his documents, reveals itself again and again in his plantation home, **Gunston Hall**, in northern Virginia. His keen powers of concentration, you'll learn, sometimes caused him to lose track of some very important details, however, such as the whereabouts of his nine children. His son, John, said, "I have frequently known his mind, tho' always kind and affectionate to his children, so diverted from the objects around him that he would not for days together miss one of the family who may have been absent, and would sometimes at table enquire for one of my sisters who had perhaps been gone a week on a visit to some friend, of which he had known but forgotten."

George Mason suffered from gout and therefore served the cause of the Revolution primarily with his pen from the confines of his study at Gunston Hall. He did, in spite of his handicap, attend every session of the Constitutional Convention in Philadelphia during the long hot summer of 1787. He made dozens of speeches and helped draft the Constitution, but when he lost the battle to include a Bill of Rights and a ban on the slave trade he refused to sign the finished document.

141

For the most part he did not travel great distances, content to travel instead in his mind. John Mason recalled, "The small dining room was devoted to (my Father's) service when he used to write, and he absented himself as it were from his family sometimes for weeks togehter, and often until very late at night during the Revolutionary War. . ." Mason's walnut writing table was salvaged from a fire in July 1880, and has been returned to the study at Gunston Hall.

It is the interior woodwork that places Gunston Hall among the most attractive of Virginia's colonial plantations. The house, unassuming from the outside, is unrivaled in its exquisitely carved interior woodwork. This work was designed by William Buckland, a 21-year-old indentured carpenter whom George Mason's brother engaged in England. He chose well, for Buckland went on to become the "taste maker" of the colonies, becoming the first to use chinoiserie in America. He used the new style in the dining room at Gunston Hall, designing scalloped frames over the windows and doors, each with intricate fretwork, or designs. The Palladian Room is Buckland's masterpiece. This drawing room was done in the 16th-century Italian style popularized by Andrea Palladio. On the wall is a portrait of Ann Eilbeck Mason, of whom her devoted husband, George, said, "She never met me without a smile."

If you think you've seen a representative sampling of Virginia colonial houses, you haven't until you see Gunston Hall. It is not only beautifully built and decorated; it also has the largest Dutch-English style garden in the United States. From the main house you gaze down a 280-foot boxwood allée, planted by George Mason, to the Potomac River overlook. Flanking the garden on raised knolls are twin gazebos. On either side of the allée on both upper and lower terraces are networks of flower beds (parterres), which though balanced are not similarly designed or planted.

The gazebos offer a view of the house, garden, river and Deer Park, which was once stocked with white-tailed deer. If time permits you can take the two-mile Barn Wharf Nature Trail which begins at the front of the house. The trail offers the chance to enjoy spring wildflowers and nesting bluebirds.

Hours at Gunston Hall are 9:30 A.M. to 5:00 P.M. daily except Christmas Day. A movie highlighting George Mason's life is shown at the Visitor Center. Admission is charged.

Bird fanciers may want to extend their day by visiting the nearby **Mason Neck Wildlife Refuge**. The neighboring wildlife refuge is open only April through November. This is the first sanctuary established for the protection of the American bald eagle. Here on this 1,920-acre refuge a wide variety of wildlife make their home. Much of the marshlands, forests and wooded swamps are inaccessible to visitors, but the peaceful protection they offer serves both wildlife and man. More than 226 species of birds have been spotted at Mason Neck. When you visit bring both binoculars and a field guide to the birds as you will undoubtedly meet some unfamiliar varieties.

Directions: From Richmond take I-95 north to Fort Belvoir Exit 54; the sign reads "Mt. Vernon–Ft. Belvoir." Continue north on Route 1, then turn right on Route 242 for both Gunston Hall and Mason Neck National Wildlife Refuge.

Lee-Fendall House and Boyhood Home of Robert E. Lee

Certain-lee

Nothing succeeds like excess. Philip Richard Fendall was not content with one Lee wife, he had three! Philip, himself, the grandson of Philip Lee of Blenheim, first married a cousin, Sarah Lettice Lee. He next wed Elizabeth Steptoe Lee, widow of Philip Ludwell Lee and the mother of Matilda who grew up to marry Henry "Lighthorse Harry" Lee. To further complicate the matter Philip's third wife was Harry Lee's sister, Mary.

Visitors will be thoroughly confused if they try to keep track of the 37 Lees who lived at the **Lee-Fendall House** from 1785 to 1903. (As a historical footnote, the last resident-owner of the house, from 1937 to 1969, was labor leader John L. Lewis.)

Philip Fendall built this rambling frame house in 1785. Both George Washington and Harry Lee were frequent visitors. In March 1789, the mayor of Alexandria interrupted dinner to tell the assembled guests that Washington would be riding through town on his way to his inauguration in New York. Lee moved from the table to a nearby desk and wrote a Farewell Address from the citizens of Alexandria to their favorite son. He would write another and final farewell to his old friend ten years later expressing the esteem in which he was held throughout the nation: "First in war, first in peace, and first in the hearts of his countrymen."

Though the Lee-Fendall House is furnished with family heirlooms spanning the 118 years of Lee occupancy, it is the way the house appeared in the 1850s, as a grand mansion, that you see on your tour. Lees were born in this home up until 1892. Favorite toys down through the years can be seen in the children's room. There is Traveler, the rocking horse, and Minerva, a doll ordered from the first Sears and Roebuck catalog. An antique dollhouse collection is also displayed.

Tours are given at the Lee-Fendall House, 614 Oronoco Street, from 10:00 A.M. until 4:00 P.M. Tuesday through Saturday and NOON to 4:00 P.M. on Sunday. Admission is charged.

Across the street is the **Boyhood Home of Robert E. Lee**. As if the Lee family tree wasn't complicated enough, there is a link between the Lee and Washington families. Martha Washington's grandson, George Washington Parke Custis, married Mary Fitzhugh on July 7, 1804, at his Oronoco Street house. Twenty-seven years later their daughter, Mary Anne Randolph Custis, married Robert E. Lee. He had spent part of his boyhood growing up in the house where his bride's parents had married.

William Fitzhugh, formerly the owner of Chatham (see selection), purchased this Alexandria house two years after it was built in 1795 by Revolutionary War hero, John Potts. In 1811 another hero of the war, "Light Horse" Harry Lee rented the house and moved here with his wife and five children. It was just prior to the War of 1812, and at that time Alexandria was part of the District of Columbia. When the British burned the Capitol in 1814 they sacked the warehouses of Alexandria. It was a tense time for all the citizens including seven-year-old Robert E. Lee, who perhaps felt it more keenly because his father had left his family and traveled to the West Indies in a fruitless attempt to improve his health. In the upstairs bedroom you can imagine young Robert anxiously watching the Potomac both in hopes of his father's return and in fear of the British. Robert lived here for ten years.

When Robert E. Lee was preparing for West Point, his father's famous friend, the Marquis de Lafayette, paid a courtesy visit on Ann Hill Carter, the widow of his comrade-in-arms, General "Light Horse" Harry Lee. The downstairs parlor, or sitting room, is called the "Lafayette Room" in honor of his October 1824 visit. This short call was followed by a dinner visit in December of the same year.

The Boyhood Home of Robert E. Lee at 607 Oronoco Street is open Monday through Saturday 10:00 A.M. to 4:00 P.M. and Sunday NOON to 4:00 P.M. Admission is charged.

Directions: From Richmond take I-95 north to the Washington Beltway. Take the Beltway which is still I-95 east to Exit 1, U.S. 1. Follow U.S. 1 into Alexandria and turn right on Oronoco Street, which is 10 blocks past Franklin Street.

Mount Vernon

There's No Place Like Home!

George Washington's great-grandfather acquired the land on which **Mount Vernon** stands in 1674. George Washington's father acquired Little Hunting Creek Plantation, as it was first called, in 1726, and at his death George's elder half-brother, Lawrence, inherited it. Lawrence renamed the estate Mount Vernon in honor of his commanding officer Admiral Vernon.

At Lawrence's death, George first leased Mount Vernon from his brother's widow, then inherited the family estate. On January 6, 1759, George married the wealthy widow, Martha Dandrige Custis, whose worth by today's standards has been calculated by some historians (who may exaggerate) as approaching six million dollars, not counting the vast acres of land she owned. Before he moved his bride and her two children to Mount Vernon, he enlarged the main house to 2½ stories.

George Washington continued to enlarge, ornament and plan the grounds of his Virginia plantation throughout the long years of his military and political service. He took an interest in the day-to-day activities of his estate amid the turmoil of war and the travail of establishing a new government. Take for example his letter in 1776 to his cousin, Lund Washington, Mount Vernon's wartime manager. The letter mixes disturbing wartime news with directions for the building of the two-story dining room addition. Washington advises: "The chimney of the new room should be exactly in the middle of it—the doors and every thing else to be exactly answerable and uniform—in short I would have the whole executed in a masterly manner."

Or consider the letter he wrote on June 6, 1796: "Tell the Gardener I shall expect everything that a Garden ought to produce, in the most ample manner." Washington also wrote: "My agricultural pursuits and rural amusements . . . (have) been the most pleasing occupation of my life, and the most congenial to my temper."

No detail was too small for him. There are 37 volumes of Washington's writings, plus letters and weekly garden reports. These precise records helped the Mount Vernon Ladies' Association in restoring Washington's home to its appearance at the time of his death, on December 14, 1799, as did a room-by-room inventory.

Bushrod Washington and John Augustine Washington, inheritors of Mount Vernon, worked hard to keep up the estate, but because it was no longer agriculturally productive it was difficult to maintain. Their concern that it be preserved as a shrine led them to approach the federal government and the commonwealth of Virginia about purchasing Mount Vernon; neither accepted the offer. Its journey back to its days of glory began on a moonlit night in 1853 when Mrs. Robert Cunningham, cruising the Potomac, saw the rundown Mount Vernon on the hilltop. She wrote her daughter, "I was painfully distressed at the ruin and desolation of the home of Washington." And she related, "The thought passed through my mind: why was it that the women of his country did not try to keep it in repair, if the men could not do it? It does seem such a blot on our country!"

The recipient of this letter, Ann Pamela Cunningham, realized her mother's hopes by founding the Mount Vernon Ladies' Association. After both state and federal governments had refused to purchase Washington's home, her group bought the estate in 1858 for $200,000. Nineteenth-century additions were removed, furniture was restored and the atmosphere of the original plantation that Washington so enjoyed was recaptured. Visitors can imagine the great man strolling the home he once called "a well resorted tavern." It was never a glittering environment of power but always the home of a gentleman farmer. The presence of George Washington can be sensed at Mount Vernon, and this is perhaps the greatest legacy the Mount Vernon Ladies' Association offers succeeding generations.

Mount Vernon is open 9:00 A.M. to 4:00 P.M. November through February and 9:00 A.M. to 5:00 P.M. March through October. Admission is charged.

Directions: From Richmond take I-95 north to U.S. 1, Exit 54. Take U.S. 1 north to Route 235, the Old Mount Vernon Highway. Make a right turn on Route 235 which will take you directly to the traffic circle in front of Mount Vernon.

Ramsay House, Carlyle House and Christ Church

Historical Triumvirate

Both the **Ramsay House** and **Carlyle House**, just five doors apart on Fairfax Street, reveal Scottish influences. The Ramsay House was built about 24 years before Alexandria was founded. Its gambrel roof makes it an unusual structure on the city's skyline. Historians believe that William Ramsay's house may have been barged up the Potomac River from the Scottish settlement at Dumfries. When it was moved to Alexandria in 1749, it was the first house in the city.

Scottish merchant John Carlyle built his grand mansion three years later, in 1752. It was inspired by an elaborate Scottish country house in a popular architectural patternbook. Its manor house design, like the Ramsay House design, was unique to Alexandria.

William Ramsay and John Carlyle made more than architectural history in the newly developing town. Ramsay served his community as town trustee, census taker, postmaster, member of the Committee of Safety, Colonel of the Militia Regiment and honorary Lord Mayor. One of his eight children would later be elected Mayor of Alexandria. His wife, Anne, raised over $75,000 for the cause of American independence. At William Ramsay's funeral in 1785 George Washington, his close friend, joined the funeral procession.

The Carlyle House found its place in history just three years after it was built when General Edward Braddock chose it as his headquarters. Braddock summoned five colonial governors to a meeting that John Carlyle called ". . . the Grandest Congress . . . ever known on the Continent." The idea of taxing the colonies to support British expenditures in the New World was first proposed at this meeting as a means of financing the French and Indian War. This concept of taxation without representation was one that the colonists would bitterly reject. When it was imposed ten years later by the Stamp Act, it became a leading cause of the American Revolution.

John Carlyle, like William Ramsay, was a merchant. His marriage to Sarah Fairfax linked him with one of the most powerful families in Virginia. He was a partner in two merchant firms and acquired great wealth.

The Carlyle House is furnished to suggest the elegant life style of the Carlyles. One room, however, has been left unfurnished and serves as an architectural exhibit room. It clearly reveals even to the untrained eye how the 18th-century work was changed in the 19th century, then returned to its original appearance in the 20th century. Carlyle House at 121 North Fairfax Street can be visited from 10:00 A.M. to 5:00 P.M. Tuesday through Saturday and NOON to 5:00 P.M. on Sunday. Admission is charged.

Although the Ramsay tartan hangs outside his home on the corner of Fairfax and King Streets, the building now serves as a visitor center. It is the ideal first stop for anyone exploring Alexandria. You can obtain maps, brochures and up-to-date information on special events, museums, shops, restaurants and hotels—plus parking passes for non-residents. Ramsay House is open daily from 9:00 A.M. to 5:00 P.M. It is closed Thanksgiving, Christmas and New Year's Day.

If time permits walk five blocks west along Cameron Street up to **Christ Church** at Cameron and Washington Streets. James Wren, descendant of the noted British architect Sir Christopher Wren, helped design the interior of Christ Church and some authorities hold that he also contributed to the exterior design. George Washington was the first member of the congregation to purchase a pew. A silver plate marks the pew he bought for 36 pounds and 10 shillings (approximately $20).

When the widowed Martha Washington died, her grandson, George Washington Parke Custis, gave the Washington family bible to Christ Church. Another prominent American family, the Lees, considers this their family church. Robert E. Lee and two of his daughters were confirmed at Christ Church.

Christ Church is open daily and there is a regularly scheduled service every Sunday. Nearly all American presidents have attended service here on the Sunday closest to George Washington's Birthday.

Directions: From Richmond take I-95 north to the Washington Beltway. Take the Beltway which is still I-95 east to Exit 1, U.S. 1. Follow U.S. 1 into Alexandria. Continue down U.S. 1 to King Street and turn right. The Ramsay House is at the corner of King and Fairfax Streets.

Urban Archeology Center and Torpedo Factory Art Center

On the Waterfront

Alexandria is one of the few cities in America attempting to preserve archeological sites within an urban environment. The city operates a lab and exhibit center at the **Torpedo Factory Art Center** where visitors can glimpse the scope of the archeological work. The mere fact that such a program exists prompts developers to be sensitive to the significance of artifacts uncovered by their bulldozers, and many builders in Alexandria have given archeologists the opportunity to examine promising discoveries before they are lost to the inroads of 20th-century progress.

Alexandria's history as a city goes back to the mid-1700s. George Washington, who considered Alexandria his home town, surveyed the city's waterfront as early as 1749 just two years after the city was founded. At that time the banks of the Potomac River rose just over Union Street, then called Water Street. When larger ships began plying the river, residents filled in the land to deeper water, extending the riverbank by 100 yards.

The city's maritime heritage is detailed at the Alexandria Waterfront Museum, scheduled to open early in 1987, located at the Trans Potomac Canal Center. Like so much of the south, Alexandria was figuratively and literally drained by the Civil War. The city built the canal after Congress granted the necessary

The city of Alexandria claims its Scottish origins throughout the
year but never more colorfully nor loudly than when the clans
gather for the Virginia Scottish Games in July.

charter in 1830. Alexandria was then linked with the Chesapeake and Ohio Canal at Georgetown. When Federal troops occupied Alexandria during the Civil War, they drained the Alexandria Canal. Although it was refilled after the war it never regained its prewar prosperity. The canal and related 19th-century maritime activities are the focus of the museum which will open in 1987.

Although there is plenty of action on the Potomac River it also serves as artistic inspiration to some 175 artists who have studios at the Torpedo Factory Art Center. An unimposing structure used during both World Wars to manufacture torpedoes and later as a storehouse for captured war records, the factory has been renovated into a bright and busy art center. Navy Seabees presented a talismen from the past when the center opened. The Seabees' housewarming present was a sickly green 3,000-pound Mark 14 torpedo case made at this factory in 1944. Now the once drab factory has a central atrium surrounded by classrooms and studios. A ceiling skylight provides natural light for some of the area's most talented artists.

More than three-quarters of a million visitors each year enjoy the open door policy practiced by most of these working artists. You can watch them at work and make purchases at prices lower than those at downtown galleries. You'll see a wide diversity of painters, sculptors, potters, fiber artists, printers, stained glass workers, jewelers, batik designers, musical instrument makers and other artists and craftspeople.

The Torpedo Factory Art Center is open daily 10:00 A.M. to 5:00 P.M. It's located on the river in the Old Town historic district just north of the intersection of King and Union Streets at 105 N. Union Street.

Directions: From Richmond take I-95 north to the Washington Beltway, go east to Alexandria. Take Alexandria exit, Route 1, and head into the city. Turn right at King Street and head down to the river where you turn left for the Factory. There is a parking garage across the street and on street metered parking.

Woodlawn Plantation and George Washington's Gristmill

By George!

At least George Washington's last birthday, February 22, 1799, was a happy one. There was a family wedding at Mount Vernon on that date uniting his foster daughter, Eleanor (Nelly) Parke Custis, and his sister Betty's son, Major Lawrence Lewis. The delighted Washington, noted for buying land not giving it away, made the newlyweds a present of a portion of his beloved Mount Vernon estate. He said the 2,000 acres would be a "most beautiful site for a Gentlemen's Seat."

The architect, Dr. William Thornton, who did the first work on the U.S. Capitol, designed a stately Georgian mansion for the crest of the highest hill on the Lewises' property. While their house was being built they lived at Mount Vernon, comforting the grief-stricken Martha Washington. In 1802 when they and their two young children moved to Woodlawn, only its wings were completed. The center portion wasn't finished until 1805.

Visiting **Woodlawn** gives you a sense of the deep grief Nelly felt at the death of the only father she ever knew. She placed his bust on a pedestal as high as Washington's own considerable height. A swath was cut through the trees so that she could see Mount Vernon, her girlhood home, from Woodlawn's river entrance.

In the Music Room you see Nelly's music on a pianoforte similar to one she played, and you hear a taped rendition of it. Her husband was more interested in hunting than harmonics. He imported thoroughbred horses and the first Merino sheep in North America. When Lawrence Lewis died in 1839, his widow moved to Clarke County to live with her son.

Woodlawn is a house that hasn't forgotten it was once filled with children. Parents needn't worry that this tour will bore the young; at Woodlawn there is a Touch and Try Room filled with old-fashioned toys and games. On pleasant days children can take hoops and stilts onto the sloping lawn. At other times puzzles, blocks, dollhouses and even quill pens will keep youngsters amused.

The Garden Club of Virginia has re-created the formal gardens. An unexpected addition to this 19th-century plantation is the 20th-century Usonian house. It is the second home of this type designed by Frank Lloyd Wright, built of cypress and not of concrete like his later models.

Woodlawn Plantation is open 9:30 A.M. to 4:30 P.M. except on Christmas Day. The Frank Lloyd Wright House is open during those hours on weekends from March through December.

The 2,000 acres that George Washington gave the Lewises included Dogue Run Farm, a distillery and a **gristmill**. The latter, a reconstruction, is open to the public.

George Washington inherited Mount Vernon after the death of his older stepbrother, Lawrence. The mill operating at Mount Vernon when George assumed ownership was, he felt, inefficient and so, in 1770, he had a new 3½-story millhouse built on Dogue Creek. This original gristmill was abandoned by his ancestors and eventually collapsed into ruins. The stone was carried off and the site covered over.

The mill you see today was brought here from Front Royal in the early 1930s and reconstructed piece by piece. It was, like George Washington's original mill, built according to the specifications of Oliver Evans, who revolutionized the milling process (see Colvin Run Mill selection). Recorded messages at the mill give visitors a clear idea of how the milling process worked and how important it was to the community. The miller's wife recounts on a tape how you can determine class distinctions from the grain brought to the mill. The "merchant trade," according to her, would bring in wheat to be ground into flour; "country folks" depended on ground corn. To prevent a mixup each customer's grain was labeled and then ground separately.

Visiting the site of Washington's gristmill reminds one poignantly that this was the last spot that the great man visited. It was on a snowy day in December 1799 when Washington was here and caught the cold from which he never recovered. He died at 10:20 P.M. on December 14, 1799.

Directions: From Richmond take I-95 north to the Woodbridge Exit. Head north on Route 1. After you pass Fort Belvoir you come to Woodlawn on the left and George Washington's Gristmill on your right, just off Route 1 on the Mount Vernon Parkway.

FREDERICKSBURG

Belmont

Artistic Environs

Expectation can tax the creative. Consider the chef who wants to have friends over for a potluck supper, the novelist who wants to dash off a quick note or the artist who wants to create a comfortable home. All must cope with the busman's holiday syndrome that never permits them to be off duty.

It's nice to report that **Belmont**, the home of American artist Gari Melchers, does not disappoint. Belmont combines the beauty of nature with the artist's own. A long promenade of boxwoods and century old trees leads down to the banks of the Rappahannock River from a lovely old white frame house, with colonnaded porches on the first and second floors. Built sometime between 1790 and 1800, the house was enlarged in 1843. Gari Melchers lived here from 1916 to 1932, the last 16 years of his life. Melchers filled his home with his own work and art that he and his wife collected while in Europe. His one structural addition was a cheerful sun porch.

Gari Melchers's father was a sculptor who came to America from Germany. He is remembered today primarily for his wooden cigar store Indians. Young Gari studied in his father's drawing classes, then traveled to Düsseldorf, Germany, and Paris, France to continue his art education. Before moving to Belmont Melchers and his wife, Corinne, spent a great deal of time in Europe. He had studios in Egmond, Holland, and Weimar, Germany.

At Belmont old family pieces mix with European antiques to form a stylish but comfortable home. An 18th-century desk from Holland has four secret compartments so well hidden that the guides have trouble remembering their locations. Oriental carpets, English Regency slipper chairs and Victorian bedroom furniture vie for attention with American antiques acquired in Fredericksburg.

Both Gari and his wife painted. There are many family portraits. Gari painted his mother when he was 24 and his father ten years later. Melchers also did a self-portrait. In the dining room there is a portrait of Mrs. Melchers and her brother. The work of both Melcherses and European artists like Frans Snyders and Jan Breugel are mixed harmoniously at Belmont.

After a guided tour of the house you're invited to walk down the path to Melchers's stone studio. More than 50 of his paintings fill the studio walls and the brush, paint and palettes create the illusion that the artist is only momentarily missing.

Belmont is open April 1–September 30, 10:00 A.M.–5:00 P.M. Monday through Saturday, and 1:00–5:00 P.M. Sundays. October 1–March 31, 10:00 A.M.–4:00 P.M. Monday through Saturday, and 1:00–4:00 P.M. Sundays.

Directions: From Richmond take I-95 north to the Falmouth-Warrenton Exit. Follow Route 17 east toward Falmouth for 1¼ miles to Route 1001 and turn right to Belmont.

Fredericksburg National Military Park and Chatham

Ministering Angels

Civil War buffs are noted for their encyclopedic knowledge of battle strategy, fighting units and field commands; but the average traveler is held in thrall by the human aspects of the battles. **Fredericksburg National Military Park** and **Chatham** are rich in stories about individuals who transcended the ordinary. Fredericksburg was a place "where uncommon valor was common place." Because of its strategic position between Washington and Richmond four major battles were fought around Fredericksburg. In December 1862, the Battle of Fredericksburg resulted in a

Union debacle; in May 1863, Lee's great victory at Chancellorsville was marred by a bullet fired by his own men that eventually cost Stonewall Jackson his life; in May 1864, the Battle of the Wilderness proved costly to both sides, and it was followed by the fearsome two-week battle of Spotsylvania Court House which encompassed the single most terrible 24 hours of the war.

Fredericksburg was first drawn into the war in April 1862 when the town was occupied for four months by Union troops. Betty Maury recorded in her diary: "Their flags are everywhere, over foundry, bank, bridges, stores, stretched in lines across the streets, tacked on trees, stuck on soldier's guns, tied to horns of oxen." When the Federal troops arrived they did a house-by-house search for weapons and confiscated five swords at the Maury house.

Residents were almost entirely Confederate supporters, and so in December 1862 when sentries were anxiously watching the Rappahannock River for signs of an imminent Union attack they weren't surprised to hear a woman's voice calling a warning across the river. "Yankees cooking big ration! March Tomorrow!" And the next day the Union guns did begin to bombard the town. When the Federal troops entered the city they left a path of destruction in their wake: shredded books, bayoneted paintings, wrecked furniture and broken china and crystal. The Confederates had retreated just a short distance outside the town and entrenched themselves in a seven-mile line. The crucial half-mile of their line was behind a protective stone wall.

The Confederates on Marye's Heights literally mowed down the Union troops as they advanced column after column in a futile attempt to take the hill. By the end of the Battle of Fredericksburg more than 12,000 Union men lay dead or wounded. The plight of the wounded so moved Sergeant Richard Kirkland, a Confederate from South Carolina, that he asked his commanding officer, General Kershaw, for permission to carry water to the Union wounded lying in agony on the hillside. Permission was granted, but he was not allowed to carry a flag of truce and he was warned that Federal troops were apt to fire at him as soon as he climbed over the wall. Cheers, however, not bullets, filled the air as Kirkland ministered to the wounded. Today on the hillside behind the original stone wall you can see the Kirkland Monument honoring the soldier who became known as the "Angel of Marye's Heights."

To gain an overview of the battle, stop at the Fredericksburg National Park Service Visitor Center. It provides a slide-movie, exhibits and a self-guided battlefield tour map for Fredericksburg, Chancellorsville, Wilderness and Spotsylvania. There is also a small Visitor Center at Chancellorsville.

Before leaving Fredericksburg be sure to visit Chatham, part of the battlefield tour. This gracious 18th-century Georgian mansion paid a high price for its choice location overlooking the Rappahannock River. In 1862 and 1863 the grounds were used as an artillery position. The house itself was a front-line headquarters for Union Generals Edwin V. Sumner and Joseph Hooker. Chatham was also a field hospital, served by Clara Barton, known as the "Angel of the Battlefield," and Walt Whitman, one of America's most revered poets.

Chatham is also noteworthy because it is the only home still standing where both George Washington and Abraham Lincoln are known to have been entertained. George Washington wrote in a letter to William Fitzhugh, "I have put my legs oftener under your mahogany at Chatham than anywhere else in the world, and have enjoyed your good dinners, good wine and good company more than any other." The builder of Chatham, William Fitzhugh, achieved such a reputation for hospitality he was exhausted by a steady stream of guests. He finally sold Chatham and moved to a smaller house in Alexandria, now known as the Boyhood Home of Robert E. Lee (see selection), where he could more readily restrict his social calendar.

You can tour Chatham and see several rooms of museum exhibits. The gardens have been restored and from the river overlook there is a panoramic view of Fredericksburg. Chatham and the Fredericksburg Visitor Center are open at no charge daily from 9:00 A.M. to 5:00 P.M.

Directions: From Richmond take I-95 north to Fredericksburg, exiting on Route 3 east into town. Turn right on Hanover Street and right again on Sunken Road to reach the Fredericksburg Visitor Center. Chatham is two miles from the center, off Route 218, east of the Rappahannock River.

Hugh Mercer Apothecary Shop and Rising Sun Tavern

Both Mixed a Mean Brew

Combine business and pleasure 18th-century style when you visit Fredericksburg, Virginia. On Caroline Street you will find both the **Hugh Mercer Apothecary Shop** and the **Rising Sun Tavern**, social centers of town during the colonial period.

The apothecary shop looks as it did the day in 1776 when Mercer left Fredericksburg to serve in the Continental army. Mercer, a Brigadier General, was killed at the Battle of Princeton. His shop, though filled with few original items, does authentically reflect the colonial practice of both diagnosing ailments and preparing medications.

Dr. Mercer obtained his medical degree in Scotland at the University of Aberdeen. He served as assistant surgeon to the army of the Pretender, Charles Edward Stuart, and provided medical assistance at the Battle of Culloden. His support for a losing cause forced his emigration to Philadelphia in 1746. Later when he moved to Fredericksburg, Virginia, he entered into practice with Dr. Ewen Clements. They placed the following ad in an issue of the *Virginia Gazette* in 1771:

". . . This day became Partners in the Practice of Physick and Surgery, and have opened Shop on Main Street, furnished with a large assortment of Drugs and Medicines just imported from London."

Dr. Mercer had become friends with several Virginians while serving in the French and Indian War. One of his closest friends was George Washington. As Washington's mother, sister and brother lived in Fredericksburg (see Mary Washington House & Kenmore selection), the two men were able to maintain close ties. It is likely that many Virginia patriots gathered with these two experienced soldiers in Mercer's candle-lit library to discuss British intransigence.

The Hugh Mercer Apothecary Shop at 1020 Caroline Street is open daily 9:00 A.M. to 5:00 P.M. A small admission fee is charged.

Just down the street at 1306 Caroline Street is the other meeting spot, the Rising Sun Tavern. Built in 1760 by Charles Washington, George's younger brother, it was originally called the Washington Tavern. Here entertainment was provided by traveling players, balls were held and many meetings took place. George Washington's Masonic Lodge No. 4 met here for several years before their lodge house was completed. The tavern also served as the stage coach stop and Post Office.

Visitors to Rising Sun Tavern see the original tavern that young Charles built; although it has been extensively restored and refurnished, it has never been structurally altered. It is a simple colonial story-and-a-half-frame house which looks more residential than commercial. The hand-beveled clapboard, steep gabled roof and narrow dormer windows look quite homey.

During renovations the original bar railing was found. This has made it possible to rebuild the bar to its 18th-century specifications. The tap room has an impressive collection of English and American pewter, and there are gaming tables reflecting the sporting nature of the tavern.

Costumed tavern wenches serve spiced tea and hand out recipes for the colonial favorite, "Stewed Quaker." There is no liquor served.

The Rising Sun Tavern is open daily from 10:00 A.M. to 4:00 P.M. From April through October it remains open until 5:00 P.M. Admission is charged.

Directions: From Richmond take I-95 north and exit on Route 3. Turn east on Route 3 and follow to William Street. Follow blue visitors signs to Princess Ann Street and turn right on Caroline Street. Continue following blue signs to Fredericksburg Visitor Center at Caroline Street. You can obtain maps and brochures on all the city attractions.

James Monroe Law Office Museum and Memorial Library

Man for All Seasons—Statesman for All Occasions

In the famous painting, *Washington Crossing the Delaware*, James Monroe is the young man behind George Washington holding the flag. Monroe did not stay in the background for long. He went on to become U.S. Senator; the American Ambassador to France, England and Spain; four-term Governor of Virginia; Secretary of State; Secretary of War; and two-term President of the United States.

It is the young James Monroe who is remembered in Fredericksburg. It was here that he began his law practice after reading law with Thomas Jefferson in Williamsburg. The office where Monroe practiced from 1786 to 1789 is still standing.

Inside you'll see reminders of Monroe's long career of public service. Perhaps the most significant is his Louis XVI desk. It was at this desk in 1823 that Monroe signed the message to Congress containing the section that became known as the Monroe Doctrine. The desk has a secret compartment that was not discovered until 1906. It held letters Monroe had received from Alexander Hamilton, Benjamin Franklin and other statesmen of his day.

James Monroe, fifth President, was the first to occupy the White House after it was burned by the British in 1814. Since all the furniture had been destroyed the Monroes had to fill the house with their own. While in France representing the United States they had acquired a great many Louis XVI pieces of mahogany and brass. Today you see the originals in this Fredericksburg museum. (The White House has copies made at Mrs. Hoover's direction in 1932.)

Among the museum's most popular exhibits are Mrs. Monroe's gowns. There is a stunning dress she wore to the Court of Napoleon and, matching in elegance, the green velvet suit worn by Mr. Monroe.

157

For scholars the museum has an extensive library on James Monroe and his pivotal foreign policy doctrine. A reconstruction of his personal library is also housed here.

You'll leave the museum through an old-fashioned walled garden with a bronze bust of James Monroe done by Margaret French Cresson.

The **James Monroe Law Office Museum and Memorial Library** is open 9:00 A.M. to 5:00 P.M. daily except Thanksgiving, Christmas Eve and Day, and New Year's Eve and Day. Admission is charged.

Directions: From Richmond take I-95 north to Fredericksburg, then Route 3 east to the heart of town. Turn right on Charles Street and you will see the James Monroe Law Office at 908 Charles Street.

Kenmore and Mary Washington House

All in the Family

Like mother, like daughter, the saying goes. If Mary Ball Washington and Betty Washington Lewis were not completely alike, they were at least very similar. Both were widowed, both lived in Fredericksburg and both had households supported in part, if not entirely, by George Washington.

Betty's husband, Fielding Lewis, was a wealthy landowner, businessman, court justice and member of the House of Burgesses. Lewis spared no expense building a luxurious Georgian mansion when he married Betty in 1750. It was one of the earliest colonial mansions to have plastered rather than paneled walls. The ornate plasterwork on walls and ceilings is considered the finest example of the art in the United States. The drawing room ceiling is a masterpiece and deservedly was included in Helen Comstock's *100 Most Beautiful Rooms in America*.

It is well that Fielding Lewis did not wait to build his bride a home; his efforts to support the Continental army bankrupted him. He used his substantial fortune to found the Fredericksburg Gunnery which manufactured and repaired munitions for the army. He also outfitted ships. His death just two months after Yorktown gave him no opportunity to recoup his losses.

The house is furnished to match the inventory taken after Colonel Lewis's death in December 1781, with additional items reflecting the belongings sold after Betty's death in 1797. One family piece is Betty's portrait in the dining room. She looked like her brother. According to one account, "It was a matter of frolic to throw a cloak around her, and, placing a military hat on her head, such was her amazing resemblance that battalions would have presented arms. . ."

Kenmore literally provides a taste of the past; Mary Washington's gingerbread recipe, so popular with George and Betty, is prepared daily and served with hot tea to visitors in the colonial kitchen. The path to the kitchen leads through the 18th-century formal boxwood gardens; spend some time exploring this re-created haven with its flanking gazebos. The brick path once led to **Mary Washington's House** just two blocks away. It is said that when Lafayette visited Fredericksburg he, too, used this garden path, and came upon the Commander-in-Chief's mother working in her boxwood garden in her apron.

George purchased this town house for his mother on September 18, 1772. As he explained to his friend Benjamin Harrison, "Before I left Virginia (to make her more comfortable and free from care) I did at her request, but at my own expense, purchase a commodious house, garden and Lotts (of her own choosing) in Fredericksburg that she might be near my sister Lewis, her own daughter. . ." Although she suggested the move Mary Washington complained often of the city noise and water. It is said she sent a slave back to Ferry Farm each day for fresh well water.

This was not the only complaint she made. She repeatedly upbraided George for his neglect. While Washington was struggling with Congress to obtain funds for the Continental army, his mother was petitioning the Virginia Legislature for a pension to offset the stinginess of her son. Embarrassed at this news, he responded that she "had an ample income of her own" and that further he had provided funds for her whenever they were requested. He was careful, however, to note them in the debit side of his detailed ledgers. In the midst of the staggering deprivations of the Valley Forge winter encampment, Washington's mother wrote to him, "I would be much obliged to you to send me forty pounds 'sic' cash for corn. . . I have never lived so poor in my life. . ."

Like Kenmore, the town house is furnished to match inventoried items, this time those made for the wills of Augustine and Mary Washington. Eighteenth-century pieces fill the rooms; only a few like the looking glass, engravings and *Book of Meditations* belonged to Mary Washington.

Mary Ball Washington lived for the last 17 years of her life in this house. She died four months after George Washington's inauguration on August 25, 1789. At her request she is buried on land that was once part of Kenmore near Meditation Rock.

Kenmore is open daily 9:00 A.M. to 5:00 P.M. March through November, and 10:00 A.M. to 4:00 P.M. December through February. It is closed on Thanksgiving Day, December 24, 25, 31 and January 1. Tickets are purchased in Kenmore's Crowninshield Museum which has a diorama that helps you see Kenmore in its 18th-century context. Hours at the Mary Washington House are the same. Admission is charged at both.

Directions: From Richmond take I-95 north to Fredericksburg, exit on Route 3 east, William Street. Then make a left on Washington Avenue for Kenmore. For the Mary Washington House continue down William Street to Charles and turn left. The house is at 1200 Charles Street.

At Sharptop, near the Peaks of Otter on the Blue Ridge Parkway, visitors marvel at the view. The Parkway and Skyline Drive through Virginia's highlands form one of America's most scenic highways.

Blue Ridge Parkway

So Near and Yet So Far Removed

It is astonishing to learn that the **Blue Ridge Parkway** lies within a one-day drive of approximately half the population of the United States living in 20 states between New York and northern Florida. More than 20 million people a year travel its 469 miles, and yet it remains unspoiled and, except on peak autumn weekends, uncrowded.

The Blue Ridge Parkway begins where the Shenandoah National Park ends at Waynesboro, Virginia, and continues to the beginning of the Great Smoky Mountain National Park in Cherokee, North Carolina. The idea of a scenic parkway is generally credited to Virginia Senator Harry F. Byrd who in 1933 suggested to President Franklin D. Roosevelt that the two national parks be connected. Construction began September 11, 1935, and the last seven-mile segment around Grandfather Mountain in North Carolina is expected to be open in 1987. This scenic parkway was designed to be savored, not rapidly consumed. The ten Visitor Centers and 275 turnouts provide ample opportunity to enjoy the scenic overlooks, explore the many trails and visit the areas of special interest.

Milepost zero of America's longest national park is at Rockfish Gap and from there both the numbers and the road climb. Elevation ranges from a low of 649 feet around the James River milepost, 63.8, where there is a Visitor Center and a restored lock of the James River Canal (see James River and Kanawah Canal selection) to a high of 6,053 around Devil's Courthouse in North Carolina.

The planners of the Blue Ridge Parkway sought to conserve not only the natural beauty of the southern Appalachia highlands but also the cultural and historical resources. Humpback Rocks at milepost 5.8, for example, features exhibits on the home life of mountain settlers. A self-guided trail leads to a restored pioneer farm where visitors get a first-hand look at what life was like for those who literally carved homesteads out of wilderness. They hewed the logs for their cabins and picked the rocks for the foundations and fireplaces. In addition to their houses, they built barns and pens for their animals and bins for their crops. The rustic cabin is furnished and has "live-in" occupants who re-create life every day May through October on this mountain farm.

Of course, on the parkway the fun is in traveling along the mountain tops gazing over the mesmerizing valleys of Virginia. This is a drive you'll want to take slowly; the 45-mile-an-hour speed limit and the winding macadam road make that a require-ment even if it's not a preference. One of the most scenic spots along the way is the Peaks of Otter, milepost 85, also one of only two spots on the Virginia portion of the parkway offering over-night accommodations. (For reservations at Peaks of Otter Lodge call (703)586-1081. In Virginia the toll-free number is (1-800)542-5927.) Rocky Knob, milepost 174, offers overnight cabins. (For reservations call (703)593-3503.) The Virginia por-tion of the parkway also has four campgrounds: Otter Creek, near the James River; Peaks of Otter; Roanoke Mountain and Rocky Knob. (For information on these campgrounds call (703)982-6490.)

The Peaks of Otter drew visitors even before European settle-ment. The Iroquois and Cherokee once used the area as a "War-rior's Path." Supplies for the Revolutionary War were carried along a valley road. From 1845 to 1859 Polly Wood operated an ordinary, or inn, for travelers through the Alleghenies. You can visit Polly Wood's Ordinary on weekend guided walks or take part in the frequently scheduled living history programs on this site.

Another location for living history is the Johnson Farm built about 1850 and farmed through the 1930s. Today it is used to re-create farm life of the 1920s. Back in 1867 Robert E. Lee climbed the summit of the Peaks of Otter; today you can ride a bus to the top of Sharp Top Summit. You can also hike one of the six trails. For an easy and short walk take the .08 Elk Run Loop, and if you want a real work-out, try the 3.3 mile moderately difficult Harkening Hill Loop.

Do save enough time to continue your drive as far as Mabry Mill, milepost 176, perhaps the best-loved spot on the entire parkway. Ed Mabry made his stake in the coal mines of West Virginia and came back to the southern highlands of Virginia to purchase land. He quickly gained a reputation for fixing things at the blacksmith shop he set up in the Meadows of Dan area. Today the ring of hammer and anvil resound from the shop Ed Mabry built. He went on to build a gristmill and sawmill. Customers claimed the Mabrys produced the "best cornmeal in the coun-try." You can test that claim yourself by buying a sample of the cornmeal and buckwheat flour still produced at Mabry's Mill.

The weathered gray frame mill with its giant wheel sits beside a stream in the sylvan setting pictured on the cover of this book.

Amateur shutter bugs and professional photographers line the stream bank vying for just the right shot. Mabry's Mill, which served the community as a mill from 1905 until 1935, now serves as the central attraction of the Park Service exhibit on mountain industry. The exhibit depicts the work of a tanner and shoemaker and, on summer weekends, other craftsmen and a blacksmith.

From beyond the Virginia border, in North Carolina, the diverse charms of Linville Falls, Craggy Gardens and Mt. Pisgah beckon. You owe it to yourself to drive all the way to the end of this magnificent mountain drive.

Directions: From Richmond take I-64 west past Charlottesville to the beginning of the Blue Ridge Parkway.

Luray Caverns

Hurray for Luray!

Once you have explored nature's handiwork beneath the hills of **Luray**, you can well imagine the awe Andrew Campbell and Benton Stebbins felt in 1878 when they discovered the labyrinth. With two helpers, young Billy Campbell, Andrew's nephew, and Trent Lilliard, they had been searching for a month for a cave in the hills outside this sleepy Virginia community in the Shenandoah Valley. They searched so long they became the butt of good-natured jokes around town. Being called a "cave rat" and "phantom chaser" discouraged young Trent, and he gave up the quest. On August 13 the searchers found a sinkhole on Cave Hill that looked promising. Digging all morning in the August heat they were cooled by air welling up from below. When they finally had an opening large enough Andrew Campbell was lowered into the cave. What he saw was beyond the trio's wildest dreams: a cavernous palace with columns of stalagmites meeting hanging stalactites, crystals that glistened like diamonds and pristine white formations to provide dramatic contrast to the onyx colored walls.

At Luray you see the caverns just as they looked when discovered. Only the walks and lights have been added. There is no artifice, no colored lights or special effects; none is needed to enhance the natural beauty of this subterranean fantasy world. The dripping stalactites continue forming just as they have for millions of years. The limestone base rock in the caverns was formed during the Paleozoic age over 400 million years ago.

The caverns opened several months after they were discovered and have been open every day since. One addition made in 1954 is worth noting: the Great Stalacpipe Organ in what is called the "Cathedral" room. *Ripley's Believe It Or Not* television crew filmed this one-of-a-kind organ. The stalactite formations have been tuned by reshaping and are played from a large organ console.

This is not the only musical attraction at Luray. On Tuesday, Thursday, Saturday and Sunday at 8:00 P.M. you can hear a free 45-minute recital on the 47 bells of "The Luray Singing Tower" built on the grounds above the caverns.

While at Luray Caverns you can also explore the Historic Car and Carriage Caravan. The 75 vehicles in this collection are all polished and ready to go. There are some real sporty models to consider, including a 1908 Baker Electric, a 1927 Bugatti, a 1927 Rolls Royce believed to have belonged to Rudolph Valentino, a 1930 Cord and a 1935 Hispano Suiza. You can also decide whether you would have preferred a Ford, Chevrolet or Dodge when you view all three manufacturers' models for 1915.

Admission covers both the caverns and the historic vehicle museum. The first tour of the caverns is at 9:00 A.M. every day, and the last tour is given at 7:00 P.M. from June 15 until Labor Day. From Labor Day to November 14 the last tour is at 6:00 P.M. After November 14 it is at 4:00 P.M. on weekdays and 5:00 P.M. on weekends.

Directions: From Richmond take I-95 north to Fredericksburg, then make a left on Route 3 to Culpeper. Continue west on Route 522 to Sperryville and Route 211 to Luray.

New Market Battlefield Park

From Classroom to Conflict

The Battle of New Market is remembered as the first and only time in history that the entire student body of an American college marched into battle. The 247 brave cadets from the Virginia Military Institute joined General John Breckinridge's troops. Together they won the last Confederate victory in the Shenandoah Valley.

This 260-acre battlefield park is dedicated "to valor on the part of all young Americans in defense of their country." Most Virginia battlefields belong to state or federal governments, but New Market was purchased by a 1911 VMI graduate and given to the college. The Hall of Valor, which should be your first stop at the park, has a movie, *New Market—A Field of Honor*, that tells the story of the VMI soldiers. Their four-day march from the classroom to the battlefield was made in a torrential downpour. Their strategy classes had never dealt with the problem of advancing across a field so sodden it sucked the shoes off soldiers' feet. Forever after, the land around the Bushong Farm has been called, "The Field of Lost Shoes."

The young soldiers become more than statistics when you read the penciled note from Cadet Merritt to his father: "Dear Pa, I write you a few lines to let you know that I was wounded. I was in the battle here yesterday..." Cadet Merritt was one of 47 cadets wounded during the battle, and ten young boys lost their lives. You'll empathize with the grief another father must have felt as you read the telegram informing him of his son's death. There is a life-size portrait of Thomas Garland Jefferson, 17-year-old cousin of President Thomas Jefferson, who died from a fatal chest wound.

A dramatic stained glass window includes among the symbols of war the names of the ten cadets who died at New Market. Diaries, photo murals, models illustrating the variety of uniforms worn during the Civil War and battlefield mementos provide a glimpse of the full scope of the war. Also in the museum's Virginia Room all of the major campaigns in the state are covered. The Hall of Valor salutes the brave of both North and South and tells more than the story of New Market. A second film covers Stonewall Jackson's Valley Campaign. Before the war Jackson was an instructor at VMI (see selections covering Stonewall Jackson House and Stonewall Jackson's Headquarters) and along with the fallen cadets, he is enshrined in the pantheon of Civil War heroes at VMI.

From the Hall of Valor you'll move outside. The Bushong Farm around which the battle raged has been preserved to give you a look at farm life during the 19th century. The original farm house was built about 1815 on land the family acquired on June 22, 1791. During the summer months you can tour two rooms of the house. Throughout the year you can see the seven restored outbuildings including a wheelwright and blacksmith shop, a bakeoven and summer kitchen. A trail leads from the house across the fatal field to the hilltops from which the Union forces made their last stand. A second trail takes you along the high bluffs above the North Fork of the Shenandoah River.

New Market Battlefield Park is open daily 9:00 A.M. to 5:00 P.M. except Christmas. The Bushong Farm House is open mid-June through Labor Day from 10:00 A.M. to 4:30 P.M. Admission is charged. Each year on the Sunday prior to May 15 the Battle of New Market Reenactment is presented.

Directions: From Richmond take I-64 west to Staunton and I-81 north to New Market. The battlefield is directly off I-81 at Exit 67.

Smithfield Plantation and
The Long Way Home

Mountain Laurels

In their brave hope of extending Virginia's boundaries beyond the Blue Ridge, a band of early settlers carved out homesteads in the Indian-dominated wilderness of what is now southwest Virginia in 1748. On July 30, 1755, the Shawnee Indians, who had heretofore ignored the vanguard of white settlers, attacked and massacred all but a few of the valley families. Two that survived were the Pattons and the Ingles.

Colonel James Patton, who had been given a Crown Grant of 120,000 acres in 1745, headed the valley's militia. A widower, aged 63, he took the responsibility of guarding the valley very seriously. When the French and Indian War began, George Washington stopped in the New River Valley to warn him of the war's potential danger to the settlers. As Washington had foreseen, the war did come to the valley. Colonel Patton died during the Indian attack. The Ingles family, who farmed a small homestead on land they had purchased from Colonel Patton, were also grievously affected.

Mary Draper Ingles's mother, Elenor, who years earlier had lost her husband to marauding Indians, was killed in the massacre. Mary Ingles, 23, and her two boys, age two and four, were abducted by the Shawnee Indians (also abducted was her sister-in-law Bettie Draper). They were forced to walk hundreds of miles to the Indian camp near what is now Cincinnati, Ohio, and Mary bore a daughter enroute. After months of captivity Mary escaped with an elderly Dutch woman. Following the Ohio River, they made their way back across 850 miles of uncharted wilderness before Mary Ingles finally rejoined her husband and brother.

This dramatic story is re-created each summer by the New River Historical Society in the outdoor dramatization, *The Long Way Home*. It is performed in an amphitheatre beside the Ingles Homestead in Radford, Thursday through Sunday at 8:30 P.M. The role of Elenor Draper has for more than 15 seasons been played by her great, great, great, great granddaughter, Mary Ingles Jeffries. Reviewers of outdoor drama give high marks to this stirring production. For ticket information call (703)639-0679 or write The Long Way Home, P.O. Box 711, Radford, VA 24141. The novel, *Follow the River*, by James Alexander Thom, also tells the story of Mary's kidnapping and her 42-day walk to freedom.

Despite the adversity, the Ingleses did not abandon the Virginia frontier although they did for a time move to a protective fort before returning to the New River Valley. Neither did the Patton-Preston family. In 1772 James Patton's nephew, William Preston, who had been visiting in the New River Valley at the time of the massacre and narrowly escaped death himself, built a story-and-a-half white frame plantation house he called **Smithfield** after his wife, Susanna Smith. Preston represented the area in the Virginia House of Burgesses and was County Surveyor, County Lieutenant, Colonel of the Militia (like his uncle) and a member of the Committee of Safety.

Smithfield Plantation in Blacksburg has been open for tours since 1965. The house is no rough country home; it is furnished in a style William Preston copied from Williamsburg. The drawing room fireplace duplicates the one that can be seen in Raleigh Tavern (see Williamsburg Tavern selection). In this formal room you'll also see a copy of the Gilbert Stuart portrait of James Patton Preston. One of William and Susanna's 12 children became governor of Virginia (1816–1819). Several terms later James's son-in-law, John Floyd, Jr., became governor (1830–1834) as did James's grandson, John Buchanan Floyd (1849–1852). Another grandson, James McDowell, also served as governor (1843–1846) but unlike the others he never lived at Smithfield.

One of the few pieces of furniture you see that belonged to the Preston family is the walnut corner cabinet in the dining room. It was made on the plantation and displays Chinese export china. The staircase to the upstairs, carved in the Chinese Chippendale pattern, also reveals the influence of the Far East. In the basement you see the winter kitchen, located within the colonial house to protect the cooks against the cold weather and the Indian peril.

Smithfield Plantation is open mid-April to November on Wednesday, Saturday and Sunday from 1:00 to 5:00 P.M. Admission is charged.

Outdoor enthusiasts may want to add two nearby lakes to their outing. Just 20 miles north of Smithfield is Mountain Lake. Claytor Lake State Park and Camping Grounds is 30 miles south.

Directions: From Richmond take Route 360 southwest to Burkeville. Then pick up Route 460 west past Lynchburg to the outskirts of Roanoke. Use I-581 to cut through Roanoke. Head south on I-81 to Blacksburg where you will again pick up Route 460 Bypass. Smithfield Plantation is surrounded by the Virginia Polytechnic Institute and State University campus off Route 314. For the Ingles Homestead Amphitheatre take Exit 34 off I-81 and go one-quarter mile on Route 232 towards Radford.

Thunderbird Museum
and Archeological Park

Tooling Back In Time

Virginia has a well-deserved reputation as the spot to visit for early American history. Few realize just how early! At the **Thunderbird Museum and Archeological Park** you can see the evidence of one of the earliest Indian occupations in North America, dating from 9000 to 8000 B.C. The Thunderbird site and associated sites have revealed much about the way of life of the Valley's earliest inhabitants. A pattern of posthole stains in the ground shows where they lived; stone tools show us how they carried out everyday tasks. Stone spearpoints, knives and scraping tools were used in hunting. Women used scrapers, knives and cutting and gouging tools in cooking and hideworking. Hammerstones and piles of stone flakes show us where these stone tools were actually made.

You can see this archeological dig as a visitor or a participant. Its summer field session gives interested non-professionals a chance to learn more about the intricacies of archeology. Week-long training sessions include basic excavation techniques, site surveying and laboratory techniques. There are also week-long family programs with sessions geared to various ages—adult field work, secondary school level excavation work in the field and a workshop for young children on nature and Indian crafts. Credit courses are offered by Catholic University's Archeological Field School.

For those who want a shorter exposure Thunderbird has day long flint-knapping workshops. These are open on a drop-in basis to anyone 15 years or older on scheduled summer Saturdays, late June through mid-August, from 10:00 A.M. to 3:00 P.M. To obtain information on the workshops or week-long sessions write: Thunderbird Museum, Summer Field Program & Workshops, Route 1, Box 1375, Front Royal, VA 22630 or call (703)635-7337.

Even if your interest does not extend to active involvement, you should visit this unique resource. At the rustic museum in the woods you'll see a narrated slide program that introduces you to the dig. The museum focuses on the Thunderbird site, an undisturbed and unmixed North American Paleo-Indian base camp, but also covers the whole 11,000 years of Indian occupation in the Valley.

A walking tour to the Corral site on one of the park's nature trails gives you a chance to watch the excavation work in progress. It is a job that requires great patience and precision. As you observe the archeologists and summer assistants you can't help feeling that "dig" isn't quite the right word—brush or spoon might be more appropriate. The soil is removed rather than dug up, and meticulously uncovered layer after layer. The place where an artifact is found is as important as the artifact itself. From the 1971 excavation discoveries, Thunderbird is building a simulated Paleo-Indian house based on the posthole pattern that has been uncovered. This structure, located on one of the museum's nature trails, is being built with tools of stone, bone and wood.

After exploring you can enjoy a picnic lunch under the trees. If your curiosity is aroused by your trip to Thunderbird you'll find books on archeology and prehistory for sale at the gift shop.

Thunderbird Museum and Archeological Park is open daily from mid-March through mid-November from 10:00 A.M. to 5:00 P.M.

Directions: From Richmond take Route I-64 west to I-81. Proceed north on I-81 to the New Market Exit, then go east on Route 211 to Luray. At Luray go north on Route 340. Several miles beyond Bentonville you will see signs indicating a left turn on Route 737 for Thunderbird.

The Woodrow Wilson Birthplace

Family Manse

Thomas Woodrow Wilson was born in Staunton, Virginia, in the Presbyterian manse on December 28, 1856, "at 12¾ o'clock at night," as his proud father recorded in the family Bible. The Bible and Tommy's handsewn baby dress, likely worn for his baptism in April 1857, are on display at his birthplace. When the Reverend Joseph Wilson accepted a call to be minister of the Staunton Presbyterian Church, he and his wife, Jessie Woodrow, and their daughters, Marion 4 and Annie 2½, moved into the manse.

The 12-room Greek Revival style brick house was less than ten years old when the Wilsons arrived in March 1855. The house was built for Mr. Wilson's predecessor, the Reverend Benjamin Mosby Smith. "The congregation has contracted to have a house built for Mr. Smith," it was recorded, "which it is said will be the best house in Staunton when it is finished. The lot on which it is to be built is one of the most beautiful situations in Staunton. . ." The total cost of construction was about $4,000. Indicating how little some things have changed over the years, there is a notation in Mr. Smith's diary about his dissatisfaction with the poor work being done by the paperhanger. The Reverend dismissed him, and with his wife's help, finished wallpapering the parlor and dining room himself.

Tommy Wilson, as the future president was called until his law school days, spent little more than a year in Staunton (pronounced Stanton). His father's success led to a call from the larger, more prosperous church in Augusta, Georgia. The Wilsons left Staunton in early 1858.

The manse has been extensively restored, giving an accurate look at life in a middle-class minister's home in antebellum Virginia. Many of the furnishings belonged to the Wilsons; others are period pieces.

The manse tour includes three floors. The kitchen, workroom, servant's bedroom and family dining room are on the ground floor. On the main floor there is the master bedroom where Thomas Woodrow Wilson was born, the pastor's study, the parlor and the formal dining room. A silver service given to Mr. Wilson by his Augusta congregation and English flatware belonging to Jessie Woodrow's family are displayed in the dining room. Upstairs there are bedrooms for the children and for guests.

Before touring the manse, visitors can stop at the Reception Center where exhibits about "Woodrow Wilson: Professor, President and Peacemaker" are shown. There is also an audiovisual program about the 28th President.

The manse gardens, one of the earliest projects of the Garden Club of Virginia, make a delightful add-on to the house tour. They were laid out in 1934 with crescent and bowknot beds on the terraced grounds. One last stop is the Carriage House where President Wilson's 1919 Pierce-Arrow limousine is displayed. This three-ton cast aluminum car was leased by the government for the White House fleet. After using the car for the last 18 months of his presidency, Wilson purchased it from the Pierce-Arrow Motor Car Company for $3,000.

The Woodrow Wilson Birthplace is open daily 9:00 A.M. to 5:00 P.M. It is closed on Sunday during December, January and February and on New Year's Day, Christmas and Thanksgiving. Admission is charged.

A new attraction is in the works for Staunton—the Museum of American Frontier Culture. Plans call for the reconstruction of an early 19th-century Appalachian farm, followed by a Scotch-Irish farm, a 17th-century English farm and a German farm. This exciting project bears watching.

Directions: From Richmond take I-64 west to I-81. Go north to Staunton, Exit 57, which is Richmond Road (Route 250). Take Richmond Road into Staunton and turn right on Route 11, which becomes Coalter street. The Woodrow Wilson Birthplace is at 24 North Coalter Street.

ROANOKE

Booker T. Washington National Monument and Smith Mountain Lake

Up from Virginia

The slide presentation at the **Booker T. Washington National Monument** is inspirational but that's not surprising. The subject is the phenomenal journey of a young boy born here in slavery who grew up to become head of Tuskegee Institute and adviser to three presidents. The 15-minute program was awarded second place in the National Parks and Recreation Association's 1984 slide show competition. The images are poignant and the evocation of the life of young Booker T. Washington striking. It sets the stage for your walking tour of this pre-Civil War plantation.

As you walk along Plantation Trail additional information is provided by audio push-button tapes. A kitchen cabin has been built near the location of the original cabin where Booker T. Washington was born. Like the original it has no windows, just crude openings, and the floor is bare earth. Booker, his brother John, and sister Amanda slept on rags piled in the cabin corner. The slide show quotes young Booker on the discomfort of a new flax shirt—like cockleburs pressed against his chest. He also complained about his crude wooden shoes.

As a child, Booker carried water, fed the livestock, took corn to the mill and swept the yard at the Big House. Though his ambition as a boy of eight or nine was to "secure and eat gingercakes," he developed more ambitious goals. After the Emancipation Proclamation he moved with his family to West Virginia. Life was still hard, but he was permitted to learn reading and writing. His day at/the salt furnace began at 4:00 A.M., and he studied the alphabet at night. When he heard about the Hampton Normal and Agriculture Institute for blacks, he was determined to attend although he had no idea where it was located or how he would get there.

Booker walked and begged rides across Virginia to reach Hampton. His experiences at this school changed his life. Because of his outstanding scholastic performance, the principal at Hampton recommended Washington for a similar position at Tuskegee. When Washington arrived in Tuskegee, Alabama, there were no teachers, classrooms, supplies or campus. He established the school and made it successful.

Booker T. Washington's roots are in the rural Piedmont farm where he was born, and he referred to his early days on the Burroughs Plantation throughout his life. In fact, his biography was called *Up From Slavery*. It is amazing to reflect as you walk the paths of this out-of-the way farm that a slave boy born here

A reconstruction of the slave cabin in which Booker T. Washington was born near Rocky Mount is a part of the National Monument commemorating his life as an educator.

ended up having tea with Queen Victoria and advising Presidents McKinley, Roosevelt and Taft.

The farm today is a working plantation with 19th-century farm buildings, hogs, sheep, chickens and fields of tobacco. During the summer months interpreters dressed in 19th-century garb are on hand. If time permits, there is a 1½-mile, well-marked Jack-O-Lantern Branch Trail to walk. The Booker T. Washington National Monument Visitor Center is open daily at no charge from 8:30 A.M. to 5:00 P.M. except Thanksgiving Day, Christmas and New Year's Day.

While in the area you may want to continue down Route 122 to **Smith Mountain Lake**, a state park rivaling Lake Tahoe in beauty and sports opportunity, according to Virginia enthusiasts. With the Blue Ridge Mountains as a backdrop, you can fish, boat, swim and camp at this 20,000-acre man-made lake. If your destination is the state park, take Route 122 to Route 608. Proceed to the intersection with Route 626 and turn right. At Route 742 turn right again for the park. If you continue down Route 626 you'll reach one of the 25 marinas on the lake—Saunders Marina (703)297-4412. You'll also pass one of the four campgrounds that provide vantage points from which to enjoy the 500 miles of shoreline. Campgrounds include Crazy Horse Campground at Moneta (703)721-2792 and 3 locations in Huddleston: Eagle's Roast Campground (703)297-7381, Pine Shores Family Camp (703)297-5433 and Whip-O-Will Campground (703)297-4459.

The well-stocked lake offers record-size striped bass and muskies. Altogether 5,000 acres have been set aside for hunting, fishing and wildlife development. Local game includes squirrel, rabbit, raccoon, woodchuck, whitetail deer and sometimes bear. Game birds include dove, quail and wild turkey. For information on the activities at Smith Mountain Lake call (804)297-6066.

History and nature combine for a full day's outing at these two different spots just 20 miles southeast of Roanoke.

Directions: From Richmond take Route 360 west to Burkeville, then follow Route 460 to Bedford. At Bedford take Route 122 south. For Smith Mountain Lake State Park turn left off Route 122 at Route 608. For the Booker T. Washington National Monument continue across Hales Ford Bridge and on down Route 122 to Hardy, Virginia. Signs for the park will indicate turn-off on your left.

Center in the Square and City Market

Action Around the Square

Years ago malls revolutionized suburban shopping; in a similar fashion Roanoke has creatively combined the city's cultural offerings into one exciting location called **Center in the Square**. When you add the adjacent **City Market** with its shops, stalls and eateries you have an especially appealing one-stop attraction.

Since Center in the Square opened in December 1983 it has been the focus of action in Roanoke. The action even moves out of this world at Hopkins Planetarium, part of the Roanoke Valley Science Museum which is one of the three museums in the complex. A regular presentation explores the universe and other shows such as *To Fly*, *Comet Halley* and *Space Shuttle* have extended runs. On the second Saturday of each month there is a live sky show lecture at 11:00 A.M. Children under four are not permitted in the planetarium.

The Roanoke Valley Science Museum has plenty of child appeal with its hands-on exhibits featuring the geology, weather and the flora and fauna of Virginia. Anyone of any age who has ever despaired at the often misleading local television weather forecast will enjoy playing anchor at the museum's studio. A weather map and other props are in place; all you have to supply is the jargon and you're ready to roll tape. Television is also featured in an exhibit on energy designed to test endurance, not imagination. You bike your way to fleeting fame; the faster you pedal, the clearer your screen image becomes.

For kids young and old the bubble machine is bursting with fun. You dip a large screen into a vat and blow enormous bubbles, something that's a lot harder to do than it looks. There is so much to see, touch and discover you may end up spending more time than you anticipated. Just don't forget there are two more museums to explore at Center in the Square plus the Mill Mountain Theatre which offers performances almost every evening.

You'll learn how the city got its name at the Roanoke Valley Historical Society's museum. The town was first called Salt Lick because animals frequented this part of the Shenandoah Valley for the rich salt deposits. Following the animals came the Indians whose shell beads were called "rawranoke" beads. The Historical Society has collected more than legends. Their displays begin with Indian baskets, bowls and beads, then moves to the belongings of settlers along the Valley Trail. Life on the frontier can be better understood after viewing such artifacts as mill equipment, a blacksmith's work table and farm implements. The turbulent times of the War Between the States and the Reconstruction period are reflected. Finally there is a collection representing 100 years of fashionable gowns from 1880 to 1980.

From the state of fashion to the state of art, Roanoke is enjoying an active artistic renaissance with galleries proliferating around Center in the Square. In fact just across the street is Galleries in the Square's Butterflies and Unicorns, an artists' cooperative. Here painters, sculptors, carvers, weavers, potters and other artists produce and sell their work. Within Center in the Square you'll find the Roanoke Museum of Fine Arts. This eclectic collection includes a Mediterranean Gallery with work obtained from the Collins collection formerly at the Metropolitan Museum, the Japanese Gallery and a comprehensive grouping of Traditional Arts and Crafts of Middle Appalachia. The museum's tea room is a charming place for a noon break.

Only the Science Museum charges admission both for the Planetarium and for the exhibit area. Hours for the Roanoke Valley Science Museum and the Roanoke Museum of Fine Arts are Tuesday through Saturday from 10:00 A.M. to 5:00 P.M., Friday 10:00 A.M. to 8:00 P.M. and Sunday 1:00 to 5:00 P.M. Hours for the Historical Museum are 10:00 A.M. to 5:00 P.M. and Sunday 1:00 to 5:00 P.M.

Surrounding Center in the Square is the City Market with two main areas of interest: the three story Farmer's Market with its Rouse-like specialty shops and ethnic food booths and the colorful street stalls offering local produce. Shops run the gamut from the chic Gallery III to old fashioned neighborhood outlets like Wertz's Country Store and the Agnew Feed and Seed. Some shops are closed on Sunday. City Market opens at 10:00 A.M., and the Farmer's Market is open in the evenings so that you can take advantage of the many restaurants.

Directions: From Richmond take Route 360 southwest to Burkeville and then Route 460 west to Roanoke. In Roanoke Route 460 becomes Orange Avenue which intersects with Route 581 south. Take Route 581 south to the Elm Avenue Exit and turn right on Elm. Go two blocks on Elm Avenue and turn right onto Jefferson Street. Turn right again at Campbell Avenue at Market Square. A parking deck adjoins Center in the Square.

LEXINGTON

George C. Marshall Museum and Library

War and Peace

George Catlett Marshall, the only professional soldier to be awarded the Nobel Peace Prize, was both a military genius and an inspired humanitarian. His European Recovery Plan rehabilitated the economies of that wartorn continent.

As the son of a Kentucky Democrat living in Republican Uniontown, Pennsylvania, young Marshall had no hope for an appointment to West Point. He chose instead to attend Virginia Military Institute, spending his spare time exploring Virginia's Civil War battlefields.

He obviously learned much about the military strategies of the great Stonewall Jackson, the legendary VMI instructor. Today at

Sightseers in Lexington may ride in style in a surrey through downtown and residential districts.

the **George C. Marshall Museum**, you'll see in an exhibit covering Marshall's years as staff officer in France, 1917–1919, a newspaper column written about him by Damon Runyan entitled, "American Sudan Drive According to Principles of Stonewall Jackson." Runyan was not the only one to discern the influence of Jackson. As early as 1913 while he was in the Philippines, Marshall was called upon to order an attack when his chief of staff fell ill. Marshall dictated the entire plan of battle without corrections. In commending the young lieutenant for his field orders, Major General J. Franklin Bell said, "He is the greatest military genius since Stonewall Jackson."

Photo murals and personal mementos trace Marshall's outstanding military leadership. The course of World War II is detailed in a 25-minute electric map presentation. For military buffs there is General George Patton's helmet, Field Marshall Rommel's map of El Alamein and General Gerow's operation of Omaha Beach.

Marshall's career as statesman and diplomat is also thoroughly covered. In the postwar years he served as President Truman's envoy to China with the rank of Ambassador and as his Secretary of State. It was in the latter capacity that he spoke at the Harvard Commencement program in June 1947 and outlined what has become known as the Marshall Plan. At the age of 70 by a special act of Congress Marshall became Truman's Secretary of Defense during the Korean conflict.

America is not the only nation to recognize Marshall's achievements. The museum displays medals from 16 countries including the George VI's Honorary Knight of the Grand Cross, Military Division of the Order of Bath. One award did not go directly to Marshall but to *Patton*, the movie about General Patton's drive across Europe. The producer of this Best Picture of the Year for 1970, Frank M. McCarthy, chose to have his Oscar displayed at the George C. Marshall Museum.

The museum has an innovative "Try on a Piece of History" program for young visitors. Through hands-on displays they learn about the life and ideals of General Marshall. The Marshall Library, containing Marshall's personal and public papers, is also open to use by researchers.

The George C. Marshall Museum is open at no charge Monday through Saturday from 9:00 A.M. to 5:00 P.M. and Sunday 2:00 to 5:00 P.M. It closes an hour earlier November through March. The library is only open on weekdays.

Directions: From Richmond take Route I-64 west to Lexington. Take Route 11 Exit off Route I-64. Just outside Lexington, Route 11 forks to the right onto Main Street. Follow Main Street to the VMI parade grounds and the George C. Marshall Museum.

Lee Chapel and Museum

Certain-lee, Master-lee!

On October 2, 1865, less than six months after the surrender at Appomattox, Robert E. Lee accepted the presidency of Washington College at an annual salary of $1,500. At 58, he was anxious for the chance to be of use to the "rising" generation.

Lee first lived in the president's house that Thomas "Stonewall" Jackson had shared with his in-laws during his 14-month marriage to Elinor Junkin, whose father was president. (See Stonewall Jackson House selection.) Soon after Lee arrived he embarked on a building program. His first project was a chapel and then with the help of his son, General George Washington Custis Lee, a professor at neighboring Virginia Military Institute, Lee helped formulate plans for a new president's house. Although unhappy that the house cost more than the $15,000 originally appropriated for it, he was pleased with several architectural details. The verandas were designed so that his wife, crippled with arthritis, could move her rolling chair around them. Lee was also happy to have his old friend, Traveller, nearby in a new brick stable adjoining the house. Reports from the 1860s indicate that Traveller certainly needed a refuge. Souvenir hunters had pulled so much mane and tail the warhorse shied away from people.

Lee's greatest enthusiasm was lavished on the chapel he had requested the trustees to build on campus. Work began on the chapel in January 1867, under the close supervision of Lee and his son, Custis. It was completed in time for the 1868 June commencement, and from then until his death in 1870, Lee attended daily worship services there with his students.

On the lower level, Lee established his office. He fashioned and furnished it, and it remains today as it was when illness forced him from his desk on September 28, 1870. The remains of Traveller are buried just outside the office. Today the rest of the lower level is a museum where reminders of both Lee and Washington can be seen. One case contains the faded christening dress of George Washington. A letter dated 1796 thanks George Washington for his gift of stock, saving the school from bankruptcy. Washington endowed the school with $50,000 of James River Canal Company stock that is still paying dividends. Students today each receive roughly $3 a year in residuals. Many of Lee's personal belongings are included in the museum collection. Historical portraits bring many famous figures from history to life. Famous paintings include the Charles Willson Peale portraits of Washington and Lafayette and the most popular Lee portrait done by Theodore Pine.

The lower level also contains the Lee family crypt where Lee is buried with his wife, parents and six of their seven children. Many visitors mistakenly believe Lee is buried in the chapel apse beneath the impressive Edward Valentine statue. Lee's widow chose the recumbent pose; she wanted to remember him as if he were sleeping on the battlefield.

Three days after Robert E. Lee died on October 12, 1870, the college name was changed to Washington and Lee University. Both the Lee Chapel and the Front Campus Colonnade are National Historic Landmarks. There is no charge to visit the **Lee Chapel and Museum**. Hours are 9:00 A.M. to 4:00 P.M. Monday through Saturday from mid-October to mid-April, and until 5:00 P.M. the rest of the year. Sunday hours are 2:00 to 5:00 P.M.

Directions: From Richmond take I-64 west to Lexington. Take Route 11 Exit off I-64 and travel south. Just outside Lexington Route 11 will fork right onto Main Street. Follow Main Street to the Washington and Lee campus. For information on this and all the Lexington attractions stop first at the Lexington Visitor Center at 107 East Washington Street.

McCormick Farm and Historic Museum and Wade's Mill

Corny But Authentic

An historic mill on the farm where Cyrus McCormick was born and a working farm where a fourth generation Virginian has restored the family grist mill make a dandy country duo.

Walnut Grove Farm, while not widely known, is picturesque, educational and historical. The oak log grist mill, built in 1778, stands beside the blacksmith shop where in 1831 young Cyrus designed and built the first successful horse-drawn mechanical reaper. Twenty-two-year-old Cyrus worked with his father, Robert, who was also an inventor and tinkerer. They tested the reaper in John Steele's neighboring grain field. It was a two-man operation. Jim Hite drove the horse and Jon Anderson raked the grain. In half a day they had reaped six acres of oats, or as much as five men with scythes could harvest in a day. Despite such a demonstration, there were no buyers when Cyrus offered his marvel for sale at $50.

The following season the McCormicks harvested their own 50 acres with the new reaper. Gradually buyers were found. Between 1831 and 1846 when Cyrus left Walnut Grove at age 36, he built and sold 100 reapers and the price increased from $50 to $100. The American Agricultural Revolution started slowly, but unquestionably this out-of-the-way Virginia farm was its birthplace.

In the blacksmith workshop, which was the only "factory" McCormick had during the 1830s, you'll see an anvil he used to build the first reaper. A working reproduction of the reaper has the place of honor among the numerous McCormick farm inventions displayed in the museum above the shop. As part of the nation's Bicentennial this old reaper was operated for a BBC program. Getting it out of the museum was like trying to take a ship from a bottle. It had to be disassembled to get it through the door and rebuilt. Then a young horse harnessed to the noisy reaper bolted and ran it into a fence. Finally an old work horse pulled it into the field for the film. The TV crew might better have used the models; the details are so exact on these scale models they look full-size when photographed outdoors. You'll see models of the reaper and binder, as well as the combined reaper and mower.

The McCormick homestead, built in 1821, now serves as headquarters for the Virginia Polytechnic Institute's Shenandoah Valley Research Station. Visitors are welcome to explore the sheep barns and other livestock areas. There is also a picnic area, and the rest rooms are in the old slave quarters. This low-keyed farm is open daily 8:00 A.M. to 5:00 P.M. at no charge. Just a half mile off I-81, it's a great place for an interstate break.

Down the road 4½ miles is **Wade's Mill**, listed on the National Register of Historic Places. Charlie Wade is a man who has come back to his roots. His great-grandfather bought the mill in 1882. Although the stone foundations date back to 1750 the original upper portion was burned in the 1870s. Charlie is the fourth generation of Wades to run the flour mill. His father shut down the operation in 1964, but the renewed interest in natural foods has prompted Charlie to gamble that his stone-ground flour will sell.

Wade's Mill produces a wide variety of flours with no bleaches, additives, preservatives or chemicals. The flours include wholewheat, buckwheat, cornmeal, cracked wheat, naturally white and a buckwheat pancake mix. These can be purchased in shops in Virginia, in D.C. Safeways or by mail. Write Wade's Mill, Inc., Route 1, P.O. Box 475, Raphine, VA 24472. You can stop by the mill Monday through Friday from 8:00 A.M. to 4:30 P.M.

Directions: From Richmond take Route I-64 west to Charlottesville. From Charlottesville take the scenic Blue Ridge Parkway south. Exit the parkway at milepost 27.2 on Virginia Route 56 to Steele's Tavern. At Steele's Tavern go south on Route 11 for about 100 yards and then turn right on Route 606 to McCormick Farm. For Wade's Mill take Route 606 four miles past I-81. The mill will be on the right as indicated by the sign on Route 606.

Natural Bridge

Don't Knock the Rock!

The key word is natural. If you ignore all of man's intrusions, the rock bridge Thomas Jefferson called "the most sublime of nature's works" still enthralls.

Jefferson's enthusiasm was in part proprietal, since he owned the bridge. It and Niagara Falls were considered wonders of the New World. **Natural Bridge** was part of a 157-acre tract Jefferson acquired from King George III for 20 shillings, or less than $5, just two years before the revolution. Once he had acquired it, Jefferson refused to sell the bridge, calling his ownership a "public trust" to make sure that it was available to the people.

The Natural Bridge is a massive geological structure rising 215 feet above meandering Cedar Creek. The bridge span is 90 feet long and 50–150 feet wide. Scientists theorize that the bridge was formed when Cedar Creek was diverted into a cave. Over time the roof of the cave collapsed, leaving the bridge as the most stable portion of the natural tunnel through the cave.

You'll rarely find a more impressive nature walk than the one along Cedar Creek. The steps down to the creek follow the smaller Cascade Creek. For those who have trouble walking there is a shuttle bus. Along your walk you will observe examples of fossil moss being formed. One noticeable outcropping is just to the left of the first wooden bench along the trail.

The arbor vitae along the trail are some of the oldest and largest specimens in the world. The Monocan Indians who used the bridge as a thoroughfare and worshiped it as "The Bridge of God" found medicinal properties in the arbor vitae foliage. As you approach the bridge along Cedar Creek you'll see how the rocks are inclined. This effect was created 200 million years ago when the Appalachian Mountains were uplifted.

Across the creek on the steep wall beneath the bridge are the initials George Washington carved when he was surveying the area in 1750. He climbed up 23 feet to leave his mark.

On the other side of the bridge you'll discover picnic tables beside the creek. If you continue your walk you'll see the saltpeter cave. Nitrates mined from the cave during the War of 1812 and the Civil War were used to make gunpowder. The cave does not appear to extend any farther than the cavity you'll observe when peering into the opening. A short distance from the cave is the barely visible Lost River.

Far more interesting is the 50-foot drop of Lace Falls just down the trail. This is the last point of interest along the Natural Bridge walking trail. If you are staying through the evening you should plan to attend the Drama of Creation. Twice a night during the summer (once nightly during the winter) the 45-minute sound and light show is presented. The musical program is technically a bit passé and some purists might prefer listening to Strauss's *Zarathustra* or an equally dramatic work on their personal cassette while watching the impressive play of lights across the great chasm. The show goes on despite the weather, so dress appropriately.

Since 1978 the Natural Bridge caverns have been open to the public. First discovered in the 1880s, these are worth investigating. The caverns have numerous flowstone cascades, deposits of calcite formed when water flows down the walls of a cave. One example, a dome-shaped mass, is one of the largest of this type of deposit to be found in the east. The caverns are also noted for their drapery-shaped deposits.

The beauty above and below make this excursion a double treat for nature lovers. Admission is charged to all three attractions—Natural Bridge, caverns and a wax museum. Children under six are admitted free. Natural Bridge is open from 7:00 A.M. daily until dark when the Drama of Creation begins.

Directions: From Richmond take I-64 west to Staunton and pick up I-81 south. Continue past Lexington to Exit 50, Route 11. Follow the well-marked Route 11 to Natural Bridge.

Stonewall Jackson House

From Square Box to Stone Wall

Jackson was nicknamed Square Box and Tom Fool by his young charges at Virginia Military Institute who thought ". . . his classes too dull, his methods too rigid and his discipline too severe." Those who survived the carnage of the War Between the States grew old bragging that they were taught natural philosophy or artillery tactics by Old Jack.

The teacher who memorized his lessons standing at his desk in his Lexington home, went on to glory by standing firm at Bull Run. He became known as "Stonewall" after that opening Civil War battle when General Bee spotted Jackson's brigade and cried, "There stands Jackson like a stone wall. Rally behind the Virginians."

But it is the days Jackson spent in Lexington before the war that are remembered at the **Jackson House**. A short slide program introduces you to the young, handsome Viriginia instructor. He was a deeply religious and disciplined military man who began each day with a cold bath and a brisk walk around town before his morning devotions. During the week he taught his classes at

VMI, and on Sunday he founded and taught a colored Sunday School. When he left for the war he earmarked part of his pay so that these religious classes could continue. Jackson regularly contributed a tenth of his income to the Presbyterian Church.

Two years after he arrived in Lexington he married Elinor Junkin, whose father was President of Washington College. The newlyweds lived on campus with Elinor's parents in what is now called the Lee-Jackson House. Their life together was brief; she died the following year in childbirth.

In 1857 after three years as a widower, Jackson married Mary Anna Morrison, and in 1858 they purchased the Washington Street house. The furnishings you see today are personal possessions and period pieces that match the inventory made following Jackson's tragic death after the Battle of Chancellorsville in 1863. The first room on the tour is the kitchen which is furnished with a six-burner wood cookstove. The Jacksons owned one like it which was valued at $50 on the estate inventory. On a 20-acre farm at the edge of town Jackson, with the help of three slaves, grew much of the food for his table. He would often supervise the preserving of his crops, keeping an eye on the kitchen slaves and lending a hand to seal jars of tomatoes.

In Jackson's study there is a desk like the one he stood before while memorizing his lessons. It is said that when he was asked for clarification by a student he would simply repeat his statement using the same words and intonation. His lectures were not lightened by explanations or discussions. In the parlor are a love seat and two chairs that belonged to the Jacksons. Representing Jackson's one extravagance is a piano like the one he purchased for Mary Anna for $500. Even though he was a devout churchgoer he was known to occasionally waltz his wife around the parlor. He learned to waltz and polka while serving in the Mexican War. Jackson's rocker is in the bedroom, and Mary Anna's nightcap sits on the cupboard shelf. An early picture of Jackson reveals just how handsome he was without his beard. Legend has it that he vowed not to shave until the South was victorious, a story that is suspect as he did carry his shaving kit with him to war. At least one British journalist described him during the war as having ". . . thin colorless cheeks, with only a very small allowance of whiskers; a cleanly-shaven upper lip and chin. . ."

The dining room was used every morning and evening for Bible reading and prayers. On Sunday evenings slaves in the neighborhood would join the Jacksons for devotions. Before ending your visit be sure to view the exhibits which focus on General Jackson, the Civil War era and life in Lexington during its "golden age."

The Stonewall Jackson House at 8 East Washington Street is open 9:00 A.M. to 4:30 P.M. Monday through Saturday and 1:00 to

4:30 P.M. on Sunday. Admission is charged. To discover other city sites associated with Jackson stop at the Historic Lexington Visitor Center just down Washington Street at number 107. You'll realize that this is a town with character when you read the historic plaque on the house next to Jackson's. It says:

N.O.N. Historical Marker
On this Spot
February 20, 1776
Absolutely Nothing Happened.

While you are exploring the 19th-century houses, inns and quaint shops, join Lexington natives at the Sweet Things Ice Cream Shoppe at 106 W. Washington Street. Opened in 1981, this shop serves homemade ice cream in homemade waffle cones—a double delight. For an extra taste treat try a waffle cone sundae.

Directions: From Richmond take I-64 west. At Staunton head south on either I-81 or Route 11. From I-81 take the Lexington Exit. If you are on Route 11 it will divide, and you should take Main Street, not Route 11 By-pass. From Main Street turn left on Washington Street for the Stonewall Jackson House.

VMI Museum

From RAT to VIP

On November 11, 1839, 23 men reported to the Franklin Literary Society Hall in Lexington, Virginia. They became the first Virginia Military Institute cadets when their sole instructor, Major Francis Smith, assumed command of the old arsenal and established the nation's first state supported military college. The history of **VMI** and its well-known graduates unfolds at the museum on the campus parade grounds.

For 146 years VMI has trained many officers who have made outstanding contributions to the military. The young cadets study in spartan surroundings as you will learn in the museum's cadet exhibit room.

The first graduates barely completed their college years before being called to serve in the Mexican War, 1846–48. A captured Mexican general's war chest with its silver goblets provides a look at what the Mexican high command considered roughing it.

After the Mexican War in 1851, Thomas Jonathan Jackson resigned his army commission and joined the faculty at VMI. He found the peacetime army too tedious and unrewarding for a man anxious to make his reputation. As a teacher of natural philosophy and artillery tactics his students found him dull, rigid and severe. (See Stonewall Jackson House selection.)

Jackson's genius became apparent when he led the Stonewall Brigade in the War Between the States. The VMI Museum dis-

Cadets parade in front of the Barracks on the campus of the Virginia Military Institute. Stonewall Jackson of Civil War fame taught at V M I and George C. Marshall was a gifted graduate.

plays the uniform Jackson wore as a teacher as well as his battlefield raincoat, a poignant reminder of his senseless death after the Battle of Chancellorsville. Jackson was wearing the India rubber raincoat on May 3, 1863, when he was accidentally shot in the arm by one of his own men. The bullet hole is clearly visible; it seems too small to have caused such a big hole in the Confederate command. After his arm was amputated he contracted pneumonia and died within a week.

It was not only teachers who marched off to battle during the Civil War. The small butternut jackets on display remind visitors how young the boys were who were sent off to join General Breckenridge's battle-worn regulars. The southern general was ordered to stop the northern push into the crucial Shenandoah Valley. The Union troops numbered 7,000 against Breckenridge's 4,500. To augment the ranks the 157 cadets at VMI were ordered out of the classroom into battle. Ten cadets lost their lives on May 15, 1864, at the Battle of New Market. (See New Market Battlefield selection.)

Jackson is only one of the illustrious professors profiled in this museum. Following him so closely that they used the same microscope, was Physics Professor Matthew Fontaine Maury, noted for his marine charts. Another faculty member, John Mercer Brooke, designed the armor for the *Merrimac*, the ironclad the Confederates called the *Virginia*. Brooke also invented a device to bring up samples from the ocean floor. One of VMI's most gifted graduates was George Catlett Marshall (see George C. Marshall Museum selection), and his accomplishments are proudly noted.

Today when cadets enter the barracks through the Jackson Arch, they are reminded of Stonewall's determination. Carved overhead are his time-honored words: "You may be whatever you resolve to be." The museum shows that many VMI graduates have followed his advice.

The museum is open at no charge weekdays 9:00 A.M. to 4:30 P.M.; Saturdays 9:00 A.M. to NOON and 2:00 to 5:00 P.M.; Sundays 2:00 to 5:00 P.M.

Directions: From Richmond take Route 64 west towards Lexington. From 64, take Route 11 Exit. Just before Lexington Route 11 forks right onto Main Street. Follow Main Street to the VMI parade grounds and the VMI Museum in Jackson Memorial Hall.

WINCHESTER

Abram's Delight

Acquired Heiferlessly

In 1682 Valentine Hollingsworth traveled to the New World with William Penn. His family continued to seek new frontiers, sometimes with tragic results. His son, Thomas, when exploring the wilderness, was killed by a wounded buffalo. But the third generation established a homestead that is still associated with the Hollingsworths.

When Abram Hollingsworth came upon the Shawnees camped beside a natural spring he declared the site "a delight to behold." He purchased 582 acres from the Indians for a cow, a calf and a piece of red cloth. Abram built a log cabin beside the spring and the area's first grist mill. The family prospered and added a flour mill and then a flax-seed-oil mill.

In 1754, Abram's son Isaac built a two-story limestone house. It's the oldest now in Winchester, having survived in part because of its 2½-foot thick walls. A wing was added in 1800 by Jonah Hollingsworth, who needed extra room for his 15 children. The house was "modernized" in 1830 in the Federal style. By 1943, when **Abram's Delight** was purchased by the city, it was in ruins. Restoration was undertaken by the Winchester-Frederick County Historical Society and upon completion, it was furnished and opened as a house museum.

Jonah's daughter Mary was the last Hollingsworth to live in the house. It seemed to be filled with more than memories for her. She spoke of hearing people singing and playing the piano in her empty home. Some of the family pieces that augment the 18th-century furnishings are an oil painting done by Mary and several Quaker quilts.

There is an herb garden and a formal boxwood garden outside the house. You'll also see a log cabin on the grounds of the same type Abram first built. You can visit Abram's Delight daily from 10:00 A.M. to 5:00 P.M. April through October and by appointment off-season. Admission is charged.

Directions: From Richmond take I-95 north to Fredericksburg. Then take Route 17 to Marshall and pick up I-66 west to I-81. Proceed north on I-81 to Winchester, Exit 80, Millwood Avenue. Head into Winchester on Millwood Avenue and turn right on Pleasant Valley Road for Abram's Delight which will be on your right.

Belle Grove

The Hite of Fashion

In what turned out to be one of the longest legal battles in United States jurisprudence, Joyst Hite retained ownership of 100,000 acres in the upper Shenandoah Valley despite Lord Fairfax's claims on the land. Joyst Hite received the land in return for bringing 100 settlers to this part of the Virginia colony.

Joyst's grandson, Major Isaac Hite, who was commissioned by George Washington, built **Belle Grove** in 1794. Isaac married

James Madison's sister, Nelly Conway Madison. When his brother-in-law, the future president, married Dolley Paine Todd they honeymooned at Belle Grove. James Madison's friend and neighbor, Thomas Jefferson, provided architectural advice during the building of Belle Grove. His touch can be discerned in the graceful symmetry of the house, in the T-shaped halls and the top and bottom opening windows. The house is built of native limestone and has a large porticoed porch.

Looking out the windows at the blue haze on the nearby mountains, you don't question how the range got its name, but you do wonder why the house isn't called Belle View. The house is furnished with many pieces made in the Valley, but few belonged to the Hite family. The parlor does have a Charles Peale Polk portrait of Major Hite.

During the Civil War's Valley Campaign, military action occurred in and around Belle Grove. In the fall of 1864 General Philip Sheridan made his headquarters at Belle Grove. At 5:00 A.M. on October 19, Confederate General Jubal Early led a surprise raid on the Union soldiers camped here. Sheridan was in Washington conferring with Secretary of War Stanton. Sheridan heard the gun fire as he returned. Confederate forces were already counting this a victory when Sheridan's timely arrival turned the tide of battle. More than 6,000 men died at what the history books call the Battle of Cedar Creek, the last major battle for control of the Shenandoah Valley.

The Confederate General Stephen Dodson Ranseur, a classmate of George Custer's at West Point, was mortally wounded and died at Belle Grove. General Custer visited him before his death.

There was a ladder to a roof top platform where Sheridan's men sent messages to a lookout on Signal Mountain. Candle smoke graffiti in the attic says, "U.S.A. Signal Corps 1864."

In the cellar you can visit the winter kitchen where you will learn the derivation of the expression, "too many irons in the fire." If cooks of the Federal period tried to use more than one cookie press the irons got too hot and burnt the cookie wafers, thus there were too many irons in the fire. Near the kitchen is an extensive herb garden to explore. Before you leave be sure to visit the large regional craft shop which specializes in needlecraft supplies.

Belle Grove is open April through October, Monday through Saturday, from 10:00 A.M. to 4:00 P.M., and Sunday 1:00 to 5:00 P.M. Admission is charged.

Directions: From Richmond take I-64 west to Route I-81. Go north on Route I-81 to Exit 77 (Route 627) and proceed west to Route 11. Then take Route 11 south for 11 miles to Belle Grove on your right in Middletown.

Stonewall Jackson's Headquarters and George Washington's Office Museum

Double Duty

In 1854 Dr. William Fuller built a Hudson River Gothic house in Winchester in rural Virginia. His wife, Victorine S. Green, used many Continental touches in decorating her new home: diamond-shaped window panes, marble fireplaces, hearth tiles and gilt wallpaper. The Fullers soon outgrew their cottage and sold it to Lewis Tilghman Moore, great-grandfather of Mary Tyler Moore, the television and screen actress.

In the fall of 1861 General Stonewall Jackson came to Winchester to plan his Valley Campaign. Lewis Moore, a Lieutenant Colonel in the Fourth Virignia Infantry Stonewall Brigade, offered his home to Jackson as his **headquarters**. The General wrote to his wife, ". . . The situation is beautiful. The building is of cottage style and contains six rooms. I have two rooms, one above the other. My lower room, or office, has matting on the floor, a large fine table, six chairs and a piano. The walls are papered with elegant gilt paper. I don't remember to have ever seen more beautiful papering. . ."

His wife, Mary Anna Morrison Jackson, joined him in Winchester at Christmas time and stayed until March 1862. (See Stonewall Jackson House selection.) You'll see the table where they enjoyed Christmas dinner, Jackson's office just as he described it and his bedroom. Photographs and personal memorabilia of Jackson and other Confederate officers are displayed. The gift shop sells rare first edition books, old hard-to-find books on the Civil War and Confederate money. The house at 415 Braddock Street is open 10:00 A.M. to 5:00 P.M. daily April through October. Admission is charged.

Just down Braddock Street at the intersection with Cork Street is the small log office Colonel George Washington of the Virginia Militia used from September 1755 to December 1756 while he supervised the construction of Fort Loudoun. The **museum** has a model of this fort built to protect part of Virginia's 300-mile frontier from the French.

Washington spent a good deal of time in his early years in the Winchester area, having come here first at the age of 16, in 1748, when Lord Fairfax sent him with a surveying team to have a look at a part of Lord Fairfax's vast six million acres of land. The office museum offers both surveying and military displays as well as Washington memorabilia. Hours are 10:00 A.M. to 5:00 P.M. daily, April through October. Admission is charged.

Directions: From Richmond take I-95 north to Fredericksburg and then follow Route 17 to Marshall where you will pick up I-66. This will connect with Route I-81. Proceed north on I-81 to Winchester, Exit 80, Millwood Avenue. Head into Winchester on Millwood Avenue and turn right on Pleasant Valley Road past Abram's Delight. (See selection.) Turn left on Cork Street and left again on Cameron Street. Continue to North Avenue and turn left for two blocks to Braddock Street and turn left. Stonewall Jackson's Headquarters is half way down the first block of Braddock Street, on the right. Continue down Braddock to Cork Street for George Washington's Office Museum on the left.

CHARLOTTESVILLE

Ash Lawn

Accomplished Protégé

Improbable but true, three of the first five of America's presidents died on July 4: Thomas Jefferson and John Adams on the very same day in 1825 and James Monroe in 1831. After 50 years of public service Monroe had hoped to retire to Highland (now called **Ash Lawn**), his rural Virginia home. His long years of government work, however, had so impoverished him that he was forced to sell Highland. The loss was undoubtedly easier to bear because earlier that year his good friend and neighbor, Jefferson, had died.

Monroe built Ash Lawn at Jefferson's urging. The Sage of Monticello wanted to create "a society to our taste." He envisioned surrounding himself with a coterie of interesting and stimulating friends. The young James Monroe, who had studied law with Jefferson after the American Revolution, was happy to oblige his mentor.

In 1793 Monroe spent $1,000 for 1,000 acres adjoining Monticello. Before he could begin building, President Washington, another Virginian with whom Monroe had close ties having served under him at Valley Forge, appointed Monroe Minister to France. In the entrance hall of Ash Lawn there is a copy of the Leutze painting, *Washington Crossing the Delaware*, which portrays Monroe holding the flag behind his commander.

Not wanting the project to languish while Monroe was out of the country, Jefferson enlisted the help of James Madison and the two of them, with Monroe's uncle, Joseph Jones, began the planning of Monroe's house. Jefferson also sent his gardener over to begin landscaping the grounds. Monroe incurred debts while he was abroad so that what he built when he returned four years later was a modest house. Monroe dubbed his home a "cabin-castle" because though the exterior was simple, the interior was furnished with Neoclassical French Empire pieces the Monroe's acquired abroad. On your tour of the house you'll see a portrait of their daughter Eliza's life-long friend, Hortense de Beauharnais, daughter of the Empress Josephine and herself Queen of Holland and the mother of Napoleon III. There is also a portrait of the headmistress of the French school attended by Eliza and Hortense. In the parlor you'll see a marble bust of Napoleon Bonaparte, a gift to Monroe. The study has a copy of the Louis XVI desk used by Monroe when he was President.

Monroe, like his friend George Washington, was taller than average. The highpost bed was big enough to accommodate his 6'2" frame. Although it is the only original piece in the master bedroom, the rest of the furnishings are of the period. You'll learn that the wooden working parts of the case clock were greased with fat. This attracted mice and provided the inspiration for the popular nursery rhyme.

Ash Lawn is operated today by James Monroe's alma mater, The College of William and Mary. Thomas Jefferson and John Tyler were also alumni. The college maintains the 535-acre estate as a 19th-century working plantation. Two dozen peacocks strut in the boxwood garden, and the abundance of nature can be enjoyed year round. Spring and summer bring flowers and herbs. Vegetables are harvested in the fall and in winter Christmas trees can be cut at Ash Lawn. Traditional farm crafts are demonstrated at special programs throughout the year.

Ash Lawn is open March through October from 9:00 A.M. to 6:00 P.M. Hours from November through February are 10:00 A.M. to 5:00 P.M. It is closed on major holidays. Admission is charged.

Directions: From Richmond take I-64 west to Charlottesville. Take Route 20 Exit toward the Visitor Center, then turn left on Route 53 past Monticello and make a right turn on Route 795 for Ash Lawn.

Castle Hill

You Can't Judge a House by Its Cover

History and the arts blend felicitously at this Albemarle County manor awaft with ghostly reminders of the past. When fire destroyed the original house, which had belonged to his wife, Dr. Thomas Walker built **Castle Hill** using large square stones salvaged from the walls of the ruins. He waited until he acquired legal title to the land in 1764 before building their home. Dr. Walker was Peter Jefferson's physician, close friend and guardian to his son, Thomas. He was also a member of the Virginia House of Burgesses from 1715 to 1794.

On June 4, 1781, Dr. Walker learned that the British were riding toward Charlottesville to imprison his ward, Thomas Jefferson.

Colonel Tarleton, known in Virginia as Bloody Tarleton the Butcher, and his cavalry broke their ride at Castle Hill. They arrived at 4:30 A.M., and Dr. Walker offered the British officers breakfast beginning with mint juleps on the porch. This lavish spread delayed the British while young Jack Jouett rode through the early dawn to warn Jefferson and the Virginia legislature 30 miles away. Though forewarned, the legislature spared time for a meeting before decamping. Jefferson also refused to allow the approaching British to deprive him of a hearty breakfast. He left Monticello with only 30 minutes to spare.

Castle Hill still bears a reminder of this dawn breakfast. Tarleton became so convivial he brought in his orderly to show Walker the tallest British soldier in America. The soldier's height was notched on the door frame—6'9½". The area around Castle Hill where Tarleton's cavalry rested is still called by some "Tarleton's Woods."

Dr. Walker had 12 children, two of whom became successful politicians. John Walker was a U.S. Senator and Francis Walker, a U.S. Congressman. Despite his large family, he took an interest in several young protégés. Dr. Walker paid for dance lessons for a number of area gentlemen including James Madison. On festive occasions Thomas Jefferson would play his violin while Madison and others danced at Castle Hill.

Castle Hill is really two houses, the older Walker section and the formal American Federal Period story brick addition built in 1824 by Walker's grandaughter, Judith Walker Rives. Judith and her husband, Senator William Cabell Rives, also designed the slipper-shaped lawn which they planted with rare trees, some acquired from cuttings the Rives obtained at the Tuileries Garden while he was Ambassador to France. Judith Walker was a novelist as was her granddaughter, Amelie Louise Rives. Amelie's books were best sellers denounced from church pulpits and banned from libraries. Amelie's first husband was the eccentric John Armstrong Chanler, an heir to the Astor family fortune. Oscar Wilde was captivated by Amelie's beauty and determined that the two most beautiful people in London should meet. He introduced her to Prince Pierre Troubetzkoy, the handsome Russian artist, who became her second husband. Many of the Prince's paintings hang at Castle Hill as do several drawings by Amelie.

A long list of distinguished political and artistic figures have been entertained at Castle Hill including seven presidents and such talents as Ellen Glasgow, Louis Auchincloss, H. L. Mencken, William Faulkner and Katherine Hepburn. The house is now owned by Wayne Newton.

Castle Hill is open daily 10:00 A.M. to 5:00 P.M. from March through November. Admission is charged.

Directions: From Richmond take I-64 west to the Keswick Exit 26. Turn right on Route 616 and right again on Route 22. Take Route 22 to Cismont where you pick up Route 231. Take Route 231 north for two miles to Castle Hill on the left.

Historic Michie Tavern

A Real Mickey

The Rules of the House are listed as you enter **Michie** (pronounced micky) **Tavern**'s front door: "Four pence (50¢) a night for a bed. Six pence (75¢) with supper. No more than five to one bed. No boots to be worn in bed. Organ grinders to sleep in the wash house. No dogs allowed upstairs. No beer allowed in the kitchen. No razor grinders or tinkers taken in."

The tavern's costumed hostess will tell you about William Michie. His father, "Scotch" John Michie, was deported to Virginia in 1716 after taking part in the Scottish Jacobite Rising. When he arrived in Virginia he began acquiring land; ultimately he handled more than 11,500 acres. The land on which his son would eventually build Michie Tavern was acquired from Major John Henry, father of Patrick, another rebel against England.

William Michie also played a role in the struggle against England. He was part of the Continental army that wintered with Washington at Valley Forge. He signed the Albemarle Declaration of Independence in 1779. After the Revolutionary War, William Michie obtained a license in 1784 to operate an "Ordinary." The rules he established for his inn at that time are those you read as you enter.

You may wonder why razor grinders and tinkers were held in such low esteem. The former were engaged in what was a dirty job, a factor that had to be considered when you slept five to a bed. Tinkers were peddlers who traveled around the countryside repairing kettles and pans. They, too, had little time for cleanliness. From their work we get the expression, "not worth a tinker's dam." A dam was the mold the tinker used to make a pot; it had to be cracked to remove the pot and so had little value.

After the guide's introduction you will make your way through the tavern. Each room has a taped explanation of the main pieces you see. There are about 50 items that once belonged to the Michie family. The first room on the tour is the gentlemen's parlor with its adjoining tap room. The tap room is one of only two original colonial bars exhibited in Virginia. Like the rest of the tavern, it is not on its original site. In 1927 it was moved 17 miles to Monticello Mountain. In the gentlemen's parlor is a glass whiskey bottle shaped like a log cabin. The bottler, E. C. Booze, put his name on every bottle of Old Cabin Whiskey; thus to this day we talk about ordering and drinking "booze." Another unusual derivation comes from the spinning wheel attachment you'll see that was invented to count thread. It was called a weasel and gave rise to the nursery rhyme about the monkey, or wooden peg, that chased the weasel.

From the gentlemen's parlor you'll move to the distaff side, the ladies' parlor. Only taverns catering to the gentry had rooms for the ladies. One of this room's most interesting displays is the large hoop skirt from the 1780s. It is fascinating to see how these old hoop frames were made. The kneeling bench with beads that reflected light at night is also worth noting.

Upstairs in the ballroom, the tape includes a tune played on the dulcimer that is on display. It was here, legend proclaims, that Martha Jefferson scandalized Virginia society by dancing the first waltz in the colonies. The ballroom also contains a large folding bed in the closet, an early "Murphy" bed that undoubtedly came in handy at this crowded tavern.

Back downstairs you see the keeping hall, or dining room. Food wasn't prepared here but was kept warm before serving. William Michie's rifle hangs over the fireplace and in front of the hearth once stood the cook's chair (now in the corner). This unusual piece has high legs in the back so that the chair tilts forward, enabling the cook to tend the fire and stir the food. Other handy kitchen items include the hand-carved cheese press, apple peeler and French-fried potato cutter.

Recordings continue as you tour the dependencies—kitchen, necessary, spring house, well house and smoke house. If you have problems with steps you may want to skip these buildings. Your tour ends beneath the tavern in the wine cellar, but you may continue to the Ordinary and enjoy a colonial buffet. Michie's hospitality didn't end with the 18th century. The Ordinary still serves fried chicken, blackeye peas, stewed tomatoes, cole slaw, southern beets, green bean salad, potato salad, corn bread, biscuits and apple cobbler. Lunch is available from 11:30 A.M. to 3:00 P.M. daily in the four dining rooms and outdoor courtyard.

Before leaving you should also tour the Meadow Run Grist Mill and General Store. It was moved 50 miles to this new location. It is an appropriate addition to the growing Michie Tavern complex as the Michies once operated a mill and country store. Above the country store is the Virginia Wine Museum that opened in April 1985.

Michie Tavern is open 9:00 A.M. to 5:00 P.M. with the last tour beginning at 4:20 P.M. Admission is charged and includes both the tavern and grist mill.

Directions: Take I-64 west from Richmond to the Charlottesville area. Use Exit 24 (Route 20). Just past the Thomas Jefferson Visitors Bureau, turn left on Route 53. Michie Tavern will be on the right just before the entrance to Monticello; both are well-marked.

Thomas Jefferson called his tea room, a projection off the dining room at Monticello, his "most honorable suite." He kept likenesses of many American heroes on display here.

Monticello

The Sage of Monticello Grew Other Spices

Monticello is one of the most interesting homes in America because Thomas Jefferson was one of the most original thinkers of his, or any, age. His home reveals the breadth and scope of his interests.

Ex-President Taft said that in Charlottesville "they still talked of Mr. Jefferson as though he were in the next room." When you visit Monticello and sense the individuality of its designer, it is easy to feel that Mr. Jefferson is in the next room.

Thomas Jefferson inherited the land on which he built Monticello at his father's death in 1759. He had played on the mountaintop as a child while growing up at neighboring Shadwell. Jefferson occasionally took time out from his law studies with George Wythe in Williamsburg and explored his Virginia hilltop, perhaps planning the home he eventually built. The year after he finished reading law, 1768, he began to level the top of his 857-foot mountain so that he could begin building. He named his estate "Monticello," or little mountain. The design, like the name, is Italian; Jefferson used architectural books to design his house, and he borrowed heavily from the Palladian style popularized by Andrea Palladio.

Like so many of the skills Jefferson acquired, his architectural artistry was self-taught. He was an enthusiastic innovator in all that he attempted. One of the features that would become a Jeffersonian trademark was the dome he added to his house. His was the first private house in America to have a dome. His skyroom is only reached by a pair of narrow staircases, so visitors cannot enjoy an upclose look at this architectural feature. Jefferson loved domes but disliked obtrusive staircases.

Another innovation was the seven-day clock Jefferson designed for the Entrance Hall. Cannonball weights indicated the day of the week. Saturday's marker is below the hall on the basement level and can be seen in the archeological exhibit area beneath the Entrance Hall. Jefferson even designed a special ladder for the weekly winding of the clock. The hall also boasts antlers brought back by Lewis and Clark from their trip to the far west, as well as mastodon bones the two explorers found in Kentucky.

When you tour Monticello you quickly become aware of Jefferson's practical turn of mind. In the study there is a marvelous device that allowed him to write with one pen while a second connected pen made a copy of the letter. Jefferson designed his bedroom so that he could have access to his bed from either the bedroom or the sitting room; the bed itself is a room divider. He also designed beds to fit in alcoves to conserve space. His practicality extended to other areas of the house, such as a lazy susan door in the dining room that allowed the kitchen staff to set the prepared dishes on the door shelves and then simply turn the door, fully stocked, for service in the dining room.

Much as Jefferson enjoyed designing, building and embellishing his mountain top home, his real passion was for horticulture. Indeed, this great leader who served as President of the United States, Vice-President, Secretary of State, Minister to France and Governor of Virginia, once said, "I have often thought that if heaven had given me a choice of my position and calling, it should have been on a rich spot of earth . . . and near a good market . . . No occupation is so delightful to me as the culture of the earth. . ."

The gardens of Monticello are not to be missed. Visitors should plan their day so that they can include an hour's escorted tour of the garden, offered daily during the spring, summer and fall. Jefferson's creativity certainly extended to his garden. As he proudly proclaimed, "I am become the most ardent farmer in the state." In his later years he would say, "Though an old man, I am but a young gardener."

He was 23 years old when he began the garden diary he would keep until two years before his death. His precise records have enabled the Thomas Jefferson Memorial Foundation to restore the landscape accurately to its appearance following Jefferson's third term as president in 1809. A grid, drawn by Jefferson in 1778, gives the exact location of 300 trees. In all, his notes and planting plans indicate the position of 900 trees. His enthusiasm for fruit trees unquestionably exceeded their usefulness. Even on his busy estate there weren't enough people to consume the fruit from 300 trees. Jefferson's orchard was one of the most extensive in America; he planted 122 varieties of ten different types of fruit.

He also enjoyed experimenting with vegetables in his massive 1,000-foot vegetable garden located on a terraced area above the orchard. Peas were one of Jefferson's favorite vegetable, and he grew 20 kinds of English pea. In total he cultivated 250 varieties of vegetable. Jefferson once said that the "greatest service which can be rendered any country is to add an useful plant to its culture."

Monticello is open daily except Christmas from 8:00 A.M. to 5:00 P.M. March through October, and from 9:00 A.M. to 4:30 P.M. November through February. Admission is charged. You can purchase a Presidents' Pass which is a discounted combination ticket for Monticello, Historic Michie Tavern and Ash Lawn.

Directions: From Richmond take I-64 west to Charlottesville. Take Exit 24, Route 20, off I-64 and follow the signs to Monticello.

LYNCHBURG

Anne Spencer House

At Home with the Arts

Anne Spencer, noted black Virginia poet, was an individualist with a questing mind and an indomitable spirit. Her Lynchburg home reflects both. Tours are conducted by her only son, Chauncey Edward Spencer, whose reminiscences of his mother add a personal dimension few other homes on the National Register of Historic Places can match.

Chauncey is quick to point out, "Mother was the intellectual." It is readily apparent that her family and friends recognized and encouraged her creative muse. Her daily routine, both before and after her 26 years as a librarian at Dunbar High School, was clearly that of a thinker and poet. Someone else did the housework and cared for her three children. She slept until 11:00 A.M., bathed until noon, then sat by the window brushing her hair and thinking, finally dressing around 3:00 P.M.. She worked in her flower garden and wrote in the garden house during the late afternoons. She would frequently stay in her garden cottage during dinner eating from a tray while she worked long into the night.

The garden house was added by her husband, Edward Spencer, to give Anne a retreat where she could work undisturbed. The name she gave her cottage-studio, Edankraal (Ed and Ann's home), reveals their close relationship. Many of her poems touch on her love of flowers and her garden oasis. A tender sentiment is expressed in the following Anne Spencer poem:

HE SAID:

"Your garden at dusk
is the soul of love
Blurred in its beauty
And softly caressing;
I, gently daring
This sweetest confessing
Say your garden at dusk
Is your soul, My Love."

Both the garden and house provide an intimate look at Anne Spencer. The house has remained as it was during the 72 years she lived here, and it rings with her vibrant spirit. Many of her poems are literally written on the walls. "Lines to a Nasturtium" is printed on a nasturtium decorated wallpaper covering a kitchen cupboard.

The house was built for Edward Spencer and his family in 1903, and he continued to work for years expanding and decorating it. He added several guest rooms; the Spencers kept an open house for traveling blacks and, in fact, for all those interested in meeting and talking with Anne Spencer. Travel for blacks in the 1920s and '30s was difficult because so few accommodations were available. Their children often referred to their home as an overground, not underground, railroad. The Spencer home became a stopover for many political and literary figures. James Weldon Johnson, Field Secretary of the NAACP, was instrumental in thrusting Anne Spencer on the national horizon. He and H.L. Mencken sought a publisher for her poems, and Johnson's friendship led to a wider circle of contacts.

Visitors to the Spencer home included Booker T. Washington, Paul Robeson, Charles Gilpin, Marian Anderson, Dr. George Washington Carver, Langston Hughes, Carl Van Vechten, H.L. Mencken, Thurgood Marshall, W.E.B. DuBois, Martin Luther King, Jr., Jackie Robinson, Mary McCloud Bethune and many others. The Rev. Adam Clayton Powell and his bride honeymooned at the Spencer home.

The **Anne Spencer House** is open by appointment only; to arrange a visit, call (804)846-0517 or 845-1313.

Directions: From Richmond take Route 340 south to Burkeville, then Route 460 west to Lynchburg. At Lynchburg turn right on Route 501, then take the Buena Vista off ramp to Kemper Street. Take Kemper Street to 12th Street and turn right. Drive two blocks on 12th to Pierce Street and turn right. The Anne Spencer House is at 1313 Pierce Street. There is an Historical State Marker at the front of the house.

Appomattox Court House National Historical Park

Surrender to Its Appeal!

In 1861 Wilmer McLean, merchant and sugar importer, lived with his family along a stream in a sleepy Virginia community. The town was Manassas Station, the stream Bull Run, and the first battle of the War Between the States was fought there. General Beauregard used McLean's home as his headquarters. Town folks say that a Yankee cannonball went through the McLean's kitchen during his stay spoiling the General's dinner. A year later the armies of the North and South clashed once more on the hills and fields around McLean's home. He decided Manassas wasn't safe and moved his family to Appomattox Court House, an obscure county seat in the central Piedmont region. It is one of the ironies of history that the war which began in Wilmer McLean's front yard ended in his parlor!

Tales about the daily life of **Appomattox Court House** villagers and how they were affected by the Civil War are an important part of the story told at this National Historical Park. You can catch the Widow Keely holding forth during the summer months from her front porch. She tells what it was like when General Lee's men straggled into Appomattox after the northern troops had burned the supply trains so desperately needed by the Confederates.

Widow Kelly is not the only character visitors get to meet. A Union and a Confederate soldier provide different viewpoints on the war's end. Not every character is available every day, but one or two personalities are on hand daily throughout the summer.

There are 27 restored or reconstructed buildings at Appomattox Court House. Your first stop should be the Visitor Center where a 15-minute chronological slide program will acquaint you with the dramatic events from April 1 through 12, 1865, leading up to the final surrender. A second program, *Honor Answers Honor* uses first person accounts to recapture the emotions felt by those on both sides of the surrender field.

After this slide program you'll be able to walk the quiet country lanes to the Surrender Triangle with a sense of what the battle weary Confederates felt as they marched between the Union soldiers and discovered that they were presenting arms. When you tour the Clover Hill Tavern you'll see some of the paroles printed for the surrendering army. The presses had to turn out 28,231 passes for the Confederates who laid down their arms.

At the reconstructed McLean House you'll learn that only the sofa is original. Not only did the war end in Wilmer McLean's parlor, the Federal soldiers took some of his furniture when they left. Some purchased pieces and others, it is said, stole them; all wanted souvenirs of Lee's surrender to Grant.

The war ended ironically on the fourth anniversary of its opening salvo. The surrender of Lee's Army of Northern Virginia took place on April 12, 1865, exactly four years to the day after Fort Sumter was fired on by Confederate batteries.

Appomattox Court House is open daily from 9:00 A.M. to 5:00 P.M. except Thanksgiving, Christmas, New Year's, Martin Luther King's Birthday and George Washington's Birthday. There is a nominal charge per car. Living history programs are given during the summer months.

Directions: From Richmond take Route 360 west to Jetersville, then Route 307 to Route 460. Go west on Route 460 to Appomattox. Take Route 24 north for three miles to Appomattox Court House National Historical Park on the right.

Point of Honor and Court House Museum

Hill Street Greys

Lynchburg, which Thomas Jefferson described as "the most interesting spot in the state and the most entitled to general patronage for its industry, enterprise and correct course," has two important hills that bring to focus a great deal of its fascinating past. The first, a residential area known as Daniel's Hill, gets its name from Judge William Daniel, Sr., who inherited the property in 1830. Its handsome Federal-style mansion, situated on 737 acres overlooking the James River Basin, was built by Dr. George Cabell, Sr., 25 years earlier.

Dr. Cabell (you'll find a street named for him) called his place **Point of Honor** because he is said to have sited his house on a dueling ground. He treated his most illustrious patient, Patrick Henry, with mercury—a remedy that neither cured nor comforted the patient. Dr. Cabell lost his life in 1823 from an injury sustained in a riding fall. His legacy, Point of Honor, remains.

Point of Honor was home to a number of prominent Lynchburg families after Judge Daniel lived there, and after the War Between the States the estate was developed as a residential community. The homes along Cabell Street are now included in the Historic Lynchburg Walking Tour Brochure, number 3 Daniel's Hill. A five-block walk down Cabell Street includes ten points of interest. But if you are short of time the most important stop is Point of Honor.

Picture a two-story house with long porches across the front on both the first and second floors. Point of Honor is not boxy but many-angled, so the porches meet octagonal bays not right angles. The polygonal rooms in these bays are light and airy because each has three large windows. You might think to look at Point of Honor that there is an architectural link with Thomas Jefferson's Poplar Forest that was being built at the same time just outside of Lynchburg. But although Jefferson and Cabell were friends there is no indication that Jefferson had any input in the design of Point of Honor.

The interior is still evolving. The wallpaper in the parlor is a copy of the 1814 original, "Monuments of Paris." The downstairs, or best, bedroom has an exact duplicate of the original bed hangings on the four-post bed. The house and restored gardens can be toured 1:00 to 4:00 P.M. Tuesday through Saturday except in January and February. A small admission is charged.

Lynchburg's second major hill was once owned by the city's founder, John Lynch. He sold the property to the city in 1805 for one dollar, and the city built a courthouse on the site in 1814. Although the structure you see today is called the Old Court

House, it is actually the second courthouse on the site, dating from 1855. Its design is based on the Parthenon, and the stucco over the brick facade was scored to give it the look of sandstone.

Inside the Old Court House is the **Court House Museum**. Its exhibits trace the development of Lynchburg from its early days as a hub of eastern markets and western mountain goods. Plans are under way to re-create an 1855 Hustings courtroom, representing the time when 12 aldermen were elected to preside over and judge legal cases. The museum is open from 1:00 to 4:00 P.M., Tuesday through Saturday from March through December. There is a small admission charge.

If you take the Courthouse Hill walking tour, you will see 14 points of interest in all. One of them, Monument Terrace, is just across Court Street. You needn't climb the 161 steps of Monument Terrace in order to appreciate this city landmark. At the top of the terrace is a Confederate Memorial and at the foot, a statue of a World War I soldier. The walking tour also takes you past four churches, a mere sampling of the city's total of 126 churches. It is no wonder that Lynchburg is often referred to as the city of churches.

Directions: From Richmond take I-64 west to Charlottesville and Route 29 south to Lynchburg. In Lynchburg continue on Route 29 Alternate. Proceed past Main Street and turn left on Cabell Street. Point of Honor is located at Cabell and A Streets. For the Court House Museum continue on Cabell Street to the intersection with Rivermont Avenue and turn left on Rivermont. Take Rivermont to 5th Street and make a right, go one block to Court Street and turn left. The museum is at 9th and Court Streets.

Poplar Forest and Miller-Claytor House

On Jefferson's Trail

The visionary design can be discerned despite the ruinous inroads time has inflicted on **Poplar Forest**, Jefferson's country retreat, 70 miles south of Monticello in Lynchburg. Although plans are in the works to restore this masterpiece, created when Jefferson was at the peak of his architectural maturity, there is much yet to be done.

Jefferson acquired the land through his wife, Martha Wayles Skelton Jefferson, whose father owned the Lynchburg acreage. Jefferson designed the house as an escape from the crush of visitors that engulfed him at Monticello. Based on a Palladian plan, the house has four equal octagonal rooms grouped around a square dining room with an overhead skylight. It was the first octagonal residence in the New World.

Work on Poplar Forest began in 1806, and in 1812 Jefferson said, "When finished, it will be the best dwelling house in the state, except that of Monticello; perhaps preferable to that, as more proportioned to the faculties of a private citizen."

Today you can still manage to see the outline of Jefferson's private sanctuary where he said he enjoyed the "solitude of a hermit." You can imagine Jefferson reading in the bright, airy rooms. The details of scrollwork, the pleasing lines and the atmosphere are overlaid with modern additions. But these will eventually be stripped away. To arrange a visit to Poplar Forest, call (804)866-1654.

When Jefferson traveled to Poplar Forest he often stopped for a visit at the **Miller-Claytor House**. You can add this stop to your outing. This modest house was the fourth house built in 1791 in the new town of Lynchburg. Legend has it that on one of Jefferson's visits he took a bite of a "love apple" growing in the yard. It is believed to be the first time that a tomato, generally considered poisonous, was eaten in this part of the country.

The Miller-Claytor House at Rivermont Avenue and Treasure Island Road in Riverside Park is open by appointment. To arrange a tour, call (804)847-1654. You can include a stop at this old home on the Rivermont Avenue, Historic Lynchburg Tour number 4. The 12 sites along Rivermont Avenue include richly embellished private residences, Randolph-Macon Women's College, the Jones Memorial Library and the Centenary United Methodist Church. The architecture runs the gamut from Beaux Arts to a Swiss Chalet style with Queen Anne influence.

Directions: From Richmond take Route 360 southwest to Burkeville, then take Route 460 west to Lynchburg. Or take I-64 west to Charlottesville; then Route 29 south to Lynchburg. The Visitor Center is at 12th and Church Streets.

Red Hill Shrine

Country Sage

No one visits **Red Hill Shrine** by accident; greater numbers should visit by design. This is the last home and gravesite of Patrick Henry, the "voice of the Revolution." Some attribute his lack of prominence to his Revolutionary role of speaker, not scribe. He left few papers or letters behind. This neglect lends irony to his gravestone inscription, "His Fame His Best Epitaph." Henry's fame has diminished, though school children recognize his famous quote, "Give me liberty, or give me death," they know nothing about the man.

This is quite an eclipse for a man once heralded as the "first national hero," the "idol of the country," and "the Noble Patriot." A visit to Patrick Henry's last home, Red Hill, in Brookneal, Virginia, introduces you to this fascinating Founding Father. Patrick Henry was the last Royal, and the first elected, Governor of Virginia. He served five terms in total. After the last two in 1793 he decided not to run again and retired at age 57 to Red Hill where he resumed his law practice. One of the few original buildings at his plantation is his old law office. The house, kitchen and smokehouse were destroyed by fire but have been reconstructed on their original foundations.

Red Hill, the final and favorite of Patrick's seven houses, is a modest 1½-story frame house. You'll explore his home with the help of a self-guided walking tour brochure. The house has three main downstairs rooms—the master bedroom, parlor and dining room. The last two of the Henry's 17 children were born in the master bedroom, and the bed is still covered by a bedspread hand-loomed by two of Patrick Henry's sisters. His old walnut wash stand is one of the home's original furnishings.

The Henry family relaxed and entertained in the parlor. Two of their daughters were married there. It was in this room that Patrick Henry died on June 6, 1799. A Chippendale corner chair is identical to the one he was resting in when he died. Another family piece is the Sheraton tilt-top tea table.

The dining room contains several family pieces. The gateleg walnut dining table and a small Hepplewhite tea table are Henry pieces. Several examples of the family's "Blue Willow" china can be seen in the 18th-century corner cupboard. Food was brought to the dining room from the out-kitchen, the next stop on your self-guided tour.

After you explore the house you may want to take the garden walk to the family graveyard. Henry was, at his request, buried at the foot of what he called "the garden spot of the world." He enjoyed reading and relaxing beneath the Osage orange tree in front of Red Hill. Today this 400-year-old tree is 54 feet high and its limbs extend for more than 90 feet. It is considered the largest specimen of its kind in the world; its gnarled roots and striated bark are an impressive and artistic sight.

Red Hill Shrine is open daily 9:00 A.M. to 5:00 P.M., except from November through March when it closes at 4:00 P.M. It is closed on Christmas Day. A small admission is charged. A 15-minute film is shown at the Patrick Henry Museum before the walking tour.

Directions: From Richmond take Route 360 southwest to the Keysville area, then follow Route 15 until it intersects with Route 40. Take Route 40 to within 2 miles of Brookneal and follow well-marked signs to Red Hill.

South River Meeting House

A Quiet Place

The history of the Lynch family and the **South River Meeting House** are entwined. John Lynch established a ferry service across the James River in 1757 near what is now Lynchburg. After the ferry prospered he divided 45 acres on the hills above the ferry house into town streets and lots. In 1786 Lynch obtained a charter that authorized the establishment of the town of Lynchburg, and he sold the lots. He earmarked some of the land for community purposes; two acres for a burial ground and a large hillside tract for the courthouse which cost the city only one dollar. At the time that John Lynch first settled in the area his mother, Sarah, had given two acres for the first Quaker meeting house. In 1791 John provided ten acres for the third meeting house, school and cemetery.

The stone meeting house, begun in 1791 and completed in 1798, is what you see today. The earlier log structures were destroyed by fire. This is an economical and ecumenical house of worship; it passed from the Quakers to the Methodists who, although they never owned the property did worship here, and then to the Presbyterians. Appearances changed with denominations, but work to restore the meeting house to its 1790s look is nearly complete.

Despite their generosity to their fellow Quakers, the founding family was not exempted from the strict discipline of their group. John Lynch's mother was "read out of meeting" because she married a non-Quaker. She was eventually reinstated in the fellowship, but two of her children were also "read out:" her oldest son, Charles, because he took an oath as a member of the House of Burgesses and John Lynch because he "too unguardedly gave way to a spirit of resentment."

It is interesting to learn that the term "Lynch Law" is derived from Charles Lynch's band of determined patriots who took the law into their own hands. Lynch organized and led a group of Virginians who protected their community from the lawless Tories. Malcontents who were captured were tried by the patriots and flogged; the sentence was never death. Although it was called Lynch Law, at the time it did not carry the connotation it does today. Colonel Charles Lynch was even commended for his service by the Virginia legislature, which at the same time exonerated him from all charges of acting outside the legal system.

Tours of this old meeting house are conducted by volunteers wearing traditional Quaker garb. You'll see that this old church is divided into two distinct meeting rooms to separate the sexes during the service. Each side conducted its own meeting, and men and women could only be "read out" by their own meeting. You'll learn how a Quaker meeting was conducted and what it was like to be a Quaker in Lynchburg in the 18th and early 19th century.

Just outside the meeting house is the church burial ground. The Quakers did not hold burial services. You'll observe that there are no tombstones; the graves are marked with simple field stones. John Lynch, who died on Halloween in 1820, does, however, have a marker on his grave. It was placed there by the city of Lynchburg.

You can arrange to visit the Quaker Meeting House from 9:00 A.M. to 4:00 P.M. daily. At least three days prior notice is needed. Call (804)239-2548.

While you're in Lynchburg you may want to visit the Thomas Road Baptist Church where pastor, Jerry Falwell, has seen his congregation grow from 31 members to 21,000. He built Liberty College on 4,000 acres overlooking Lynchburg. In 1971 Lynchburg Baptist College had 100 students; it expects to have 50,000 by the year 2000.

Directions: From Richmond take Route 360 southwest to Burkeville, then take Route 460 west to Lynchburg. From Route 460 take Candlers Mountain Road (Route 128) west. At Wards Road and Candlers Mountain Road intersection continue straight ahead; the road becomes Sheffield Drive. Turn right onto Fenwick Drive from Sheffield Drive and right again on Fort Avenue. The South River Meeting House is at 5810 Fort Avenue.

Acknowledgments

A special thanks to Sue Brinkerhoff of the Virginia Division of Tourism whose helpful assistance made my journeys through Virginia easier and more productive.

Others who provided friendly assistance to my research for *The Virginia One-Day Trip Book* include: Linda Rider Royall of the Metropolitan Richmond Convention and Visitors Bureau, Diann Stutz of the Norfolk Convention & Visitors Bureau, Al Louer of the Colonial Williamsburg Foundation, Stevie Dovel of Lynchburg, Bernadette Plunkett of Prince William County, Kathy Grook of the City of Portsmouth, Sergei Troubetskoy of Petersburg, Mike Ramsey of Roanoke Valley Convention and Visitors Bureau and Martha Doss of the Lexington Visitor Bureau.

I would also like to thank Evelyn Metzger, my publisher who, as always, has worked to achieve the best possible book.

Finally, I'd like to thank my husband, John, who traveled with me on my many Virginia forays and never complained when I made just one more stop, and one more. . .

Virginia Calendar of Events

JANUARY

Mid:

Fredericksburg. *Religious Freedom Day.* (703)373-1776.
Stratford Hall. *Robert E. Lee's Birthday.* (804)493-8038.
Boyhood Home of Robert E. Lee and Lee-Fendall House. *Lee Birthday Celebration.* (703)548-1789 or 548-8454.
Stonewall Jackson House. *Birthday Celebration.* (703)463-2552.

FEBRUARY

Early:

Williamsburg. *Antiques Forum.* (804)229-1000 ext. 2372.
Virginia Beach. *Mid-Atlantic Sports & Boat Show.* (804)446-2432.

Mid to Late:

Fort Ward Park. *Revolutionary War Encampment & Skirmish.* (703)839-4848.
Alexandria. *George Washington Birthday Parade.* (703)549-0205.
Fredericksburg. *Washington Birthday Celebration.* (703)373-1776.
Mary Washington House. *George Washington Birthday Party.* (703)373-1569.
G.W. Birthplace National Monument. *George Washington Birthday Celebration.* (804)224-0196.
Winchester. *Washington's Birthday Celebration.* (703)662-6550.

MARCH

Early:

Woodlawn. *Needlework Exhibit.* (703)557-7881.
Virginia Beach. *Mid-Atlantic Wildfowl Festival.* (804)425-1530.

Mid:

Norfolk Botanical Gardens. *Camellia Show.* (804)588-3446.
Gunston Hall. *Kite Festival.* (703)550-9220.
Fredericksburg. *Fine Arts Exhibit.* (703)373-9411.
Alexandria. *St. Patrick's Day Parade.* (703)549-4535.
Norfolk. *St. Patrick's Day Celebration.* (804)627-7809.

Late:

Oatlands. *Loudoun County Day.* (703)777-3174.
Williamsburg. *Garden Symposium* (or early April). (804)229-1000 ext. 2372.
Norfolk. *Children's Easter Festival* (or early April). (804)627-7809.
Natural Bridge. *Easter Sunrise Service* (or early April). (703)291-2121.
Arlington National Cemetery. *Easter Sunrise Service* (or early April). (202)695-1622 or 475-1430.

APRIL

Early:

Boyhood Home of Robert E. Lee. *George Washington's Visit.* (703)548-8454.

Chincoteague. *Decoy Carver Festival.* (804)336-6161.

Norfolk Botanical Gardens. *Shower of Flowers Show.* (804)588-3446.

Scotchtown. *18th Century Craft Day.* (804)227-3500.

Monticello. *Thomas Jefferson Birthday Celebration.* (804)295-8181 or 295-2657.

Lynchburg. *Festival of the Arts.* (804)528-1986.

Alexandria. *Market Day.* (703)830-4242.

Gloucester. *Daffodil Show.* (804)693-3422.

Mid:

Norfolk Botanical Gardens. *International Azalea Festival.* (804)622-2312.

Alexandria. *Seaport Festival.* (703)549-1000.

Carlyle House. *Celebration of General Braddock's Visit to Alexandria.* (703)549-2997.

Oatlands. *Point-to-Point Races.* (703)777-3174.

Charlottesville. *Dogwood Festival.* (804)295-3141.

Yorktown. *Concord-Yorktown Day.* (804)887-1776.

Statewide. *Historic Garden Week.* (804)644-7776.

Middleburg. *Spring Race Meet.* (703)687-6964.

Late:

Ash Lawn. *James Monroe's Birthday Celebration.* (804)293-9539.

Stratford. *Coaching Days.* (804)493-8038.

Alexandria. *Candlelight Tour.* (703)549-0205.

Roanoke. *Wildflower Pilgrimage.* (703)342-5710.

Blacksburg. *Brush Mountain Arts and Craft Fair.* (703)552-4909.

Petersburg. *Poplar Lawn Art Festival.* (804)861-4611.

MAY

Early:

Chincoteague. *Seafood Festival.* (804)787-2460.

Occoquan. *Mother's Day Weekend, Geranium Day.* (703)491-7525.

Mary Washington House. *George Washington's Farewell to his Mother.* (703)373-1569.

New Market Battlefield Park. *Reenactment of the Battle of New Market.* (703)740-3101.

Jamestown Island. *Jamestown Day Celebration.* (804)229-1733.

Richmond. *Art in the Park.* (804)353-8198.

Gunston Hall. *George Mason Day.* (703)550-9220.

Winchester. *Shenandoah Apple Blossom Festival.* (703)662-3863.

Norfolk. *Fitness Fest.* (804)627-7809.

Chesterfield. *May Fest.* (804)748-1623.

Mid:

Ash Lawn. *Kite Day.* (804)293-9539.

Fredericksburg. *Market Square Fair.* (703)373-1776.

Sully. *Plantation Daily Life.* (703)941-5008.
Meadow Farm Museum. *Spring Agricultural Fair & Militia Review.*
(804)788-0391.
Norfolk. *Ghent Art Festival.* (804)441-5266.
Dumfries. *Charter Day & Historic Dumfries Craft Show.*
(703)670-5478.
Blandford Church. *British Encampment.* (804)733-7690.

Late:

Middleburg area. *Virginia Hunt Country Stable Tour.* (703)592-3711.
Fredericksburg National Military Park. *Memorial Day Program.*
(703)373-1776.
Belle Grove. *Needlework Exhibition.* (703)869-2028.
Roanoke. *Festival on the River.* (703)342-2640.
Arlington National Cemetery. *Memorial Day Ceremony.*
(202)693-1174.
Scotchtown. *Patrick Henry's Birthday Celebration.* (804)227-3500.

JUNE

Early:

Belle Grove. *Needlework Exhibition.* (703)869-2028.
Fredericksburg. *Great Rappahannock River White Water Canoe Ride.*
(703)373-1776.
Oatlands. *Antique Car Show.* (703)777-3177.
Fort Ward Park. *Sundays at Fort Ward.* (703)838-4848.
Norfolk. *Waterside Harborfest.* (804)627-5329.
Portsmouth. *Seawall Festival at Portside.* (804)397-3453.
Fredericksburg. *Art Festival.* (703)373-1776.

Mid:

Sully. *Antique Car Show.* (703)941-5000.
Gunston Hall. *Arts & Crafts Celebration.* (703)550-9220.
Ash Lawn. *An Evening with the Monroes.* (804)293-9539.
Alexandria. *Waterfront Festival.* (703)549-0205.

Late:

Virginia Beach. *Boardwalk Art Show.* (804)425-0000.
Radford. *The Long Way Home.* (703)639-0679.
Charlottesville. *Summer Festival of Plays.* (804)924-8966.
Norfolk. *Tidewater Scottish Festival & Clan Gathering.* (804)464-4990.
Ash Lawn. *Opera Festival.* (804)293-8000.

JULY

Early:

Red Hill Shrine. *Independence Day Picnic.* (804)376-2044.
Norfolk. *4th of July Great American Picnic.* (804)627-7809.
Jamestown Festival Park. *Jamestown Summer Celebration.*
(804)229-1607.
Meadow Farm Museum. *Old Fashioned 4th of July.* (804)788-0391.
Maymont. *Old Timey 4th of July.* (804)358-7166.

Fredericksburg. *Heritage Festival.* (703)373-1776.
Yorktown. *Old Fashioned Fourth.* (804)898-3400.
Chesterfield County. *July 4th Extravaganza.* (804)748-1620.
G.W. Birthplace National Monument. *July 4th Celebration.*
(804)224-0196.
Colvin Run Mill. *Old-Fashioned 4th of July Celebration.*
(703)941-5000.
Roanoke. *Down By The Riverside.* (703)981-2889.
New Market Battlefield Park. *19th Century Folk Day at New Market.*
(703)740-3101.
Boyhood Home of Robert E. Lee. *Custis-Fitzhugh Marriage.*
(703)548-8454.
Ash Lawn. *Colonial Crafts Weekend.* (804)293-9539.
Stratford Hall. *Open House.* (804)493-8038.

Mid:

G.W. Birthplace National Monument. *Colonial Crafts Festival.*
(804)224-0196.
Fort Ward Park. *Civil War Reenactment Weekend.* (703)838-4848.
Quantico. *Scale Model Air-Craft Rally.* (703)640-2606.
Gadsby's Tavern. *Children's Day.* (703)838-4242.
Culpeper. *Virginia Wineries Festival.* (804)644-0912.
Chippokes Plantation State Park. *Pork, Peanut & Pine Festival.*
(804)866-8585.
Belle Grove. *Shenandoah Valley Farm Craft Days.* (703)869-2028.

Late:

Alexandria. *Virginia Scottish Games.* (703)549-0205.
Chincoteague. *Pony Roundup and Penning.* (804)336-6519.
Jamestown Festival Park. *Saint James Day.* (804)229-1607.

AUGUST

Early:

Lynchburg. *Jefferson's Tomato Faire.* (804)528-1986.
Shenandoah National Park. *Hoover Days.* (703)999-2243 ext. 39.
Oatlands. *Children's Day.* (703)777-3174.
Virginia Beach. *Folk Arts Festival.* (804)467-4884.
Galax. *Old Fiddlers' Convention.* (703)236-6355.
Petersburg. *Neighborhood Walking Tours.* (804)861-8086.
Roanoke. *Hot Air Balloon Festival.* (703)981-2531.

Mid:

Gadsby's Tavern. *Tavern Days.* (703)838-4242.
Fort Ward Park. *Reenactment of the Battle of Fort Stevens.*
(703)838-4848.
Leesburg. *August Court Days.* (703)777-0519.
Flying Circus. *Balloon Festival.* (703)439-8661.
Meadow Farm Museum. *Civil War Reenactment.* (804)788-0391.
Abram's Delight. *Ice Cream Social.* (703)662-6550.
Manassas. *Civil War Reenactment.* (703)361-7126.

Late:

Virginia Beach. *East Coast Surfing Championship.* (804)424-1697.
Sully. *Quilt Show.* (703)437-1794.
Middleburg area. *Virginia Wine Festival & Vineyard Tour.*
  (703)754-8564.
Roanoke. *Beach Party.* (703)981-2889.
Williamsburg. *Publick Times & Fair Day.* (804)229-1000 ext. 2372.
Charlottesville. *Universal Galleries Arts & Crafts Show.*
  (804)973-9331.
Belle Grove. *Draft Horse & Mule Day* (or early Sept.). (703)869-2028.
Jamestown Festival Park. *Craft Day.* (804)229-1607.

SEPTEMBER

Early:

Gunston Hall. *Car Show.* (703)550-9220.
Oatlands. *Needlework Exhibition.* (703)777-3174.

Mid:

Lynchburg. *Festival by the James.* (804)528-1986.
Fredericksburg. *Quilt & Loom Show.* (703)373-1569.
Meadow Farm Museum. *Harvest Festival.* (804)788-0391.
Richmond. *International Festival.* (804)353-4389.
Hopewell. *Hooray for Hopewell Festival.* (804)458-5536.
Charlottesville. *Charity Fair.* (804)977-4583.
Norfolk. *Oktoberfest.* (804)672-7809.
Manassas. *Virginia Crafts Fair.* (703)690-3088.
Edinburg. *Old Time Festival.* (703)984-8521.

Late:

Occoquan. *Craft Show.* (703)491-5984.
Meadow Farm Museum. *Colonial Muster.* (804)270-1886.
Lynchburg. *Kaleidoscope Festival.* (804)384-5818.
Virginia Beach. *Neptune Festival.* (804)490-1221.
Richmond. *Harvest Moon Festival.* (804)257-1013.
New Market. *Arts & Crafts Show.* (703)740-3213.
Portsmouth. *National Hunting & Fishing Weekend.* (804)393-8481.
Alexandria. *Old Homes Tour.* (703)951-1982.

OCTOBER

Early:

Fredericksburg. *Rose Show.* (703)373-1776.
Waterford. *Home Tour & Craft Fair.* (703)882-3018.
Morven Park. *Carriage Drive & Competition.* (703)777-2414.
Gunston Hall. *1st Virginia Regiment of the Continental Line
  Encampment.* (703)550-9220.
Front Royal. *Festival of Leaves.* (703)635-3185.
Charlottesville. *Bacchanalian Feast/Albemarle Harvest Wine Festival.*
  (804)296-4188.
Petersburg. *Nostalgiafest.* (804)733-2402.

Mid:

Chincoteague. *Oyster Festival.* (804)336-6161.
South River Meeting House. *Quaker Wedding Reenactment.*
   (804)239-2548.
Boyhood Home of Robert E. Lee. *Lafayette Visit to Lee House.*
   (703)548-8454.
Richmond. *National Tobacco Festival.* (804)288-9124.
Woodlawn. *Fall Festival of Needlework.* (703)557-7881.
Sully. *Harvest Days.* (703)437-1794.
Luray. *Page County Heritage Festival.* (703)743-3915.
Lynchburg. *Historical Appomattox Railroad Festival.* (804)352-5547.
Front Royal. *Festival of Leaves.* (703)635-3185.
Roanoke. *Fall Foliage Festival.* (703)981-2889.
Yorktown. *Yorktown Day, A Fall Festival.* (804)898-3400.

Late:

Belle Grove. *Quilt Exhibition.* (703)869-2028.
Portsmouth. *Olde Towne Ghost Walk.* (804)393-2011.
Norfolk. *Halloween Celebration.* (804)627-7809.
Blue Ridge. *Folklife Fest.* (703)365-2121 ext. 416.

NOVEMBER

Early:

Science Museum of Virginia. *Model Railroad Show.* (804)257-1013.
Gadsby's Tavern Museum. *Washington's Review of the Troops.*
   (703)549-0205.
Oatlands. *Christmas at Oatlands.* (703)777-3174.
Berkeley. *The First Thanksgiving Festival.* (804)644-1607.
Blacksburg. *YMCA Arts & Crafts Show.* (703)961-6468.
Fredericksburg. *Craft Show.* (703)373-9411.

Mid:

Fredericksburg. *Needlework Exhibit.* (804)271-1662.
Roanoke. *Crafts Festival.* (703)342-5760.

Late:

Richmond. *Civil War Show & Sale.* (804)271-1662.
Chincoteague National Wildlife Refuge. *Waterfowl Week.*
   (804)336-6122.
Boar's Head Inn, Charlottesville. *Thanksgiving Hunt Weekend,*
   Blessing of the Hounds Feast. (804)229-1607.
Jamestown Festival Park. *Thanksgiving Festival.* (804)229-1607.

DECEMBER

Early:

Fredericksburg. *Christmas Candlelight Tours.* (703)371-4504.
Norfolk. *Historic Homes Holiday.* (804)622-1211.
Mariners' Museum. *Christmas at Sea.* (804)595-0368.
Virginia Beach. *Christmas in the Country.* (804)481-4057.

Colvin Run Mill. *Traditional Christmas Celebration.* (703)759-2771.
Ash Lawn. *Cut Your Own Christmas Tree.* (804)293-9539.
Stratford Hall. *Christmas Celebration.* (804)493-8038.
Meadow Farm Museum. *Yuletide Fest.* (804)649-0566.
Science Museum of Virginia. *Joy From the World* (all month).
   (804)257-1083.
Charlottesville. *Yuletide Traditions Celebration.* (804)293-6789.
Morven Park. *Christmas Celebration.* (703)777-2414.
Alexandria. *Scottish Christmas Walk.* (703)549-0205.
Lynchburg. *Christmas Tradition, Point of Honor.* (804)847-1399.
Abram's Delight. *Candlelight Tour.* (703)662-6550.
Lexington. *Holiday in Lexington.* (703)463-3777.
Fort Ward Museum. *Victorian Christmas Open House.* (703)838-4848.
Norfolk Botanical Gardens. *Christmas Flower Show.* (804)588-3446.
Scotchtown. *Candlelight Tour.* (804)227-3500.
Woodlawn. *Carols by Candlelight.* (703)557-7880.
Alexandria. *Old Town Christmas Candlelight Tour.* (703)549-0205.
Maymont. *Christmas Open House.* (804)358-7166.

Mid:

Arlington House. *Decorate Arlington House.* (703)557-0613.
Petersburg. *Christmas Homes Tour.* (804)733-7041.
Chesterfield County Courthouse Complex. *Legendary Christmas.*
   (804)748-1623.
Fredericksburg National Military Park. *Battle of Fredericksburg
   Commemoration.* (703)373-1776.
Sully. *Christmas Candlelight Tour.* (703)437-1794.
Fort Ward Park. *A Civil War Christmas.* (703)838-4848.
Stratford Hall. *Special Christmas Celebration.* (804)493-8038.
Williamsburg. *Grand Illumination.* (804)229-1000 ext. 2372.
Rising Sun Tavern. *Christmas Open House.* (703)373-1776.
Maymont. *Christmas Open House.* (804)358-7166.
Gunston Hall. *Carols by Candlelight.* (703)550-9220.
Belle Grove. *Christmas Candlelight Tour.* (703)869-2028.
Jamestown Festival Park. *Twelve Days of Christmas.* (804)229-1607.

Late:

Yorktown Victory Center. *Christmas in the Encampment.*
   (804)887-1776.
Boar's Head Inn, Charlottesville. *Merrie Olde England Christmas
   Festival.* (804)296-2181.
Woodrow Wilson's Birthplace. *Birthday Open House.* (703)885-0897.
Alexandria. *Scottish New Year's Eve, Hogmanay.* (703)549-0205.
Norfolk. *Waterfront New Year's Eve Festival.* (804)627-7809.
Roanoke. *New Year's Eve Party at Market Square.* (703)981-2889.
Charlottesville. *First Night Virginia.* (804)296-8548.

Note: Telephone numbers do change. To obtain up-to-date information on events call the Virginia Department of Economic Development at
(804)786-2051.

Index

About the Author

Jane Ockershausen Smith has been writing about Virginia for more than a decade. Many Virginia attractions are included in her four previous One-Day Trip Books, but this is the first in the series that focuses exclusively on one state.

Though she grew up across the Potomac River in Maryland and over the years spent many weekends exploring in her neighboring state, this enthusiastic investigator was surprised by the abundance of both old and new sights she hadn't yet seen. In her travels she was especially pleased to discover that the legendary Virginia hospitality was as real and warm as ever. "I've never had so much fun doing research for a book," she says.

A full time travel writer, Jane Smith writes a feature column for *AAA World* and contributes frequently to *Mid-Atlantic Country* and the *Journal* Newspapers. Her articles have appeared in *The Washington Post*, *The Washington Times*, *Washingtonian* Magazine, *The Baltimore Sun*, *Chicago Tribune*, *The Oregonian* and *The Buffalo News*. She is a member of the Society of American Travel Writers and the American Society of Journalists and Authors.

TO HELP YOU PLAN AND ENJOY YOUR TRAVEL IN THE MID-ATLANTIC AREA

THE WALKER WASHINGTON GUIDE $7.95
The seventh edition of the "Guide's guide to Washington," completely revised by Katharine Walker, builds on a 25-year reputation as the top general guide to the capital. Its 320 pages are packed with museums, galleries, hotels, restaurants, theaters, shops, churches, as well as sites. Beautiful maps and photos. Indispensable.

ADVENTURE VACATIONS IN FIVE MID-ATLANTIC STATES $9.95
This all-season guide to making the most of free time in PA, MD, VA, WV and NC features hiking, biking, cross-country skiing, trail riding, sailing and canoeing; also archeological digs, mystery weekends, craft and specialty workshops, and lending a hand and elder-hosteling. Tips on planning, costs, equipment and special attractions included.

WASHINGTON ONE-DAY TRIP BOOK $7.95
101 fascinating excursions within a day's drive of the capital beltway—out and back before bedtime. The trips are arranged by seasons and accompanied by calendars of special events, map and notes on facilities for the handicapped.

PHILADELPHIA ONE-DAY TRIP BOOK $8.95
And you thought Independence Hall and the Liberty Bell were all Philadelphia had to offer? Norman Rockwell Museum, Pottsgrove Mansion, Daniel Boone Homestead, Covered Bridges and Amish Farms are among 101 exciting one-day trips featured.

ONE-DAY TRIPS THROUGH HISTORY $9.95
Describes 200 historic sites within 150 miles of the nation's capital where our forebears lived, dramatic events occurred and America's roots took hold. Sites are arranged chronologically starting with pre-history.

THE MARYLAND ONE-DAY TRIP BOOK $10.95
From Baltimore's famed aquarium to rugged mountain wilderness and the world's largest concentration of wintering Canada geese, the newest one-day trip guide shows, county by county and season by season, how to explore the unbelievable variety of things to see and do in 190 excursions.

Also:

Florida One-Day Trips (from Orlando). What to do after you've done Disney. **$7.95**

Call it Delmarvalous. How to talk, cook and "feel to hum" on the Delaware, Maryland and Virginia peninsula. **$7.95**

One-Day Trips to Beauty & Bounty. Year-round nature trips in and around Washington: gardens, arboretums, farms, parks, conservatories. **$8.95**

Footnote Washington. Tracking the engaging, humorous and surprising bypaths of capital history by one of the city's most popular broadcasters. **$8.95**

Mr. Lincoln's City. An illustrated guide to the Civil War sites of Washington, as readable as it is informative. **$17.95**

Walking Tours of Old Washington and Alexandria. $100,000 might buy you the original Paul Hogarth watercolors reproduced here in full color, but then you'd be missing the engaging text and the convenience of taking it all along as you step back into the distinguished heritage preserved in our Capital's finest old buildings. Usable art; exquisite gift. **$24.95**

Order Blank for all EPM books described here. Mail with check to:

EPM Publications, Inc.
Box 490, McLean, VA 22101

Title	Quantity	Price	Amount	Shipping
_____	_____	_____	_____	$2.00 each book
_____	_____	_____	_____	_____
_____	_____	_____	_____	_____
_____	_____	_____	_____	_____

Subtotal _____

Virginia residents, add 4½% tax _____

Name _____   Shipping _____

Street _____

City _____ State _____ Zip _____

Total _____

Remember to enclose names, addresses and enclosure cards for gift purchases.
Please note that prices are subject to change. Thank you.